COGITO
media group

CHARLES
MANSON
NOW

CHARLES MANSON NOW

Marlin Marynick

Edited by Elizabeth Licorish

Published by Cogito Media Group
Copyright ©2010 Marlin Marynick

ISBN: 978-2-923865-06-5

Cover design: Francois Turgeon
Text design and composition: Nassim Bahloul

Cogito Media Group
279 Sherbrooke Street West
Suite#305
Montréal, Quebec
H2X 1Y2
CANADA
Phone : + 1.514.273.0123

www.cogitomedias.com

Printed and Bounded in the United States of America

Publisher's note: Charles Manson will not receive any of the proceeds from the sale of this book. Please note that some of the names and events have been changed to respect the privacy of certain people mentioned in the book.

Table Of Contents

ACKNOWLEDGMENTS

This book would not have happened without the efforts of the following people. I would like to thank:

Robert Daniel Pytlyk, whose friendship and direction really made this book possible.

Karen Ammond, President of KBC Media and my publicist, who helped make this book a reality from concept to completion.

Bill Gladstone, my book agent from Waterside Communications, who has been more than an agent: he has helped guide this project and worked with me throughout this process.

Pierre Turgeon, who believed in an unknown author and this book.

Francois Turgeon, who is such an incredible, cooperative art director.

Gratia Ionescu, whose patience, guidance, and assistance were so valuable.

Elizabeth Licorish, my editor, who truly knows how demanding this process was: I couldn't have done this without her.

Mark "Hollywood" Hatten, who was my sounding board through all of this. You rock, dude!

Mary Chambers, for all her help.

Laurie Elyse, for all the connections and friendship.

Michael Wright, for his invaluable honesty and insights.

Gerry Krochak, for all his help. One day, we'll work on a book together.

Kelly Champagne, my transcriber, who was so efficient and organized.

Mike Ash, for being there and tending to all the little things.

Richard Caithcart, for dealing with all of my technical, computer problems.

A very special thanks to everyone at Cogito Media Group.

Much gratitude to my family, friends, and co-workers, who had to put up with me while I worked on this book.

LIST OF CHARACTERS

John Aes-Nihil: filmmaker, photographer, owner of the largest archive of Manson materials and information, recognized in Manson circles as the "authority."

Kenneth Anger: experimental filmmaker, who worked with Anton LaVey during the '70s, and for whom Bobby Beausoleil worked as a character in one of his movies.

Susan Atkins: member of the Manson Family, took part in the Tate/LaBianca murders, for which she was sentenced to life in prison; died in prison from brain cancer in 2009.

Bobby Beausoleil: member of the Manson Family, was dealing LSD; convicted of the murder of Gary Hinman, serving a life sentence in Oregon State Penitentiary.

Mary Brunner: member of the Manson Family, participated in the Hinman murder for which she received immunity after turning state's evidence, convicted for a shootout and served a six-and-a-half-year sentence.

Kenny Calihan: inmate at Corcoran Prison, close friend of Charles Manson.

Clem: an original family member who was working as a musician, has since disappeared into obscurity.

Abigail Folger: heiress to Folger coffee fortune, murdered at the Cielo Drive residence by "Tex" Watson, Susan Atkins, Linda Kasabian, and Patricia Krenwinkel.

Graywolf: first met Manson in 1969 after the murders, reconnected with him ten years ago; one of Manson's close friends and confidantes outside of prison.

William Harding: collector of items made or owned by America's most notorious apprehended criminals; he befriends the inmates with whom he corresponds.

JD Healy and Cathee Shultz: founders and owners of the Museum of Death in Los Angeles.

Gary Hinman: murder victim of Bobby Beausoleil, Susan Atkins, and Mary Brunner.

David Hooker: inmate of Corcoran Prison, close friend of Charles Manson.

Linda Kasabian: member of the Manson Family, turned state's evidence against the Tate/LaBianca murderers for which she was granted immunity, testified during the trials.

Paul Krassner: author, source for the Manson/Polanski home movie information.

Patricia Krenwinkel: member of the Manson Family, took part in the Tate/LaBianca murders, for which she was sentenced to life in prison; serving her sentence at California Institute for Women at Frontera.

Leno LaBianca: murder victim of "Tex" Watson, Patricia Krenwinkel, and Leslie Van Houten.

Rosemary LaBianca: wife of Leno LaBianca, murder victim of "Tex" Watson, Patricia Krenwinkel, and Leslie Van Houten.

Anton LaVey: founder and high priest of the Church of Satan.

Stanton LaVey: grandson of Anton LaVey.

Bill Nelson: author, became obsessed with the Manson murders.

Roman Polanski: film director, Sharon Tate's husband.

Matthew Roberts: DJ in Los Angeles, research on his biological parents indicates he could be the son of Charles Manson.

Jay Sebring: Los Angeles hairdresser, one of the victims murdered at the Cielo Drive residence by "Tex" Watson, Susan Atkins, Linda Kasabian, and Patricia Krenwinkel.

Donald Shea: aspiring actor, worked on the Spahn Ranch, murdered by Steven Grogan and "Tex" Watson.

Star: young woman who befriended Manson because of his philosophy on the environment, lives with Graywolf.

Sharon Tate: actress, pregnant wife of director Roman Polanski, resident of the house on Cielo Drive, murdered there by "Tex" Watson, Susan Atkins, Linda Kasabian, and Patricia Krenwinkel.

Donald Taylor: controversial author of One Gay Man, claimed to have a relationship with Charles Manson.

Terry: Matthew Roberts' biological mother.

Leslie Van Houten: member of the Manson Family, took part in the LaBianca murders for which she was sentenced to life in prison; serving her sentence at California Institute for Women at Frontera.

Vicki: at the age of fifteen, in 1969, first met Charles Manson, friends with him since then, has relationships with several of Manson's friends and associates.

Charles "Tex" Watson: member of the Manson Family, took part in the Tate/LaBianca murders for which he was sentence to life in prison. He is currently serving his prison sentence in Mule Creek State Prison in Ione, California.

Dedicated to the memory of Danny and David Stephenson.

FOREWORD BY CHARLES MANSON

Here's what I wrote for you, man, are you ready?

When you're raised up in a prison you learn all the tricks, and you figure out all the reasons why everything happens. You know the game better than they do. So you are a warden, you are more of a warden than the warden is. He calls you into his office, but it's actually your office. He's over there because you allow him to be there, you understand everything that goes on. What happens is you become the president, you become everybody. I was Richard Nixon, I was the mop and broom and the toilet. There wasn't anything going on that I didn't know about. So what happens is you've got a group of people, let's say one hundred million, and all those people they only know so much. You can add everything that they know and it's only gonna fill a certain amount of the bucket. You can't get any more than you get, I mean there is a limit, on the physical level anyway, there are numbers, weights, judgments, laws, rules, all of that.

When you're raised in a federal prison, the prison becomes your mind, because people come in, and people go out. People get jobs, and they serve a function, and abide by certain rules, and regulations, then after awhile everything is turned around, and there is nobody there but you! 'Cause you're in the room, and there are ten people in the room, and one person comes in and leaves, and another comes in and leaves, then two come in, and one leaves, three leave, and one comes in. *Pretty soon everything turns around, and you're the only one left, and you've been there and the room has turned over ten times. There is nobody else there! You're there all by yourself 'cause you see how everybody else's mind works, when they come into the room. They don't know what's going on. They say, "What's going on?" and the only thing they know is what they were told. So, pretty soon you see what it means when you say, "Three Dog Night." It means when you come to prison and you stay the fifteen years, all the dogs of the world are dead when you come back out, there is no dog that was alive when you were out last time. The three dog night would mean you were in prison three times, three times all the dogs.*

You watch it on the line all your life. You watch people come in and go out, come in and go out, the worms crawl in, the worms crawl out. You go and you try and talk to these people. You can't talk to them because they're so scared that they don't want to hear it. They don't want to hear nothing. All they want to do is draw their paychecks and go back and forwards and live in their lunch buckets. And there's no communication unless you can pile enough bodies up and I don't think even Hitler did that, did he? No, I was going to say I don't think there's any way you're ever going to turn the tide. I don't think it will turn around because they're not going to accept a Jesus, the real one. Because they got that Jesus in their head that they want to be whatever their victory is.

So when you're in prison, and the cops come up to you, you look up to them like they're your father, because they're retired veterans, and they are retired warriors. You're raised up by police 'cause you don't have no family, so all the cops become your dad. You're on the inside of the system, the president is your father, the government is your father, and the army is your brothers. The reality is, you are God on the inside, everything is in your mind, and you are the son of all things. When you raise a child in a prison, it's not a prison to that child, it's just the child's home. You can't break what's already been broken, you break the child, you beat the child into submission. The child submits to everything you are doing, he becomes more of what you are doing, than what you are doing. You've got all kinds of people doing all kinds of things in prison and they're coming off on you like, well, you fucked up, and you're no good, you did this, and you're just a throwaway child. You live for what they think because you think they are your parents, for years they're your parents. You look up to them, and think they are your heroes, then you get older, and you become everything they were. Then a new group comes in and they don't like you 'cause you're not looking up to them like they are your parents anymore, you're looking at them like they are your children, because they've become your children now. Then when they become your children, they feel uncomfortable with that. When you become the authority then they become befuddled, bewildered, they don't know, and the ones that raised you are already dead. So the guy says, "You go work in the kitchen." You say, "Fuck you." He says, "Well, you're not getting out of the hole then." You say, "Good, I like the hole." He says, "Well, you're not going to get out of prison." You say, "What prison? You're the one who has to come here, you can't live without this. I can live without this, I can live without it."

So, then they kick me out of prison. They say, "Your time is up, we gotta let you go." They can't deal with me so that's what [they] do. I'm not in prison, that's my home, man. "Get the hell out of here! We don't want you in here no more 'cause you're fuckin' things up, 'cause the kids are not looking up to us like we're father now and they're giving us trouble, and you're causing trouble!" You get to the point where people are destroying themselves, they would cut their own wrist, and you see them committing suicide, before they could accept the truth about themselves. Go to the nut wards and they got them filled with the criminally insane. You know what crazy is, you see it every day, man. Do you realize that everybody in the hospital in Vacaville that forced medication on me, and had me strapped down, and played all that stuff on me are all dead? In other words they did it to themselves. What you are trying to put on me is what you're thinking; it ain't got a fuckin' thing to do with me. They put me on the "no mind list."

They said "You're on the "pay no mind' list." They tell everyone "Leave him alone, and don't pay attention to him, don't listen to him, don't even mention his name, don't say nothing about him, just get rid of him, get him away from us, because we can't stand him." So, I go outside, and I go over to the music and the Grateful Dead is playing, and they put me on the witness program. Not because I snitched on somebody or betrayed a trust. I didn't snitch on nobody, and I didn't betray a trust, but they've got me on the Federal Witness program. They say, "Leave this man alone, do not put him in jail in any direction whatsoever, he's the devil, and we can't control him, and we can't whip him, we can't beat him. He anticipates everything we're going to do. So stand off of him, 'cause he'll destroy everything you fuck with him with . If you do something against him it's going to turn back on you a thousand fold." And so, I'm out there walking around, here comes the State of California and the Italian Mafia, district attorney. They said I killed people. "I ain't killed those people! I didn't have a fuckin' thing to do with killing those people!" That's your kids. Mr. Richard Milhous Nixon. That's your government, that's not my government. My government is George Washington, your government is Abraham Lincoln. That has nothing to do with me, I'm from the South. I've got enough fuckin' brains to realize that I'm stupid, and I've got enough intelligence to understand that I don't know anything, that God is great, and God is bigger than me. I'm not as big as God, but all the fuckin' assholes that got me locked up, they think they are God.

Charles Manson
Corcoran State Prison, California, 2010

A MEETING WITH MANSON

"Get down!" Charlie commanded, a sneer on his face.

He had the guards' full attention, two of them, in the center of the room, standing in the circular area that acted as a security desk. Charlie crouched down, ready to leap at any second. I was taken by how agile he was. He met the gaze of the guards full on, trying to determine if he should continue. "I'll kill you," he shouted. "Can't you see this gun? I'm serious!"

We were in the visiting room at Corcoran California State Prison, a place Charles Manson has called home for more than twenty years. Over the past few years, I'd developed a relationship with Charlie; this was our first visit. He had not been to the visiting room for almost a year and now, it seemed, he was making up for lost time. Charlie had begun acting out a bank robbery for this intimate audience: the guards and me.

This was live theater at its best. Charlie squatted down and moved around with an urgency, an intensity that caught us completely by surprise. The scene took about ninety seconds to complete. When he finished, he sat down and took a few moments to catch his breath. "Ah, I feel pretty good. I just can't breathe," Charlie laughed to himself. I was speechless.

Charlie likes to philosophize and talk about the deeper meaning of things, about ultimate reality. Often, he uses extreme examples to exemplify a point. During this visit, he tried to show me how he experiences reality. The bank robbery scene was intended to exemplify a concept Charlie called "level seven" which, he later explained, meant conquering fear. Level seven is a degree of heightened awareness, the level at which Charlie says he lives. I interpreted Charlie's one-scene play as an illustration of being in the moment–mindfulness, and presence, that sort of thing.

Charlie and I share a lot of the same insights, but we've come to them from completely different worlds. I'm normally pretty good at putting myself in other people's shoes. But I can't imagine enduring sixty-three years in prison. I've often wondered how I'd handle seclusion, isolation. I don't think I'd fare too well. Charlie's spent most of his incarceration in solitary confinement, where he is forced to be with himself, with his thoughts, forced to confront his demons, forced to develop insight from a depth unknown to most men. Charles Manson is, without a doubt, the most complex person I've ever known.

We developed a relationship over the telephone, gradually, in intervals lasting fifteen minutes, the length of a collect call from Corcoran. Almost immediately, I realized I didn't really know this guy at all. I had assumptions, sure, but most of them were unfounded. Sometimes Charlie is kind, empathetic, and funny. Other times he's vile and mean; he can be a real condescending asshole. It's almost impossible to discover the real Charlie. Yet this is exactly what I have tried to do.

Charlie often has a unique way of getting a point across, as the following actual transcripts from our phone conversations shows:

MANSON: I got a gun, right?
ME: Okay.

MANSON: You see me standing there with a gun?

ME: No?

MANSON: You do, you can't imagine that I'm standing there looking at you right now. I mean my voice is there, don't you realize that my body could be there just as easy?

ME: All right, I get it.

MANSON: If I got a gun and I'm standing there with a gun and I tell you, you know, "Get off of that chair, stand up," would you stand up?

ME: Yeah, of course.

MANSON: Then I tell you, "Then if you don't do what I said I'm going to blow your brains out, you understand me?"

ME: Yes.

MANSON: Do you think that I would lie to you about anything?

ME: No.

MANSON: Then you can understand what I'm saying. I say, "Well then, here, take this gun." And I'm handing you the gun, could you reach out and take this gun in your hand? Would you feel safer that way?

ME: Absolutely.

MANSON: In other words, can you face your fear in what I'm saying. Okay, so you got the same options. If I don't do what you say you can shoot me, right?

ME: Okay.

MANSON: I've been in that all my life. There's two guns up here on the tower that tell me what to do. And when they tell me what to do, I do what they say to do, because if I don't do what they say to do they will shoot me. Does that communicate?

1

THE WONDER YEARS

I was an odd kid.   Unlike most boys my age, I wasn't interested in sports. My heroes were Houdini, Robert Ripley, and The Elephant Man. I had a tremendous interest in things like sideshows and magic, and, while the other boys in town tossed footballs and climbed fences, I collected bugs. More important, I tried to save them. After a heavy rain, I'd run outside to rescue worms from the gutter, gently scoop them up and return them to the grass with a prayer that they'd tunnel themselves back to their homes in the dirt below. I adorned my childhood bedroom with prized natural artifacts unearthed through countless explorations of the outside world; deer antlers, feathers, even wasp nests decorated my space. I loved to catch, study, and spend time with the tiny, complex life forms I could gather up in the palms of my hands, things like minnows, frogs, and snails. But I was ultimately most fascinated by the enormous, the fantastic, or the extinct: terrifying things that aren't supposed to exist. I could contemplate dinosaurs and sea monsters for hours on end.

I grew up in Saskatchewan, in the middle of the Canadian prairies. As a kid I developed a love for seashells and a fascination with the ocean, even though the closest ocean was fifteen hundred miles away. When I learned that marble is actually comprised of millions of compressed shells, I fantasized about visiting the Parthenon in Greece and the Coliseum in Rome, not because they are two of the largest, most impressive structures ever made by humans, but because they are comprised from some of the smallest gems in nature. I haven't outgrown my childhood affection for simple treasures like seashells, and small clusters of my collection are displayed in almost every room of my home. Once, I toured Graceland, where I was delighted to discover Elvis had decorated so much of his castle in vases filled with seashells. The man could have owned anything in the world, yet he showed off his shells as though they were some of his most valuable possessions. Propped up against one of the vases in the display was a small, stuffed teddy bear.

I love a great underdog story and I began to tell my own when I was just three or four years old. Babysitters would later relate that they'd been "freaked out" by the tales I'd spin as a toddler. Most stemmed from an epic creation story I'd constructed about my own family, a carefully detailed account of its origins as an underground tribe, which was hated by rival tribes, and hunted if any member dared venture above ground for food.

I spent summers visiting my grandmother in the small town of Bateman, Saskatchewan. She was most supportive of my storytelling and loved to share some of the narrative she'd collected from her own experiences. I was fascinated by a story she told of her emigration from Holland to North America, a trip during which a passenger caught a strange fish. The creature was the ugliest thing anyone on board had ever seen: it possessed the torso of a monkey and the tail of a fish. Listening to this story as a child, I could have sworn the animal in question was a mermaid. On board, the fish writhed and hissed at everyone in sight. The passengers tried to keep the fish alive, but it died, and they had no choice but to throw it back into the ocean. I couldn't believe that they hadn't released it sooner. I always thought that story was incredibly sad. I still do. Years later I saw P.T. Barnum's Fiji mermaid in a museum, and it looked exactly as I'd imagined the creature from my grandmother's story.

I loved to be in Bateman, walking along quiet dirt roads on which you could hear a car moving three miles away. Everything about that time and place was beautiful. My cousin Kent, who was nearly the same age, accompanied me on all my adventures. Kent knew all the kids in town, and together we always found a gang with which to make slingshots, climb roofs, or hunt for buried treasure. We loved the band Kiss, listening to rock 'n' roll, pretending to drive anywhere and everywhere from the ripped up seats of some broken down car.

One lazy summer afternoon, my Uncle Roy unexpectedly sped up the road in his rusted out green Ford truck to take me home. He told me my mother had been in an accident and was badly hurt, that it was important we get back home immediately. I didn't want to go with him. I didn't trust him. My grandmother urged me to leave, however; she told me my mother needed me and I could come back later. I still remember the crazed look in Roy's eyes as he drove, way faster than he should have. He was preoccupied, and I knew whatever was going on in his head would disturb me.

From an extremely young age, I'd seen my relatively sane family members drink themselves into delirium, and it scared me. I hated being around drunk people, and I did whatever I could to avoid them. I usually retreated to my room, listened to records, or read books. I thought that getting inebriated was what older people did. Yet, each time I watched an adult slip into drunkenness, I'd worry the fix would never wear off, that he or she would never return to normal, whatever that was. And, while almost every adult I knew got wasted and stupid, there was something different about Uncle Roy when he drank. He never did anything to me, and, at that age, I couldn't really pinpoint why he seemed to be the worst, most pathetic drunk. But I began to associate everything about Uncle Roy – his creepy, perverse sense of humor, the glazed, psychotic look that could take over his face – with everything awful about alcohol.

We drove the hundred and fifty miles back to my parents' house in record time. Everything moved as if it had been set to fast forward. During the ride, I kept my face fixed on the passenger side window. I was staring into the ditches on the side of the highway, watching colors blur, browns into greens, nothing really in focus. In truth, I don't remember seeing or processing a single thing. I got out of the truck and walked up to the house, and saw the back door gaping open as if someone had carelessly forgotten to close it. Inside, I was shocked to see, for the first time in my life, my dad shaking and sobbing. In the basement, past the green tile steps, my Uncle Steve washed blood off the wall. There was so much blood, all of it thickened in a dark, red stain that, no matter how forcefully he rubbed, didn't seem to get any smaller. I watched as Uncle Steve kept his eyes riveted to his work, wiping furiously until the center grew larger, spread outward, and finally began to dissolve. I realized that I hadn't known what complete shock felt like until this moment,

My father wept as he told me my mother had been in a car accident and was taken to the hospital. I could tell he was lying, probably because he had never lied to me before. I asked him why Uncle Steve was washing blood off the wall, but he just stuttered and cried more. I went to my room. I didn't feel safe. I was doomed. I assumed things would only get worse. My brother and I shared bunk beds, and as I fell onto the bottom one that was mine, I tried to rationalize everything in my brain, produce an answer for what I'd just seen. My mother lived eight hours more before she died. As I lay there, I prayed and made promises, but I somehow knew she was dead, even while she kept breathing.

My mother didn't die in a car accident. That day, she'd walked down into the basement and shot herself. Throughout my childhood, which she'd made exceptionally happy, I don't remember seeing my mother sad. There was no indication she would do what she did. My mother was beautiful, and whenever people spoke of her they always said how lovely she was. She was a homemaker who sewed her children's clothes from scratch. When I was small, I had very bad feet and a difficult time walking, and she would lift me up and carry me around. It took tremendous patience, physical and emotional strength for my mother to get me through that time. She had a lot of love, and when she left us, it felt completely out of the blue. It didn't sink in that she was gone until the next day, when I answered the phone to hear a man say he was sorry for my loss and would I authorize the donation of my mother's eyes, so someone else could see? I didn't understand what he was asking and I hung up on him mid-sentence. But that was the point that I realized my mother was really gone. I was eight years old.

I didn't go to her funeral. My dad didn't think I could handle it. I was too young, and it had been difficult enough to lose a few pets. I was the type of kid who found a dead bird on the road and made a point to give it a proper burial. My dad did allow me to read the note my mother had left in her delicate blue handwriting, on a plain, white, crumpled piece of paper. It was a short note. I think it said something like, "I'm in a better place." She wanted us to go to church. I don't know what happened to the note, but I can still remember holding it and reading it over and over again, as if it were the most important thing in the world.

Because it was the last thing she'd asked of us, my siblings and I went to Sunday school. I'd been to church before and had learned some things about religion in school. But I didn't know much, and what little I'd been taught hadn't made much sense. Class was held in the basement of Rosemont Church where we recited the scriptures, learned the order of the gospels, and sang songs. Every week our teacher brought us little gifts, things like bookmarks, prayer cards, or stickers. We sat solemnly at long tables and were expected to be serious and studious. Above all, we had to stay silent, something at which I have never been very good.

One day, a quiet, timid boy approached me and summoned the nerve to ask, "Did your mom really shoot herself in the head?" I just looked at him. I couldn't speak, couldn't think anything except that he already seemed sorry for what he had said, very aware he couldn't take any of it back. When I didn't answer, he looked down in embarrassment. Behind him, I noticed three older boys, laughing nervously, trying to shake off the awkwardness that had ruined their joke. I could tell they'd put him up to it. That day in class I would learn that suicide was the worst sin a person could ever commit. It was considered murder, and if you did it, you would go to Hell for all of eternity. That day was my last day at Sunday school.

The idea of my mother burning in Hell gave me nightmares. In the middle of the night, I'd wake up to see a witch watching me from my bedroom door. She wore a black gown that seemed much too large; it completely covered her feet and her hands. She was ugly, hideous, older than any person I had ever met, transparent with a colorful, static quality, like the texture you'd see on a television when it wasn't set to a station. There was a consciousness about her, an energy that mocked me, terrified me. She gave off her own light in a room that was completely dark, but sometimes I could feel her before I saw her. She didn't have a voice, but somehow she'd send me thoughts. She'd project ideas like, "You're such a bad kid," and, "You make me sick." Or she'd repeat the things I'd say in my head. I would see her and think, "Oh shit" and she'd send each word back. I could tell she hated me, and, seeing the look of disgust on her face, I'd literally piss myself with fear. She never blinked, never opened her mouth, never appeared or disappeared; she was just there, unless she wasn't. She hung around for months like this, until one night, I summoned the courage to move toward her, slowly, with one arm extended and the other shielding my eyes. Eventually I made it through her, all the way to the door, and when I turned around, she was gone. She never came back.

I learned that my mom had previously been hospitalized with depression, that she'd had a nervous breakdown once while I was visiting my grandmother. I was told that she just couldn't stop being sad. After she died, the drinking in our house increased tenfold, and during these somber occasions I'd learn small bits about the things my mother had kept secret. It was said that Uncle Roy had signed my mother out of the hospital against her doctor's advice. I listened in on whispered rumors that Uncle Roy had raped my mother and another one of his sisters. I heard he'd given her drugs. After her funeral, I went through her purse and discovered a bunch of pale green, pink, and white capsules. I threw them into the toilet, crying as they dissolved, because it scared me to think someone else could have taken them and wound up killing themselves too. It wasn't hard to piece things together. I believed it when people gossiped that Uncle Roy had blood on his shoes the day my mom died. I could imagine him encouraging her to pull the trigger.

My father couldn't cope with the loss of a wife and sudden single parenthood. His life had been difficult. He lost a sister he adored to leukemia when she was just fourteen. His father, a machine gunner in the Polish army during World War II, had been captured by the Germans and retrained to fight the Russians. The Germans told him if he ever surrendered, the Russians would torture him so badly he'd wish he were dead. When he was in Siberia, his machine gun froze, and he began desperately dousing it in whiskey, trying to loosen it up. The Russians outnumbered him, and they began screaming at him to surrender; he yelled back that he wouldn't succumb to torture. Finally, a Russian soldier attacked him and stuck a bayonet into his skull. He had been shot four times. His life was saved in a Russian hospital, and at the end of the war he was released. But he was left with terrible, chronic pain as a result of his injuries, and he hanged himself in the neighbors' barn when he returned home. My grandmother died less than a year later of cancer. My father had to quit school in eighth grade to help support his family.

My dad started drinking a lot and became, more or less, a functioning alcoholic. He'd done construction work most of his life and he worked hard to take care of us during the week. But every weekend was a party and he would get wasted in such a way that I knew he still hurt over my mother. We had several live-in baby sitters and, occasionally, relatives would help take care of us. All three of my closest childhood friends had fathers who were alcoholics, and we helped each other when things got out of control at one of our homes. I would stay at a friend's place if my dad was too drunk, and they would stay with me if things got a little too dysfunctional with their families.

Throughout the rest of my childhood, Uncle Roy showed up once in awhile. He'd stumble around our house, collecting various discarded bottles of alcohol, so that he could drain the very last drop from each into a terrible looking concoction he'd chug in two or three huge, sloppy gulps. He'd be extremely sick from withdrawal as he tried to gather enough alcohol to stay drunk for just a few more minutes. One morning, I watched him perform this desperate ritual as I got ready for school. He shook and staggered around, clinking with the bottles he clutched to his chest. "Hey," he muttered almost inaudibly, though he was clearly intent on getting my attention. His eyes were bulged and bloodshot, barely focused. "Promise me something," he strained to say, slouching over and slobbering out the sides of his mouth, "Don't ever drink, okay?" I remember thinking to myself that I wished he would just die already. "I won't drink," I said, and, with that, he finished off the last of his homemade sludge and I ran off to school.

I own only one photograph taken of me before my mother died. In it, I seem healthy, alive, and vibrant. When I lost her, I became withdrawn. I hadn't heard of suicide before. It didn't make any sense, and what I couldn't understand left me scared. I was terrified my siblings and I would be put into foster care. Relatives would whisper things over my head. They'd question my father's ability to care for us and offer to take us in. No one ever talked directly to me about the nature of my mother's death. I was never able to grieve properly because I wasn't given the opportunity to make sense out of it. It hurt to see my father suffer, to see my four-year-old little sister left without her mom. It took me a long time to realize what an effect her death had on me. She was the most important person in my world.

When I was ten years old, I discovered a beat up copy of *Helter Skelter*, the bestselling book about Charles Manson and the infamous 1969 Manson Family murders. Its pages found me from a dirty corner in an abandoned house in which I was playing, a rotting, wooden structure, filled with dirt and leaves that had blown in through broken windows lined with shards of glass. The book was cracked and blistered with age, withered and yellowed from sun exposure, and broken in many places along its spine. It smelled rank with mold and mildew.

The first time I opened that book, I knew it was evil. It scared the hell out of me, but I couldn't stay away from it. Every time I tried to read it, I'd have to stop because I'd become sick with anxiety. I knew that I was peering into a very dark unknown and it terrified me to think of what I might find inside. I'd heard on television that Charles Manson was one of the wickedest men alive. His story had scared me, even though, then, Charles Manson seemed confined to the television set. But looking through the pages of the book, staring at his image, I felt compelled to confront him.

At Sunday school, I'd learned about the coming of a false prophet, who would fool everyone by pretending he was Jesus, then ultimately deny salvation. Suddenly, everything started to make sense. Charles Manson was the Antichrist. I was sure of that. I knew from Sunday school that once a person was possessed the only way to save him was to catch him sleeping and pound a stake through his heart. You could see it in his eyes. But you couldn't do that to Charles Manson. I knew he was in prison. He had even been on death row, but somehow they couldn't kill him. Because he could hypnotize people to do whatever he wanted. Just by opening the book, I believed he knew me, and could thus read my mind and brainwash me too. He would try to make me do horrible things. Manson made people shave their heads and commit murder. He had to be evil, because he always made his followers write on the walls in the blood of the people they killed. That was the sign. Charles Manson was my boogeyman.

The most horrifying thing inside *Helter Skelter* was a photo of Charles Manson with a swastika carved into his forehead. It fascinated me to think of how that mark came to be, sliced inside the space between his eyes. I pictured him staring into a mirror, carving the twisted symbol into his own flesh with some makeshift knife he'd shaped by tediously filing the end of a plastic toothbrush to a point. In my imagination, he'd stand there, grinning like the ultimate madman, as drops of blood dribbled down his face and fell with silent plops onto the cold, concrete floor of his prison cell.

I knew about asylums and mental hospitals Surely Charles Manson must have lived in such places. I pictured him pacing on all fours behind bars, like an animal in a cage, surrounded by keepers who would poke him from the outside with sharp sticks, teasing him, tormenting him for their own amusement. I could see him wrapped in a straightjacket in a padded cell, like a doomed insect cocooned in the web of a hungry spider.

He was the Godfather of Madness in all of his glory. Something told me he was the only human being alive with the power to make sense of the pain and darkness in my own life. Somehow he held the key. I never imagined he'd someday share it with me.

the plans

Fear Me!

My background is bastard, maybe, I don't know, lies, fear, confusion, prison, juvenile hall, boy's schools, Catholic reform schools, Father Flanagan's Boys Town, all the different throw away places where nobody's liked or wanted. It's just one big fight going on between everybody doing everything that they can get away with. It's pretty much freedom to its full extent, like total anarchy. What do they call it, iconoclast, something like that? It's kind of like everybody goes for what they know and you learn what you can the best way that you can and try to figure it all out before someone gets to you because, like, you already got nine scars on your left eye and five on your right and one of your ears tore half off and you got a bunch of scars and broken bones. You've been fighting ever since you can remember how to bite and scratch. You've finally whipped everybody in the world and they don't want to submit to you. You tell them do what you're told, and they say no. You say, why not, I did what I was told. You've got to put fear in somebody doing something and then you stand back and look at the fear that you put there and say if you don't do what I tell you to do I'm going to invoke all that.

When I Was Young...

When I was four years old I went to visit my mother in prison. Her brother, my uncle, took me, and I was standing on the tier in front of my mother's cell and she was doing the laundry in the toilet. That's how they do it in prison and I seen she had two big mops in this big cell block, and it was over sixty years ago. And I'm still in the cell block here mopping the floor. Now my body goes up from the bottom up. That's where all the rock chain gang music started. The bottom, everything starts at the bottom and grows up This is why I have so much trouble right now because there are a lot of people that understand that The plant can't survive if you cut the root so what they've done is they've cut the root, they've cut my root, that way I can't grow as well. You know, in other words they've found out that the way to keep me down is to cut me off from going up, but they don't realize that when they do that they're cutting themselves off. But they really don't care because it's a vindictive, like a hate thing, people have going. They accuse you of having the hate and causing the war but actually it's them, it's not you. It's them that's keeping you from doing it that starts the war, keeps the war going. And it was what they are doing to you what they're actually doing to themselves. They'll cut you back across confusion and tell lies and throw your mail in the trash and spray poison in your stuff and cause you trouble and move things around and they think they're doing it to you, but actually, you can't really do anything that don't come back to you.

Well, there's nothing else you can do. You're nine years old and they say you set the school on fire. I say, no I didn't. They say, yes you did, we know you're lying. I say, no I'm not lying, I didn't even know the school was on fire. Yeah, you set the school on fire. We're sending you to juvenile hall. You go to juvenile hall if you set the school on fire. You think you can get away with that? You can't set the school on fire. I said I didn't set the school on fire. Don't tell that lie. He's always lying. You gotta watch this kid, man. He needs to see a doctor. You need a sociologist. I just graduated college and I get paid to help you. I'm helping you with your problem. What's my problem? Well, you're introverted. You've got an inferiority complex. I said, what do you mean? Well you're short and you feel you're not as good as everybody else. I do? He said, yeah. I said, okay. I'm really stupid then. How tall are you? What's that got to do with it? Well, evidently, you got a short man complex because you recognize it in me so it must have been inside of you first, doesn't it? Doesn't everything come from within?

They use to have this one guy in reform school, he had a big magnifying glass and he was always looking for crabs, and he'd get all the kids, all the young men, and take their pants down, then he'd come around with his magnifying glass, and look for crabs, and then all the guys with the big Roscoes all seemed to end up in his residence. I think he was picking out what he wanted to play with. He was kind of a weird man, he used to have a room he called the bear den. Anybody who got packages from home, he'd put them in the bear den, and then pass them out to everyone. He was all real honest, and square with it. He'd call up all the kids to his desk, and give them the keys to open up the bear den, they would open up the bear den, get out the stuff, and pass it to all the kids, then he would lock the bear den down, and it went real cool, real good 'til it got to me. He gave me the keys, and I slipped the key off to the backdoor, and I was gone! I've always been one step ahead of the whole damn thing. I was just trying to get away. That's what I was doing in the desert, trying to figure out how the fuck can I get away from these motherfuckers, I can't stand them, man. My grandmother started that shit you know, everyone started chasing me. I've been running my whole life. I was always running off, stealing everything, every time I got the chance I was on the road. They'd catch me in Iowa, bring me back to Indiana, then they'd catch me in Salt Lake, and take me back to Indiana. Every time you ran away they'd beat your fucking ass, shave your head, work you like a dog. The beatings weren't that bad, 'cause I kept doing it.

11

THE PSYCHIATRIC NURSE

*A*s a child, I loved going to school and I had a lot of great friends. It had always been easy for me to connect with people and I formed a lot of close and diverse friendships with all sorts of kids, like the rockers, the geeks, the jocks, and the bad kids. I was more of a rocker kid myself and I was, and still am, completely in love with music. When I was eight years old, I discovered Kiss and Alice Cooper. I began to devour rock magazines, and soon I knew everything about my favorite rockers. My bedroom walls were plastered with their posters. To me, they were living comic book heroes. I spent every Halloween dressed as either Alice or a member of Kiss. Something about the madness in their music fascinated and moved me. Gene Simmons blew fire and spit blood, and Alice had his head lopped off every night by a guillotine. It was theater, and I loved it.

When I was fourteen, my dad moved the family to a small acreage just outside of Tisdale, a rich, agricultural area in northeastern Saskatchewan. We lived in the middle of nowhere, with the closest neighbor almost a mile away. While I loved nature and being outdoors, this level of isolation was a little too much. I read a lot, wrote letters, and listened to music; those things were my only means of escape. It was quite a culture shock for my siblings and me. I think my father decided to move because he saw his life getting out of control in Regina. But the reasoning behind the relocation didn't extend much past the idea that the grass is always greener on the other side. My dad established a cement business with my uncle, and everything started to look pretty good for all of us. Things slid backward a bit when Dad began working with a few other relatives who liked to drink.

I'd always been a somewhat shy kid, but my new town and my new school gave me a whole new set of reasons to keep quiet. I can remember climbing onto a school bus filled with strange faces and immediately feeling like an outcast. Those kids were neat and clean cut and they stared at the new guy with long hair as though they'd never before seen a kid like me. And they probably hadn't. It seemed wise to grab the empty, isolated seat behind the bus driver. As we sped off, the collective commenced trying to figure out which student could name the most herbicides off the top of his head. I thought, "You are so fucked." And I was.

By the time I reached high school, I'd completely retreated within myself. I would often go to school and return home without saying a word all day. I could go for days in complete quiet, and the longer each silent streak lasted, the more my isolation felt like a game. If I could answer a lecture question with a nod or a shake of the head, if I could contribute my name to the attendance sheet with merely a wave, I felt a huge sense of relief. I truly didn't want to talk to a single student or teacher. I was bullied, ridiculed, and ruthlessly stereotyped. I was clearly depressed. Each night in my dreams, I'd test drive new and terrible ways to kill myself. I'd jump from a building, put a pistol into my mouth, or hang myself from a tree.

Things went that way until I got to grade eleven. I wasn't friends with any of my peers, but the younger kids seemed to gravitate toward me. I was an outcast, and I think they identified with that.

Eventually I came out of my shell and I actually enjoyed going to school. I found amusement in the ways people reacted to me. I have fond memories of my algebra teacher, Mr. Pitzel, completely losing it after seeing a picture that I'd hung in my locker of Blackie Lawless drinking blood from a skull. Mr. Pitzel was one of my most influential teachers; he illustrated what I never wanted to become: a complete asshole. Because I was so quiet, everyone assumed I was addicted to drugs, gay, evil, etc. I was content to let them believe whatever they wished.

When I finished high school, I refused to attend the graduation ceremony, despite incessant requests by the school's principal to reconsider. I explained to him that I didn't really feel any sense of accomplishment; I hadn't forgotten how I was treated when I first started. Because I didn't accept my diploma in cap and gown, the school decided to withhold it from me. To this day, I have no physical proof that I completed grade twelve. As soon as I could escape that time and place, I moved back to Regina, where I have lived ever since.

Back home, it was difficult to find work. I started playing in a band and I refused to cut my hair. Twenty-five years ago, no one would hire a guy with long hair. I ended up taking a job as a dishwasher, because that's all there was. Eventually, I got the chance to apprentice as a pastry chef. I loved to cook, in part because of the eclectic, eccentric group of people attracted to the lure of a sweltering hot, pressure-cooked kitchen. A lot of ex-cons end up working in restaurants, as do musicians, alcoholics, transients. I became friends with a guy named Floyd who would share all kinds of wild stories while he worked at the prep table beside me. He professed a belief in the fine art of robbery and explained that a thief's success depends on a pristine, precise ability to read people. "You need to keep calm and in control," Floyd would say. And so, according to Floyd's philosophy, the most successful robber nurtures the very same quality as the most successful brain surgeon: command of the situation.

While I climbed the ranks in the restaurant business, my older brother began pursuing his education in psychiatric nursing. He had been working construction jobs until he decided he wanted to do something completely different with his life. I supported this decision, and I became fascinated by the stories he'd share. At one point, he told me that, even if I had no desire to pursue a career in psychiatry, the experience of taking classes and learning about myself would prove well worth it. I decided to take his advice, and as I pursued my own education, I fell in love with the field.

For the past fifteen years, I've enjoyed a career as a registered psychiatric nurse. During that time, I've worked in jails, hospitals, and community programs and facilities. I've counseled people suffering with major mental health disorders (schizophrenia, depression, bipolar disorder), as well as murderers, psychopaths, junkies, and sex-offenders. Among the eccentric and the insane, I've met some of the most extraordinary, beautiful people. Through them, I've discovered what a strange teacher life can be, because, often, as the caregiver in a nurse-patient relationship, I am the one who learns the most. Many people associate psychiatry with *Silence of the Lambs* or *One Flew over the Cuckoo's Nest*. But, in truth, mental illness can happen to anyone and it's a lot closer to most people than most people are willing to believe. All of us experience loss, with which we have difficulty coping.

Lots of us are overrun with thoughts that won't let us sleep at night. Horrifying things happen to ordinary people, and tragedy can overshadow the rest of people's lives. I've always known I had much more in common with a psychiatric patient than I had with a president of a bank.

While I completed my education and training, I dreamed of one day working at The Regional Psychiatric Centre in Saskatoon, a secure, forensic mental health hospital operated by Correctional Service Canada. The facility holds some of the most dangerous, criminally insane inmates in the country. Many of the prisoners are legendary psychiatric patients, and so I felt extremely lucky when I achieved a practicum on the women's unit. At the time, Saskatoon had recently received many new, extremely violent inmates transferred from Kingston Penitentiary, and the Saskatoon unit had to be divided in two, separating those inmates who would literally kill each other if they ever got the chance.

Working in Saskatoon, it became clear to me how profoundly people's mental health is influenced by their experiences. The first patient assigned to me was a woman I'll call Mary, a timid, soft-spoken woman in her early thirties, with long black hair and chiseled features. Mary wasn't able to make eye contact with me when we spoke. This habit was common among the unit's other women, most of whom had been victims of atrocious sexual abuse. Diagnoses are difficult, but someone like Mary is more likely to be consumed by "behavioral" problems than by mental illness. She was depressed and anti-social and she suffered with addiction and low self-esteem.

Mary had been a prostitute. She'd pick up men who were drunk because they were clearly the easiest to rob. In seducing them, she would instruct them to remove their clothes and convince them to allow her to tie them up; it would be more fun that way, she'd say. Once she'd secured their hands and feet, she'd take their wallets and leave them, bound and exposed. Once, Mary picked up a man who was not quite as inebriated as she'd hoped. Before she could restrain his last limb, he intuited her plan, broke free, and began to beat her. In defense, she smashed his face with a wine bottle, and when the bottle broke she used the shards to stab and slash his body. Mary told me she couldn't talk to men, she had been abused her whole life, and, even though she thought I was a nice guy, I still scared her. The only thing I could do was thank Mary for her honesty and request a new patient.

I worked with a woman I'll call Ivy full-time for two months straight, and to this day her story remains one of the saddest I've ever known. When I knew her, Ivy was in her late twenties. She was tomboyish and wore her straight black hair short around her plump features, her round cheeks and her tiny, upturned nose. Like Mary, Ivy had worked extensively as a prostitute, and she'd also been abused. She told me that, typically, the more rich and powerful a man was, the more deviant he liked to be. It was completely normal, she said, for a lawyer dressed in a "fancy" suit to pick her up and reveal later that he was wearing women's underwear. Ivy had been incarcerated after her pimp forced her to participate in a botched armed robbery. But she'd been damaged long before then.

Ivy was diagnosed with schizophrenia and she believed she

was possessed by demons. Her body was riddled with wounds, thousands of self-inflicted scars that completely covered her limbs. Ivy had been involved in a cult since she was a small child and she told me gruesome stories about the way she'd acquired the cult's beliefs. As a young girl, she'd once been forced to single-handedly abort a fetus as part of a sacrificial ritual. Ivy told me the baby was "stretched out" on a tree and that, over time, it completely disappeared. When I asked her where it went, she replied, simply, "The birds ate it." Ivy believed that she gained strength by allowing demons to enter her, that the more demons one had the mightier one became. Because she possessed so many demons, Ivy said, she had super powers: mind-reading capabilities, extraordinarily heightened intuition, and immortality. She truly believed that if someone were to shoot her, the bullet would simply hit her and harmlessly drop to the ground.

Ivy wanted to be loved more than anyone I ever met. This quality may have fueled her illness, because her need to please predisposed her to becoming other people's prey. Ivy had a son and she was devastated when he was immediately removed from her at birth and put into care. She would spend hours in her cell just staring at the little boy's picture; I'm pretty sure that photo was the only thing she had left of him. Ivy didn't have any friends or family to speak of. She eventually developed a relationship with her cellmate, but they would often fight viciously and Ivy always got the worst of it. A year or so after I stopped working with her, I was shocked to read about Ivy's death in the newspaper. Late one night, Ivy's lover strangled her and then tried to string her up to make it look as though Ivy had committed suicide.

I met Billy on the medical unit at the Regina Correctional Centre. At first encounter, Billy seemed akin to a hypothetical cross between a vampire and a rabid dog. I had never heard a human being create the kind of noises Billy made. He would spend his days crouched, barefoot and shirtless, on the table that was the only piece of furniture in his prison cell. He was emaciated and it was painful to look at the bones protruding from his chest. From his perch, he would howl, hiss, and mutter obscenities. Needless to say, Billy was an incredibly angry young man; he'd been sentenced to six months for ripping the family cat in half and eating it in front of his foster parents. They were completely traumatized, and needed extensive therapy after the event.

My first attempts to communicate with Billy were met with a series of sharp *fuck offs*. It took a great deal of time and persistence on my part, but eventually he came around. Once he asked if I could bring him an elastic band for his hair, and when I did I was shocked to see how appreciative he was of such a simple gesture. I learned that Billy's biological family was beyond dysfunctional and that Billy had been the victim of horrific abuses. Billy's foster parents had taken him in with the best intentions, but Billy was too far gone by the time they received him. After the cat incident, they were unable to allow him back into their home.

Somewhere, deep inside Billy, there was a frightened little kid. He hated to let this part of himself show through, but I could see it clearly while he wrestled with all of the horrible memories from his past. Billy told me that his older brother had killed his father before he ended up killing himself. Many of the prisoners at the Correctional Centre had witnessed countless suicides and yet they still stuck around, dysfunctional, ill, and angry, but surviving. I rarely wonder why some people kill themselves; it's those that don't I find fascinating.

I eventually moved on to work at the Regina Mental Health Clinic, where I've been part of the crisis response team for the past ten years. Billy became one of my first patients at my new job. He was homeless at that point, and finding him a place to live was next to impossible because, well, he scared the hell out of everyone. My experiences with patients have taught me that psychiatry is just as personal as it is clinical. I've formed many close relationships with my patients. I care about them, and my desire to help them doesn't cease with the end of my workday or their release from a facility. A lot of the way I understand a person can't be pinned down to his or her diagnosis, or life story, or even the way he or she speaks or behaves. I can remember driving Billy around, and literally feeling this intense energy coming out of him. I'd tell him, "Calm down, man. I can feel you over here." He'd always laugh. At that point, Billy was back into solvents. He had a girlfriend who was extremely malnourished, wide eyed, and had such awful tremors from sniffing lacquer thinner that she could hardly walk. I can still see Billy pushing her around in a shopping cart; all they had was each other. I helped Billy and his girlfriend get bus passes. He loved riding buses, spent all day transferring from one to another. When Billy went missing one day, everyone assumed he was dead. But three or four months later, he called me from a shelter in Ontario. He wanted to let me know he was all right. He said I was his only real friend, and he believed the right way to treat a friend was to let him know when you're okay. I never heard from him again.

There is often truth to madness, and mental illness is largely the process by which people attempt to make sense of their relationships with their environments. Many patients struggle to overcome their pasts, and yet many more need help coming to terms with the present. Every week I get calls at work from elderly people who believe they are being poisoned. Their bodies are breaking down, their short-term memories are deteriorating, and when it becomes too difficult to accept these changes as part of the aging process, many people create myths in their minds to explain what is happening to them. And so the ninety-year-old man who habitually misplaces his glasses may eventually become convinced that his neighbor breaks into his house and moves them around out of spite.

I worked for a time with a retired foreman who was known simply as "The Captain." He had a very old fashioned sense of sophistication and throughout the entire ten years I knew him he wore the same suit jacket every day, a sort of self-imposed uniform. The Captain had been emotionally wrecked when he was arrested and charged with trying to break into a building. He told me that he had lived in the same city his whole life and was single-handedly responsible for the town's growth and expansion in the previous twenty years, and that he would never attempt to commit such a crime. I asked him how he could achieve so much by himself, and he explained that, even though he was "retired," he was busier than ever, telepathically transmitting plans to the mayor's office or various construction companies and keeping tabs on each organization's schedule to ensure all projects were completed on time. He told me that if a house was ready to have its foundation poured, he would use his mind to instruct the cement company to send in the cement trucks. For years before he was arrested, The Captain walked through town, checking local businesses to ensure they were locked and secured. He took great pride in his work.

I got called in to assess Sarah, a retired schoolteacher, whose house had been completely overrun by mice. There were hundreds of them, scurrying through the walls and the ceilings, leaving behind enough droppings to coat the floors. When I told Sarah that this was no way to live, she didn't appear the least bit perturbed. "Ah, what's a few mice?" she said. "They're not bothering anyone." On the way to the hospital, Sarah confided in me that she had been buying large bags of peanuts to feed the mice because, to her, they were pets. Once, Sarah asked me if I wanted any life advice. When I told her I was always looking for advice, she solemnly suggested, "Never think your co-workers are your friends, because when you retire, they'll all go away, and you'll have no one." In light of Sarah's situation, her point was well taken.

I began receiving calls from concerned neighbors about a woman who'd flail her arms about for hours in front of her apartment window. She'd been performing the ritual regularly for months, so when I visited her home to do a mental health assessment, I was curious about what I'd find. I discovered that Dianne had been retired for several years. She'd been a telephone operator her entire adult life and she was extremely proud of a plaque she'd earned in honor of her exceptional service. She told me the story about how she'd been presented the award by the premier of the province at her retirement. It was her favorite story, and she'd recite it without fail each time I visited. Dianne had been standing on a small foot stool at eight o'clock every evening, and for the following three hours, she would direct traffic, coordinate all the lights, and send her energy out to ensure everyone's safety. She considered these hours her shift and she took her job very seriously. During one visit, I noticed Dianne was wearing an elaborately knitted sweater, constructed of beautiful, thick stitches. I asked her where she got it and she told me she'd made it when she was younger, before she forgot how to knit at all. She invited me to look at all the other sweaters she'd made and as I handled all the luxurious garments I noticed each had a major department store tag stitched onto the back.

Sometimes, the origin of a person's mental illness isn't traceable to a tragic set of circumstances or a sudden loss of purpose. During fifteen years counseling patients and inmates, I've encountered all sorts of obsessions, delusions, and hallucinations. And I've become desensitized to things that most people would find profoundly disturbing. The first time I talked to a man about the voices he was hearing in his head, I was completely blown away. Now, a lot of the outrageous fury and lunacy I experience becomes ultimately just part of a day's work, to be filed away in the dark recesses of my memory. I've met people who swear they've seen Jesus. I've met people who believe they *are* Jesus. And even more who believe *I'm* Jesus.

I'm often asked, "Who is the craziest person you've ever known?" Back then, I would have immediately recalled a man known, infamously, as "The Claw." I never could have prepared myself to encounter such a person because, in most ways, The Claw didn't resemble anything remotely human. The Claw was in his fifties, round and balding. He had an extremely odd-shaped, spherical skull, which sat on his shoulders in the absence of any significant stretch of neck. His ears were large and prominent, like an animal's, and his face was masked by a mass of thick, gnarled scars. I am almost certain he hadn't bothered to look at his reflection in the previous few decades; if he had, I'm positive he would have scared himself.

His mannerisms were oddly timid for such a frightening figure He kept his head slung low, and would peep up from beneath his brow only when addressed. Even then, only half of his expression would be apparent, because his left eye always remained closed. The Claw's behavior, of course, was significantly more bizarre than his countenance. Most of the staff members and inmates at the Regina Correctional Centre had fantastic stories about The Claw, because he had attained mythological status, even living among some of the strangest people alive. He drank solvents, cleaning products, really anything he could get his hands on. And he would eat everything he could put into his mouth: coins, pens, measuring spoons. If you happened to leave your car keys within his reach, The Claw would somehow manage to swallow them in seconds.

The Claw's most distinguishing feature had earned him his nickname. His hand had been severely disfigured in an incident during which he'd held an unwilling Rottweiler by the tail and licked the dog's genitals while masturbating. The dog was desperate to get away and resorted to chewing off most of his molester's hand and arm in order to free himself. What remained of the limb was fashioned into a makeshift appendage that strongly resembled a claw.

The Claw was an extremely high-risk individual. He couldn't be trusted unsupervised, by himself or with others. He was kept in a locked room, with a small rectangular window, through which he had to be checked on every fifteen minutes. Despite this rigorous monitoring system, he somehow managed to get hold of a plastic knife, and with the flimsy utensil he cut off his penis, spraying blood all over his cell. He put the severed appendage on the end of his index finger and began showing it off like a finger puppet. The Claw seemed really happy then, very satisfied with his achievement.

The clinical definition of psychiatric nursing is "therapeutic use of self." In hindsight, I clearly see how I ended up in psychiatry. I've always found it easy to connect with people. Establishing a connection requires giving someone your complete attention, without judgment. That is all you have to do; it's that simple. I've always been interested in people, thankful and humbled by the diverse men and women who have let me into their lives. There is an intimacy to what I do, a connection, and a higher level of sharing. Unlocking the secret to understanding psychiatric patients is actually about suspending the need to help them. The goal is to empower people, so that they can gain enough strength to carry themselves through their own pain. To give your complete attention to a person as he or she exists is the greatest gift you can give. It can be enough to change everything.

I believe anger brought me to psychiatry. I've always advocated for the "underdog" and I hated watching people suffer, it made me angry. That great poet and philosopher Johnny Rotten once said, "Anger is an energy." and I believe that anger lead me to psychiatry, that was the motivating force. I've always advocated for the "underdog" and I hated watching people being taken advantage of. I couldn't stand seeing people suffer, or watch them being abused, it made me angry. At the deepest level, there is a spiritual element to every relationship, and within the realm of my relationships with my patients, I have truly been tested. I've worked with people who have done things so sick and vile, people for whom any other sane human would wish death, people who have no redeeming qualities, people who don't seem to be people at all. I've looked into eyes that reveal nothing, eyes that scare the rest of the world. But all of these people were innocent children once, before something descended on their sanity. The innocent parts may be gone forever, but I can't forget that they were once there.

I've met some of the most extreme, intense, complex people on the planet. But neither these individuals nor their stories could remotely prepare me for the most complicated encounter of my life. I was about to become friends with Charles Manson.

...nels + chose to Low
...tay coal + not gift...
...the subjugated p...
...in to all that do or...
...ing to prove they me in...
...s — I see your photo...
...but you realize c...
...T FROM under a t...
...45T Commitments ar...
...rdin Bond + Bond in...
...in Chambers of Cour...
OUTLAW say + p...
...exein us juluy + homa...
...LAW Croak + Go...

They Represent the Law?!

I'm 1967 in Frisco from Alcatraz; this was during the hippie trip. There used to be Bohemians, and they were "hip" 'cause they were shooting dope in the hip, and that's what they call hippie. I was standing on the corner with a gun in my pocket. I'm not playing. I'll do whatever it takes to survive. Don't go messing with me. I'm going to do whatever I do. Now I see this woman on the street corner, this guy comes along and I see she got a baby in her arms and he just knocks her down. The baby falls in the gutter. He throws her dress up, goes up in her, fucks her, wipes his dick off on her dress, and walks on down the road. The cop's standing there on the street corner. I said "Hey man." He said, "Yeah?" I said, "Why didn't you do something about that?" He said, "Well a lot of political pressure around here. I'm not going to get involved." I said, "Oh, is that right? I just got out of prison, man. I got put into prison for doing less than that, been there for years and you're letting that happen." I said, "Well, man, you're supposed to be the father figure here, man, you're supposed to be looking out for these people." He said, "They're not my children, my children are at home, if they didn't want to get raped then they should stay at home. If they get raped, that's good, maybe they'll go home then."

He wasn't doing his job. He didn't give a fuck about those people. For me, I say, well, I can do something about it, but I'll end up going to prison, and the people that I help would end up pointing the finger at me. So, I mean, there is nothing I can do without me sacrificing my life, and I said, you know, I've already done most of my life in prison, why should I go to prison to save somebody's chastity, you know, getting raped, they can just wipe that off. Sex to me is no big trip, I don't feel that someone got violated, and it's a terrible thing, I just thought clean it off, that's all that is. So, I don't have any moral convictions in that respect. I do have a thing if a person gets paid to protect somebody from being hurt by somebody else, that's something they should do. People that turn their backs on somebody that's being abused, and they don't help, when it's their turn to be abused, they ain't got no bitch coming.

They're doing wrong and they know they're wrong and they don't want it to catch up with them. They know it's coming for them but they just don't know how, how to deal with it. That's why they're always trying to get me. Like getting me is going to stop it. What it is, is what they put in motion. Do you understand that? People put stuff in motion against themselves and then they turn around and say it's somebody else that's making it happen. There's nobody else that's making it happen. They're making it happen to themselves. As long as the law, the people representing the law, as long as they abide by the law they represent, they're in a safe zone, nobody has any power over them, but when they break the law and they're representative of the law then they have the outlaw that's going to get them. If you go to work and you sin against somebody else, like, I'll give you an example. A guy becomes a correctional officer and he comes in and he reads an inmate's mail and he finds out that his wife doesn't like homosexuals. So his wife comes to visit and he's in the visiting room and he sees the wife and the wife has got a young daughter. He likes the young daughter and the wife so he locks the kid up and when the next visit comes he says, "I'm sorry, your husband was caught in a homosexual activity."

She gets mad, and he says, "Your husband's life is at stake, I'll meet you at the hot dog stand and I'll explain it to you, but I may lose my job if I get caught doing this because I'm taking a chance." So the woman goes over to the hot dog stand and the cop picks her up in his car and says her husband was caught sucking on somebody else and he's been a faggot all down the line. So she cuts him loose and starts going out with the cop and the guy hangs himself in the cell when his wife sends him a Dear John letter... that really happened, that happens every day, you know, it happens all the time. That's all this is. All you're hiring these people to do, they come in, they're not coming in here as fine men upholding the law. They're doing anything they can get away with; only thing that's holding them is that they know they'll get their goddamn throats cut if they fuck around too much, man. If they do it too much then somebody is going to step out from somewhere and stab them to death, that's what's going to happen to them. You can't get away with this shit. You get away with it for so long and it's going to catch up with you. You're no better than anybody else, just because you're highway patrol.

If you're highway patrol and you're molesting people on the way to school, one of the parents is going to get upset when their little girls come back with blood all over their dresses. That's what I learned in Mexico. In Mexico, if you transgress against another man's family and he comes and he takes your life, they don't take him to trial. They give him an apology for the behavior of an asshole that didn't abide by the rules and regulations that he should have abided by. Then if you come up and you won't snitch, the Mexican cops will beat your motherfuckin' ass and make you tell. They'll hook you up to electronics and bury you in shit, if necessary. You're gonna get right, or get wrong, so it's just the same thing. It should be like that everywhere but it's not. You come across the border; they're rats on this side of the fucking line, man. It's one big fucking snitch-out. When I got back from Mexico I was put in prison for white slavery, and smuggling guns, and, uh, unlawful flight to avoid prosecution. I was sent to federal prison for ten years, and she filed for divorce. We wasn't even married, but they granted her the divorce. Remember when Nixon jumped up and said, "Manson is guilty?" Well, that's because he was standing in that divorce court, because he was riding on my criminal court. A lot of people don't know the way a court works. See, the civil court and the divorce court run on the criminal court. Different chambers of justice, and honor, run like upside down, and backwards.

III

NOTHING TO LOSE

These days, I'm employed as part of a crisis response team, performing emergency outreach work for the mental health clinic in my city. I do a lot of community assessments and take a lot of phone calls, most of them from people who are overwhelmed, anxious, or depressed. In these cases, it's my job to reacquaint patients with the present, help them prioritize their lives, and encourage them to work through their troubles. Many people tend to live in anticipation, agonizing over what may happen next in their lives, obsessed with that over which they have no control. In simplest terms, people suffering with anxiety are consumed by thoughts of the future. Those overwhelmed by depression often dwell too much on the past. Of course, some find themselves tossed back and forth between the two, preoccupied with the past, in constant dread of the pending.

The longer you perform crisis work, the less you perceive people's circumstances to be problematic. It becomes easier to see that everything is the way it is, because that's the way it is. And you come to recognize a sort of perfection in the way life exists, in the acceptance of the things that can't be changed. You come to appreciate the power of a simple shift in perception, realize that if only people could see things from a slightly different angle, many dilemmas would cease to exist. You learn to assess problems without regarding them as such, because in naming something a problem, you give it power. Acceptance is the most difficult thing to achieve, but my work has taught me it's most vital to life.

A few years ago, my life was lined up perfectly. I was in love with an amazing girl, I had the best friends in the world, and my band, Plastic Bastard, was working on doing a Canadian tour with my hero, Alice Cooper. I remember at the height of my happiness driving back from seeing the Groovie Ghoulies in Saskatoon with my friend Brian. The Ghoulies were one of our favorite bands and they even let us write up their set list that night. With Brian fast asleep in the passenger seat, I drove under some low lying fog and felt alive, energized. Through the fog, I witnessed the brightest falling star I'd ever seen. But as I thought about making a wish, I felt a twinge of dread that everything good was going to change.

I have a deep love for everything odd, especially those gems once possessed by my idols. It's easy to see, then, why eBay has become one of my favorite time killers. I've collected artifacts owned and worn by my heroes since I was a kid. When I was nine or ten years old, my Uncle Ernie used to take my friends and me to Stampede Wrestling matches, where we'd try to meet all the wrestlers and ask them to sign our programs. When I got into music, I'd jump at the chance to see the bands that toured through my city, especially those that hosted in-store record signings. I began accumulating autographs scrawled on records, photos, set lists, anything to which you can take a pen. I probably own well over a thousand signatures.

I own clothing worn by Kiss, Alice Cooper, Randy Rhoads, Kurt Cobain, The Ramones, and Hank Williams, and there is a story behind each piece I've acquired. I own a lounging robe worn by Marilyn Monroe, a garment she generously gave to a maid who complimented her on how beautiful she looked in it. I own three of the locks Houdini used to train for his elaborate underwater escapes. I've amassed quite a few exotic movie props—swords and shields from great epic Hollywood productions, like Ben-Hur and The Ten Commandments. My home is a tribute to these legends, a cross between a Ripley's museum and a Hard Rock Cafe.

While surfing eBay one day, I came across a vendor selling some of the more select celebrity items I've discovered on the Internet: a shirt that had supposedly been worn by Elvis Presley, a snip of James Dean's pubic hair, and several letters and postcards from Charles Manson. Even by my standards, these things were pretty fucked up. I couldn't believe the authenticity of the listings, so I emailed the seller to ask how he'd obtained such unique items. In no time, he wrote back and assured me that he knew all the people whose relics he sold, that he was writing a memoir about his Hollywood relationships. He wanted to pass these artifacts on to someone who would appreciate them. He was also hoping to earn a few extra bucks to buy an urn for the ashes of his beloved terrier, which had recently passed away.

The seller wrote that he had limited Internet access and asked me for my address so he could explain his story more efficiently. Fascinated, I complied, and a week later I received a neatly typed, sixteen-page letter from Donald Taylor, a man who claimed to have had sex with more than five thousand men, among them Elvis Presley, James Dean, Lenny Bruce, Orson Wells, and Charles Manson. In his letter, Donald went into great detail about his escapades; his story was completely over-the-top. Interestingly, he also mentioned he had been friends with Betty Grable and Marilyn Monroe. Donald's package included his phone number, and the first time I called him, our conversation lasted well over two hours. Of course this was, according to most people's standards, a strange and somewhat suspicious introduction to a very strange and suspicious man. Donald was eager to talk to me, perhaps a little too eager. I believe that timing is everything, and so he wrote, and I called, and he met me when he had finished writing his memoir without a clue how to publish it.

I found Donald fascinating; he possessed a wealth of information and told the most amazing stories. During one phone conversation, Donald told me his existence was sort of "serendipitous." He said he had worked his whole life in the service industry and, thus, met many celebrities. Since he was "a world class slut," he took whatever opportunities he could to meet and mingle with the stars; he was essentially a groupie. Donald relayed his story in a soft-spoken, southern accent. His facts were consistent and extremely specific. I got the impression that he was pretty lonely, which seemed to make sense for a man who had attempted to associate almost exclusively with famous figures, now all either dead or distanced. Donald loved to talk about his adventures and he seemed thankful I was such a receptive, interested audience. He assured me that he knew his story sounded unbelievable and that he had trouble believing it himself.

I then learned that Donald had found a San Francisco publisher interested in releasing his memoir, minus the material surrounding his relationship with Manson. Donald refused to scrap the Manson story because he believed that Manson was one of the most important and influential people he'd ever met. When we began communicating with each other, Donald promised to send a completed manuscript to me in no time at all. He was counting on my opinion. And three weeks after that conversation, I received a package from him in the mail.

I began reading the enclosed manuscript immediately, but I

could get only about four or five pages in. I was stunned to find that the book was composed almost exclusively of some of the most disturbing, poorly written gay porn anyone could possibly imagine. The author's voice seemed in stark contrast to the personality I had talked to so extensively on the phone. In the letter he sent me, Donald talked about the general nature of his relationships and the impact they'd had on his life. But his book was geared only toward shock value, filled with tasteless, graphic accounts of incest, coprophagia, and rape that functioned to disturb instead of enlighten.

While Donald's manuscript was a disappointment, his correspondence with Manson was fascinating. Don sent me several letters, postcards, and photos he'd received from his infamous friend. He hoped that, since I worked in psychiatry, I would find them "interesting." He'd tried in vain to sell the items together on eBay, hoping to acquire "at least" fifty dollars for everything. But eBay pulled the auction before anyone could bid, citing strict guidelines around selling "murderobilia."

To hold Manson's writing in my hands, the paper he'd handled and entrusted with his most personal thoughts, was nothing short of amazing. It felt as if the letters had been lifted from another time and place; Manson had written them from his jail cell, a world contained within a world I could hardly imagine. Atop the stack of letters sat a postcard with a picture of a Gambel's quail on the front. I carefully turned it over and read the first words:

"Always is always, always and that's forever in ALL WAYS."

I let the words resonate in my brain. That line had the qualities of a riddle: tempting, taunting. "Always is always,

always": a circular arc of thought, which ran like an idea falling onto itself. The subtle word play intrigued me; it seemed more like wisdom than nonsense. I read on:

"Whenever I think of what you think you are, and are not – I could never say more, because you already know why, and never less because you're on that side of the top, under and around the all of all ways and forever even when I don't spell it or tell it – it's in my own words."

I was struck by the lyricism of these lines and the immensity of the ideas they contained, like the thought that one person could read another's mind. I've met mystics who have experienced themselves as everything and perceived life as happening for them instead of to them. I wanted to pass Manson's ideas off as the products of sheer insanity, but they seemed so thoughtfully, deliberately cryptic that I couldn't dismiss them.

Naturally, I had assumed that anything written by Charles Manson would be written out of anger. But as I read through the stack of letters, I was shocked to find no trace of the fury I had come to associate with the notorious face. I had perceived Manson to be misanthropic; I believed that he truly hated people. But, if this were true, it would make no sense for Manson to write letters at all. I realized how little I knew about him. I began researching and reading other things Manson had written, keeping in mind that the man had a grade three education and had spent most of his life in prison, most of his life sentence in solitary confinement. As I learned more, I started to realize how complex Manson was. I wanted to explore how ideas, which sound so philosophical, could come forth from the mind of a guy who referred to himself as a "stupid hillbilly," a man the rest of the world deemed criminally insane. His words seemed like carefully constructed answers to some of life's most difficult and complicated questions, yet they were free-written, at the spur of a moment, according to whim. I got the sense that the heaviness, the density of his writing came naturally; it was simply the only way he could communicate with anyone.

The post card was signed "Gone, EASY."

Marilyn Manson once said, "When you are alone, you write; when you have friends, you form a band." This is exactly what I have experienced in my own life, exactly what I have witnessed others experience in theirs. It's useful to add that writers and musicians are, for the most part, not exactly the most stable people. It takes a certain level of abandonment to create meaningful art. So, it's easy to see why, when you work in psychiatry, you encounter an incredible amount of creative expression. I've seen a lot of extremely bizarre pieces of writing throughout my career. I was once asked by a psych patient to "hand deliver" an elaborate scroll he had constructed, complete with a red ribbon, to the Queen. The calligraphy on this piece was amazing. I've seen five-page mathematical equations intended to illustrate the nature of the universe. I worked with one man who wrote complete books of poetry and left them in the local library's after-hours drop box. He was frustrated because he couldn't understand why the work he submitted wasn't being published and stocked on the shelves. When I inquired about him, the confused librarians showed me a large stack of his manuscripts, which they had compiled over the previous few years. They had no idea what to do with it.

One of my schizophrenic clients, Barry, completely rewrote the Bible in his own hand writing eight times; he was halfway through his ninth edition when I met him. He was well enough to receive treatment at home, but he was often non-compliant, so he was placed on a community treatment order, which legally obliged him to receive an injection of antipsychotic medication every two weeks. My job was to follow him into the community and give him his injections when they were required. As we got acquainted, he told me he found his work peaceful, that the process gave him better insight into the word of God. He was completely obsessed. The only thing that mattered to him was that he had enough paper and ink to work on his writings. He would often isolate himself, forget to eat, grow weak, and deteriorate. His manuscripts filled boxes upon boxes, stacked on top of each other on almost every surface in his apartment. When I accepted a new job, I took a trip to his home to say goodbye and wish him well. He opened the door, looked at me, and then quickly glanced at the baseball bat in the corner before returning his gaze to my face. I made a quick exit, and Barry landed himself back in the hospital.

I showed Manson's letters to my friend and colleague Dr. Kumar, a psychiatrist. He described the letters as "disjointed and nonsensical," and even though he was unable to utilize them in making a diagnosis, he felt that Manson must suffer from some sort of psychotic disorder. As I became increasingly acquainted with things Manson had written, I was reminded more and more of a particular patient with whom I'd had the privilege of working.

It's been about five years since I've seen Dwayne; he eventually ended up in long-term care, a sort of group home setting. He was a brilliant man, an engineer, but he suffered what is commonly known as a "nervous breakdown" when his wife left him. He couldn't cope, and his life started to fall apart, most visibly at work. His colleagues tried to compensate for the deficit in his performance, but it eventually became too obvious that Dwayne wasn't well, and they had to take him to the hospital. Dwayne didn't respond well to psychiatric medications. On them, he would arch back like David Lee Roth, a fixed grimace on his face, and bellow so violently that sometimes he couldn't catch his breath.

I can still remember watching him write from the table in his hospital room, papers everywhere. I would often have to wait a few extra minutes for him to finish. He wrote on any and every surface available, mostly messages about what it meant for people to be kind to one another. He often put words together in ways that made no apparent sense, yet sometimes the combinations just clicked, and, after reading a particularly lyrical phrase, I would sometimes find myself thinking, "This would be the perfect name for a band."

It is very difficult to accept being diagnosed with a mental health disorder. Very rarely do people with mental illness seek help. When they do, it is normal for patients to start a prescription, begin feeling better, stop taking their medication, and relapse. A lot of this has to do with the terrible side effects associated with these medications. I can remember going to the psychiatric unit to take Dwayne out on a pass for a cup of coffee. Dwayne had just received his medication, and the nurse had to make sure he took some water with his pills because Dwayne was an expert at "cheeking" them. Immediately after, Dwayne excused himself to go to the washroom. Outside the door, I could hear him hacking and coughing. I knew what he was up to. When he came out, I asked him if he'd taken his medication. He looked at me, confused. "Of course not," he said. "What do you think I am – crazy?"

People with mental illness or emotional problems often have difficulty explaining their experiences; it is hard for them to find someone in which to confide, someone who understands them. So I often encourage patients to journal in order to express what they would ordinarily internalize about their illnesses. But Manson's writings, like Dwayne's, were completely devoid of any acknowledgment of mental illness. Both of their writings functioned, not as coping mechanisms, but as tangible discourse with a world they expected to receive and appreciate their ideas, even though their values differed starkly from those commonly held by most people. My fondest memory of Dwayne stems from his return to the psychiatric unit after being away on a pass. In his hand he held a fresh, crisp, brand new five-dollar bill. He asked the nurse at the desk if he could use the pencil sharpener, something he'd done at least a dozen times before. When granted permission, Dwayne rolled the bill up, tightly, pressed it into the pencil sharpener, and watched as the machine ground the money into fuzzy bits of green dust.

Even more incredible than Manson's letters was the feeling that their content lent much weight to Donald's story. I trusted that the two did indeed know each other on an intimate level. I couldn't believe I had made such a connection by chance, and I wouldn't believe the extreme places that connection would take me. Life was about to take off on the crazy train, because as my friendship with Donald developed, everything else began to fall apart.

When I told my girlfriend Sheila about Manson's letters, she wasn't impressed. In complete disgust, she said, "I can't believe you'd allow something like that in your house! What's wrong with you?" I was taken aback by her reaction. "It's not like I bought a Gacy painting," I said. "Manson never actually killed anyone." I reminded Sheila that I worked in psychiatry and so I naturally found Manson fascinating. She was silent. I knew Sheila would be dumping me soon, and the thought was devastating. Things had been falling apart for a while, and the closer I tried to get, the farther she pushed away.

Sheila was the most important person in my life; we had worked together for years and we were great friends. We had started spending a lot of time together while she was going through a really rough breakup with someone else. She was fun to be with, and so fucking cute; I could hardly handle it. It was an awkward transition, but after a year or so, we ended up in a relationship. She had two amazing daughters and she was a great mother. One of her girls was an aspiring writer, and the other one was a rocker who just loved music. I never had the opportunity to tell them how much they meant to me.

I was hardly myself those days. My friend Dave died from cancer and his brother Danny, my best friend and roommate of seven years, also died from cancer, six weeks later. Shortly after I lost these important people, Sheila gave me the "It's not you; it's me" speech, and said she needed some space. Basically, she had found someone else. It was too much.

Danny and I had been in several bands together over the years.

Almost daily, for as long as were roommates, we'd end up in our basement, making noise. He was a drummer, and I was sort of learning how to play guitar. We promoted and set up shows for hundreds of bands; our lives completely revolved around music. It was normal for us to catch bands four or five nights a week and Dave was usually right out there with us. Both Danny and Dave toured with bands, selling merchandise, and doing whatever promotional work they could. Dave was starting to turn his love of music into a career, touring with international bands like Into Eternity and Edguy. He never learned how to play an instrument, but his friends wanted to take him out on tour anyway. It was impossible to go to a show and not run into Danny or Dave; they were always there.

After both were diagnosed with cancer, I wanted to do a benefit in their honor. But they resisted. I reminded them how many benefits they'd done, how many bands they'd helped out, how everyone now wanted to do something for them. Every local band wanted to participate and our newspaper carried a front-page story about the event. When the show finally took place, Dave had died and Danny was very sick. Danny was able to make it to the show, and watching him give his final goodbyes to those closest to him broke my heart. It was the last show my band ever played and the hardest set I have ever had to get through. Emotionally, I felt completely drained. I gave up on music midway through recording my band's second album. I had made it through the vocals of eight of our fourteen songs when my voice just left me. We never did finish that record.

It's difficult to get help when you're in the helping profession, not that I was looking for it. I'd never felt so lonely, so compelled to dive into that loneliness and make sense out of what I was feeling. I experienced myself as disconnected, displaced. I'd become a textbook case of depression. I never considered stepping outside of myself and asking for help; I believed that what I was experiencing was only grief, part of a natural process we all find ourselves in sooner or later. Danny and Dave were both younger than me, and their deaths functioned as a wakeup call in my life. I became acutely aware that we're here for a very short time.

Eventually, a couple of my colleagues sat me down and told me I should seriously consider taking a leave from work. I tried to argue, but they were right, and I knew it. My work demands a certain level of focus, of which I didn't possess much. It was hard for me to connect with anyone, or feel any empathy after losing so many of the most important people in my life. I had thought about taking some time off, but I never did. Sitting around the house was the last thing I wanted to do; I needed to keep busy.

Danny was a super guy. Lots of our friends toured, and the only time we'd see them is when they'd stay over, it was pretty routine to have band people crashed all over our house. Before Danny passed away, one of his friends, Buck, found himself sort of homeless after his girlfriend kicked him out. Danny asked me if it would be all right if Buck stayed at our place for a few weeks, until he "got his shit together." Those few weeks turned into a few years, and even now I highly doubt that Buck has his shit together.

Buck is a brilliant graphic artist, who worked meticulously for hours in front of his computer, fine-tuning the details of a CD cover, or perfecting some other project. He is an extremely talented artist and he had a ton of great ideas. Buck is pretty scattered, and it's difficult for him to follow through with anything. I was grateful to have him around, though. He was the only guy I knew who would go along with some of the crazy things happening in my life.

When I told Buck about Donald Taylor, he thought it would be great if we all entered into a business partnership together. We decided to create a website and sell Donald's manuscript as an eBook entitled One Gay Man. Almost immediately after the launch of the book and the website, we were contacted by Howard Stern's people; they wanted Donald on his show.

Buck and I decided to accompany Donald to the Howard Stern taping in New York City, and we brought along a few friends to help film a documentary about the trip. We shot in NYC, Tennessee, Los Angeles, and Las Vegas, but we never produced anything from that footage – for good reason.

Howard said that none of his other guests had "ever said so much." At the end of Donald's interview, which chronicled his alleged exploits with Hollywood's crowded closet, Howard asked him if he would be willing to take a lie detector test to prove his story. Donald was startled. "No," he said; he didn't care if people believed him or not. By the time Donald made his way back to the green room, he was completely flushed, as if he were in shock. He wanted to leave, immediately. We had planned to stick around until the end of the show and then go for drinks. I was choked to leave so soon, because Perry Farrell, one of my favorite songwriters, was one of the show's other guests. I'd always wanted to meet him.

I'd begun to doubt Donald's story. His ability to recall details repeatedly in exactly the same way eroded his believability. His stories began to feel like speeches, and his speeches began to sound like scripts. He was also starting to fall too deeply in love with the limelight, turning into a bit of a diva. Our documentary was not successful; Donald wasn't able to act at all natural, so the crew gave up and wrote the project off as an adventure. Donald left us a few days earlier than expected.

Since I had some extra time in my itinerary, I tried to get in touch with Szandora and Stanton LaVey. My band had approached Szandora about doing an album cover and had been completely thrilled when she accepted. At the time, she was one of the top fetish models in the world. Certain people have an energy that runs a lot deeper than beauty and Szandora is one of those people. Stanton LaVey, then her husband, is the grandson of Anton LaVey, founder of the Church of Satan and author of the Satanic Bible.

I was able to get in touch with Stanton first, and he told me that everything was messed up, that he and Szandora were going through a divorce. We met for drinks at El Coyote in Los Angeles, a landmark Mexican restaurant that's been around since the '30s. As we sat down, Stanton told me this was the restaurant where Sharon Tate ate her last meal. He explained that, every year on the evening of "the murders," he and his friends gathered there. The tradition had become a holiday of sorts.

I couldn't get past how much Stanton looked like his grandfather. Like most kids who were into heavy metal, I was introduced to Anton's philosophy and the Satanic Bible in high school. Stanton told me he was "born into evil." I got the impression that he was a complex character, very intense. I could philosophize with the guy for hours on end about pop culture, music, and art. We hit it off. He had very strong opinions and he was passionate about his beliefs. I liked that. Stanton had a confidence about him, his own unique brand of charisma. He told me that the three most influential people in pop culture were Anton LaVey, William Burroughs, and Charles Manson. Anton LaVey and Charles Manson had been friends. Stanton told me that one day he would share their secrets with me.

Death

Death Row

When you're on death row, there's a bell in the chapel that rings every day, and after you're there for a couple of years, you begin to realize the bell you hear every day never ends. Nothing begins and nothing ends, it goes on forever. It's like a big sound wave going out into the universe. It's really weird, everybody wanted me dead, isn't that far out? They were lined up spitting on me, going through all my things. I went to death row. Do you know what they told me? "We don't want you out here, don't come out here, don't come on the row." I said, "What do you mean we, are you pregnant? I only see one of you. Are you telling me you don't want me on the tier, I'll deal with you." See, when he said "we" that puts me one down right, so I come out on the tier and there's three of them, and they are moving on me. This is serious business, and they've got their reasons for what they are doing, that I don't see.

Then, somebody stands up with me and says, "I can't let this happen on my tier." And the three said, "What do you mean?" He said, "If I let you gang up on this guy, then you're going to be ganging up on me," and he said, "I'm not going to let you gang up on anyone around me." Then another guy on the other side of the tier stood up and said, "I'm standing with that too, I don't want you ganging up on nobody on my tier. If you got one thing you want to say to this man stand forward, other than that we're not going to let you gang up on him." So, that's what saved me right there, man.

One guy stepped forward and I said, "What's your problem, man?" He said, "We don't allow snitches on this tier," and I said, "Man, snitching ain't never been on the front page of the paper, my whole life has been right there, if I would've ever snitched on anybody, it would have been right there in the open. My word is my bond, my life. I don't snitch on nobody, dig?" He said, "Well, we were told." I said, "You take it back to wherever you got it, 'cause whoever is giving you that garbage is trying to front your life off."

So, we went on down the road, and I was left with that lesson, and two or three times in my life on this tier that I'm on, things have happened where I could have ganged up on somebody, but I held down, stood down from that. I don't do that because my life was given to me by someone, so I try to pass that on in my life, as being a part of my life. I don't think we should gang up on people. That's why we got courts, that's why we got laws, rules, and regulations for our survival. Any time that you don't give the laws, and the rules, and the regulations to the most low-life fucking Manson in the world, then what you got is something coming from the will of God 'cause the laws are made for survival. That's why all those men died on all those battlefields to make those traditions. We live in the shadows of those traditions. That's what I tried to explain. I was on the witness program, the State of California should of never bothered me. They should have stood down off of me. I didn't have anything to do with that, that wasn't my play. I'm not saying that I'm a good man, that I'm not a crook. I'm not saying that I haven't buried a few people. That doesn't have anything to do with what happened there. What happened there wasn't my play, it wasn't in my lane.

I'm not saying I'm not worse than that. I'm probably a thousand times worse. Tex [Watson] was a child, you know. Whenever I do something, I don't ever get caught. People don't know what I do. I don't let them know what I do. If I let you know what I do then I can't do it. I'm the sons of liberty in the graveyard. That's my gang. My gang is crooks. That's my family, that's my cult. That's what we were convicted for. You just seen a little bit of it. You didn't see what was really going on. See, with what really goes on I don't need to break the law. The law's kind of stupid actually. You know, I'm not conspiring with nobody to do anything.

Can you imagine the Pharaoh conspiring with somebody to put a prick in the pyramid. He put his brick in the pyramid with his mind. Conspire? Tex wrote in his book, "I think that's what he wanted me to do." He was right. He was a good soldier. He did exactly what he was supposed to do, and did it well, man. Yeah. He did one mistake, they say, and I don't believe he made a mistake. They say he left one fingerprint. I don't believe it. He was too perfect under my guidance, man, to leave a fingerprint, and they said he left a fingerprint and I said I don't believe that. He didn't make a mistake. Tex did not make a mistake. There's no such thing in my kingdom.

IV

HOW IT ALL STARTED

When we returned home, Buck received inquiries from various tabloids about Donald. We booked Donald on more radio shows and his story took off exponentially with each interview he gave. But we were still stuck on how adamantly Donald had declined a lie detector test on the Howard Stern Show, so we gave him an ultimatum: Do the test, or we're done. He complied.

Kendall Shull is arguably the world's leading polygraph expert. Shull served with the FBI as a special agent for twenty-five years, and was chief of the entire FB polygraph program when he retired. If anyone can tell if you are lying, Shull can. We contacted Shull and he agreed to test Donald at his personal facility in Knoxville, Tennessee. Donald was very quiet on the drive to Knoxville; it was obvious that the looming lie-detector test was getting to him. In desperation, he tried to talk us out of the whole idea. "How many other authors have to go through this?" he demanded indignantly. I explained to Donald that he really had nothing to fear, that this was a formality that had to be dealt with sooner or later.

When we arrived at our destination, Shull greeted us, explained the entire process, then asked to be alone with Donald so that he could conduct the test. The polygraph test took four hours, and centered mostly on the question, "Did you have sex with Elvis Presley?" In short, it soon became very apparent that I had driven two thousand miles and strapped a seventy-two- year-old man to a polygraph machine to determine if he had indeed blown Elvis when, with almost completely certainty, he had not.

Donald pretended to sleep for the entire duration of the long ride home.

Things were finished with Donald. There was no longer any reason to believe the rest of his story.   Yet, I still felt there had been a legitimate connection between Donald and Manson. I looked over the stack of correspondence again and couldn't convince myself that the letters weren't legitimate. It was clear that Manson's letters were intended for Donald; they addressed Donald's questions and communicated an intimacy that seemed specific to a certain sort of relationship. Each letter was addressed to Donald in the same child-like scrawl and stamped with the postmark from Corcoran Prison.

To stay sane after such a letdown, I began journaling and even started to piece together the beginnings of a book. I wanted to write about people's connections to one another, how important those connections are, and how their dissolution directly influences depression. Because it's been my experience that the pain a person experiences during depression is really the ache of being separated from the whole –life, love, God, whatever you want to call it. I was heavily influenced by the uncompromising truth of writers like Tony Parsons, Karl Renz, Leo Hartong, and was very drawn to they're teachings. They were able to speak from a depth that really resonated within me. I knew I had to meet these people. So, I planned a six week trip to Europe. My time in Europe changed me; I had never before spent so much time both alone and in the company of so many wonderful people. Tony, Karl, and Leo met with me, and with brutal honesty were able to help me see the simplicity of life. Away from everything, I was able to confront myself and my feelings. Never in my life had I cried so hard or felt so humble, so alive, so thankful. I was worried about returning to Canada. I thought my old, less self-assured mindset might come creeping back, and I'd end up depressed again. But I didn't.

One Friday afternoon after my return, I received an unexpected letter from Corcoran Prison. An inmate named Kenny Calihan, who claimed to be a friend of Donald Taylor's, had written to me in order "to introduce" himself. Kenny said that he got my address from Donald, who had filled him in on the adventures we'd had while promoting One Gay Man. Kenny knew about the letters exchanged between Donald and Manson. He told me that several of the inmates at Corcoran had read Donald's letters at some point; he assured me that most everyone found them to be "hilarious." He explained that the prisoners routinely pass around each other's mail and retrieve old messages from the garbage. And, because no other inmate in the history of the American prison system has ever received as much mail as has Charles Manson, his letters are both most coveted and most easily attained. Kenny said that he has been friends with Charles Manson since 1992. I couldn't believe what I was reading.

I immediately called Donald and asked him why the hell he'd given my address out to inmates. Donald answered, calmly, that he didn't think I would mind. He had been writing to Kenny for a few months and had determined Kenny was a pretty good guy. Donald told me that Manson was serving a year's sentence in the hole for something related to getting caught with a knife, a very serious offense. Donald had become acquainted with Kenny through a letter Manson himself hadn't been able to read. Kenny handled much of Manson's mail, as would a secretary of sorts.

Two weeks later, another unsolicited letter from Kenny arrived in my mailbox. Enclosed was an autographed photo of Charles Manson. Kenny apologized for writing, but said that he couldn't resist, since Donald had written so extensively to him about me, and Kenny had gotten the impression I would be a cool guy to talk to. Kenny would write one more time before I made the decision to write back. He asked for my phone number, because he promised he could get Manson to call me as soon as Manson got out of the hole. It took a few days of serious introspection before I decided to send along my phone number. It had been at least fifteen years since I'd participated in any meaningful conversation through letters. It made more sense to talk on the phone.

It was incredible to think I might have scored the opportunity to talk to Charles Manson. I began to go through his letters once more and decided it would be fascinating to include some of Manson's more mystical ideas in my book. The aim would be to assist people in feeling a sort of connectedness to all people, even those they find evil or repulsive. I wanted to collect a few of his more insightful quotations and list them anonymously, hiding the author's identity until the reader turned the page to find that the man who'd harvested his or her empathy was really Charles Manson. Of course I highly doubted that Manson would ever call me; I wasn't even sure this Kenny character knew Manson.

Kenny called. And called, and called. The first phone bill was shocking, because inmates have to call collect, and it can cost upwards of twenty-five dollars each time they do. It does not take long for those charges to add up. To a prisoner, a phone number is a precious lifeline. Some inmates are meticulous in negotiating their real world relationships and are usually very careful not to "burn up" a phone number. Kenny, on the other hand, would call constantly, sometimes ten, fifteen times a day. I'd deliberately give Kenny my work schedule to ward off some of his excessive phone calls, but he would call me anyway, even when he knew I wasn't home. I think he did this in order to look important in his prison unit, as if he were doing business, as if he had people to talk to. Once, he called at an hour he expected me to be out, and when I picked up the phone, he asked, "What are you doing home?" I doubt Kenny has any idea what it's like to pay rent and manage responsibilities. And it is impossible to reason with him. I'm sure he struggles with some obsessive-compulsive behaviors and he has no attention span. For all of these reasons, he can be a bit exhausting. But, and this is a big but, I think he means well.

Kenny's criminal history is, remarkably, pretty unremarkable. He started out serving time in the California Youth Authority around the age of twelve for petty crimes like theft. After spending most of his adolescence bouncing in and out of jail, he joined the Marine Corp in an attempt to turn his life around. But after his time in the service ended, he fell right back into his old life and discovered methamphetamine, his drug of choice. Kenny also got into cocaine and a "little bit" of heroin. In 1988, Kenny ended up in the San Bernardino County Jail, sentenced to eight years for three counts of burglary. After his release from San Bernardino County Jail, Kenny ended up in Nevada, where he got caught up in a suspicious death investigation. According to Kenny, he had gone to a girl's house to hang out, not knowing there was a dead body in the building. The girl had been responsible for the care of an elderly lady, who eventually died from neglect and whose corpse sat in the home, untouched, for twenty-one days. When the girl got busted, Kenny got taken away too. Since Kenny was an informant against the Mexican Mafia, and had a contract out on his life, he made his new home in Soledad California Prison on the PHU (Protective Housing Unit). But, due to California prison budget cuts, the Soledad PHU eventually closed, and Kenny was transferred to Corcoran PHU, where he's been ever since. Kenny told me several stories about the celebrity prisoners he's hung with during his time at Corcoran: "I use to hang out with Juan Corona. I've known him since 1990. I'd kick it with Sirhan Sirhan, but he didn't talk much, kept to himself. Pat Kearney, the "trash bag" killer, was cool though; he was a mathematician, a really smart guy."

Kenny was eager to tell me everything he knew about Manson. They'd met, he said, in 1992, just as Manson got out of the hole, where he'd been kept for almost five years. Kenny insisted this was for Manson's own safety and not for punishment. "He was almost killed when that guy set him on fire," Kenny remarked. "Crazy, huh?" Kenny was of course referring to the incident that took place on September 25, 1984, inside the California Medical Facility at Vacaville. Manson was severely burned when a fellow inmate, Jan Holmstrom, poured paint thinner on him and set him afire because Manson, allegedly, had verbally threatened Jan and objected to his ritual Hare Krishna chants. Manson sustained second- and third-degree burns on over twenty percent of his body. I asked Kenny to tell me what Manson was really like. "Manson is really intelligent," he said. "He's pretty sharp and he's got a good mind, but he plays stupid sometimes, plays dumb even though he has a good memory." Kenny said he saw Manson as "kind hearted," but laughed heartily as he quipped, "Charlie says he don't lie, but he lies every day."

Kenny taught me a lot about the politics, the inner workings of such an immense prison system. He would call me daily and his letters took over my mailbox. Kenny had no problem asking for favors. He was in constant need of stamps and obsessed with acquiring them. I eventually learned that, in prison, stamps serve as currency. Inmates are not allowed to have any money, so the merchants among them expect to be paid in postage. Inmates sell all sorts of "favors" just to get their hands on stamps. When Sirhan Sirhan was transferred out of Corcoran's PHU, Kenny told me that Sirhan was being placed into population so he could be "executed" by other inmates. Kenny also mentioned that when they stripped Sirhan's room, they discovered he had more than one hundred cans of tuna under his bed. Fish too is money in prison; a can of tuna costs one dollar at the prison canteen. This was all new to me.

When I was a kid, I imagined Manson living in a cage like the most terrifying animal at the zoo. As an adult, even after reading his letters, it was hard to get a sense of the environment from which he wrote. Through Kenny, I acquired a better sense of the place Manson called home. It was strange to think that, when he wasn't in the hole, he actually interacted with other inmates, even called a few his friends. Kenny got me to talk to some of the other inmates on PHU. One of the more interesting characters was a man named Ernesto, who claimed to run most of East Los Angeles from his jail cell. Ernesto told me he was high up in the Mexican Mafia, that he'd left a path of dead bodies behind him while he killed his way to the top. Ernesto claimed that he was also a porn star, an author, and an FBI informant on gang relations. Ironically, he said he felt a duty to prevent kids from joining gangs, and he was working on a book that disclosed the dark secrets of gang life.

One day, Ernesto suddenly stopped calling. Kenny told me Ernesto had attacked another inmate, and was consequently almost beaten to death with a broken mop handle. Ernesto was thrown into the hole. I told Kenny about Ernesto's stories. "What?" Kenny laughed, "That's all bullshit. Ernesto was never in a gang; he's a little guy. FBI? No way, not a chance." I soon became incredibly aware of how difficult it would be to uncover the myth about Manson through his friends. Most of these inmates couldn't even come to terms with the myths they'd created about themselves.

During one of our many phone conversations, Kenny informed me that Manson would soon be released from the hole. I asked Kenny to tell me exactly what had happened to land Manson there in the first place. Kenny said that Manson had been receiving constant death threats from an inmate everyone liked to call "Skipper." Kenny said Manson had every reason to be careful. He got hold of a piece of aluminum tubing from another inmate's arm brace and fashioned it into a knife. While Manson served out his time in solitary confinement for his weapons violation, Skipper got caught with drugs in the visiting room and was transferred to another prison in San Diego. Crisis averted.

Kenny promised that Manson would call me as soon as he could. Of course, I didn't really believe this, but then again, stranger things had happened.

On the evening of November 4, 2008, as I dozed on the couch to the drone of the television, the phone rang in three short bursts, the signature sound of a collect call from Corcoran Prison. I assumed it was Kenny, calling for the tenth or so time that day. I was reluctant to pick up the phone, but I answered anyway and listened to the familiar recording that preludes any phone call from a prisoner.

"Global Tel Link. This call and your telephone number will be recorded and monitored. I have a collect call from..."

There was a momentary pause, and then I heard Manson's voice for the first time.

"Charles."

The monotone recording returned.

"...an inmate at California State Prison, Corcoran One, in Corcoran, California. To hear the cost of this call, dial or say, 'nine.' To accept, dial or say, 'five.'"

I pushed five, held my breath, and waited a few seconds for the call to go through. After a momentary click, I was connected.

ME: Hey, how are you doing?
MANSON: It's a beautiful day. Of course there is only one day, right? Who is this?
ME: This is Marlin.
MANSON: Oh yeah, the Canadian. So, what are we doing?
ME: What do you mean?

MANSON: What do you want from me?

ME: Nothing.

MANSON: Come on. Everyone wants something. You wanna interview me because you're writing a book?

ME: Well, I think you have a lot of insights into things. Sort of spiritual...

MANSON: Spiritual. Ha, yeah. Geraldo made millions interviewing me, they all did. ABC, NBC, all of them want a piece of me. Every day I get letters. They promise you everything, and then they twist your words. Make it into a bunch of bullshit. Fuck 'em. I stopped doing interviews years ago. Marlin, right? Like the fish?

ME: Yeah.

MANSON: I'm going to call you, "Walking Hawk." That's better than Marlin.

ME: Walking Hawk?

MANSON: Yeah, um, there's a hawk that flies around here; I see him out on the yard. I've never seen him on the ground. I don't know what I'm talking about. I'm pretty stupid. I'm one year old.

He paused. I was pretty much speechless.

MANSON: Without air you are nothing, everything we do is for the air, dig?

ME: Yup.

MANSON: Do you know about ATWA?

I did. ATWA stands for Air, Trees, Water, Animals. It is Manson's personal philosophy regarding his war against pollution.

ATWA can also mean "All The Way Alive." It's Manson's mission statement, a belief system he developed more than forty years ago.

ME: Yeah.

MANSON: Do you like bugs?

ME: Yeah, especially crickets.

MANSON: The cricket is too big for a spider to take on. I'm more like a bug than a person. I was thirty-two years old before I knew a tree was a living thing; can you believe that? Thirty-two years old. The prison has been my mother. I've been in jail for sixty-two years.

He paused, and I sat on the other end of the line, stunned.

MANSON: So, what do you do?

ME: I'm a psychiatric nurse.

MANSON: A psychiatrist?

ME: No, a psych nurse. I'm part of a crisis response team. I do emergency, outreach stuff for the mental health clinic here.

MANSON: A psychiatrist? You force people to take Thorazine?

ME: No, I would never do that.

MANSON: Force 'em down and stick 'em.

ME: No, I've never done that.

MANSON: They kept me drugged up on that stuff for a couple of years. You drool like a rabid dog. Your mind can't form a thought. I couldn't get off the floor. It was the only drug I couldn't get over. I couldn't get past it, you know? And they say they are helping people. I'm sure you help people, right?

There was more than a twinge of sarcasm in Manson's voice. I knew all about this. Thorazine was developed in the early 1950s. At the time, it was considered a breakthrough medication, the first of the antipsychotic family of drugs. It was used often on patients with psychotic disorders. It has very potent sedative properties, and was used to sedate patients to a point where they were no longer a threat to themselves or to others. It was widely used in asylums and prisons as a "chemical restraint." With modern advances in medicine, Thorazine is rarely used today.

ME: I try to. I know what you are saying; that's horrible. I'm sorry you had to go through that. Do you see a psychiatrist now?

MANSON: Nah, not for a few years. There is nothing wrong with me. The last one brought a gun here to the jail and blew his fucking brains out all over the parking lot. His wife was sucking on some black dick. There are thirty dead doctors at Vacaville, they are all in the GRAAAAAVEYARRRRD!

ME: And you're the crazy one?

MANSON: Yeah, yeah.

Manson laughed a great deal at this.

ME: I remember a quote of yours, "It's just a pile of shit anyway, so why not try to grow some flowers in it?"

MANSON: Yeah, I said that. "My nose is a rose with a

kamikaze zero…"

Manson said something about dragons flying into the sun, and laughed hysterically as he told a story about how Stonehenge was made by women carrying these huge stones on their backs.

The call was interrupted.

"You have sixty seconds left in this call."
ME: Thanks for calling; I appreciate it.
MANSON: ATWA warrior.
ME: Yeah.
MANSON: Take care, peace.
ME: Peace.

Click.

That first phone call was a blur. Afterward, I sat in silence, holding the phone, trying to make sense of what had happened. I couldn't believe I'd actually talked to Charles Manson. Really, I had been listening; he had complete control of the conversation. He hadn't sounded like a guy who was seventy-three years old. Instead, he'd seemed much younger. His southern drawl was there, but he also spoke with a bit of a California accent every once in awhile.

I tried to call a few friends to tell them what had happened, but no one was around. It didn't really matter; how could I explain? Charles Manson called me. What the hell was I getting into?

prison

I'm Not In Jail!

I really know what I'm doing but only for myself, to myself, by myself. Any time when I have anybody else or anything else comes in play it's always I don't know what they know. If they're not around and they're not there, then I know everything. It's only when I have other people that I can't know everything. Unless I conquest. Unless I take it, sit down, shut up. Be me, be me or die. See, all these great minds, I listen to them every once in a while, once in a while they get on top of it and really super minds. They have some super minds in this world. And they're really smart for what they know, but they don't know everything because they don't know nothing. If you don't know nothing that's everything. You can't start until you end. We've got to end before you start, but they're always talking about, well, start, there's no such thing as start. You're not born, you wasn't born and you don't die. You've been here for billions of years, man, to recognize in real life, the observation power is just your whole existence. When you observe what you observe, you see what needs to and what is and what's coming and what's going and you say, you know, stop fossil fuel. That's a command.

If you don't do it you're all going to die because fossil fuel is destroying your atmosphere. That's in motion. It was put in motion in World War I. So that's how far behind stopping pollution you are. Well, the irony is—are you ready for this, sweetheart? I'm not in jail. There's no such thing in my world. In other words it is all jail. The whole damn thing. My body's in prison, I'm trapped in my body, man, sometimes. Other times, I can leave and go anywhere I want to, you know, and so there's no such thing as prison. Prison's a joke, it's actually a joke. You can lock somebody up in solitary confinement and they can sit there laughing at you. Because, like it's all in the mind, everything's in your mind, man. You know all that suffering and all that, I mean we all suffer, you know, like we suffer for what we do. I'm suffering for smoking. I smoked for years. I knew it was wrong and I did it anyway. Now I'm suffering for it but it's actually not suffering. I'm just putting my body through these breathing things, you know, and if I don't get up in the morning I probably wouldn't even notice it. I'm not afraid of dying. Dying's the last thing that I'm afraid of.

They are in the minds of all the people that are in jail. I'm not in these people's minds. They come up to me and say, "You dirty son of a bitch, I'll break your neck." And, you know, that's like water on a duck's back. That doesn't touch me. I'm not upset or afraid with that, you know. I just go along with whatever, and when they sit down, I just sit down, you dig? If they stand up, I just sit down. And if they fuck with me, I just lay on them. You know. I don't ever tell them I'm going to or I don't. I may give out one, two, three little warnings about something but, like, generally I don't even bother [with] that because I'll run if I can. I'll get away, you know. I'll say excuse me and then I'll go to the toilet and I won't come back. You know, I'll just flush myself down the toilet because I'm a piece of shit anyway. I don't have all that pride thing and that ego trip.

Wagon

Well, you're not going to find too many people that remember the wagon. I remember wagons, when we used to go to town in a wagon and here was the conversation: "Those doomsday machines will destroy us all." They called them doomsday machines and they said they would contaminate all the air and the argument was, well, it will dissipate, and the bigger minds said there's no such thing as dissipate. Once you bring something into existence, it's here. You are going to have to deal with it. You can't bring something into existence and then say it's not here. Once it's here there ain't no getting rid of it because there's no such thing as getting rid of it. That's what leads me to my particular no death theory. [If] you can't get rid of anything then how the hell can you die? You don't die, you just change forms. Forms are changing. You're going to be here. Even if you don't breathe air, you're still going to be here. You just are destroying one form and placing another in its place. What that form would be I got ideas, but… you can't prove anything anyway. But they won't give Manson no say so over his own life. Everybody's got me captured and that's their reassurance that everything's going to be okay because they know that that place is secure I guess, whatever the [place,] you know, and you got a bunch of kids in here, they've got locked up for fighting and biting and carrying on. But it has no authority.

Change For a Dime?

I went into the bus station when I got out of prison in Ohio and I asked for change for a dime. The shoeshine man said, "What you want change for a dime for?" This was before they had nickel phones. I said, "I want to make a phone call." He said, "By God man, where you been, on the moon? Phone calls ain't been a nickel for years. Phone calls for a nickel?" In my mind, they were a nickel and every time I call somebody long distance, my mind just seems to go back to where phone's just starting and how marvelous the technology is. I mean,

I know it's way ahead of that but in my mind it's like I'm still primitive. In phone calls and stuff like that. So I think, I mean talking to Canada, that's far out. It really is if you think about that, you could dial a number, and talk to somebody on the other side of the world. That's pretty far out. I suppose we can do a whole lot more wondrous than that, I mean, you know. It looks like we have the intelligence to stop the damn pollution. It shouldn't be a big thing. It should be just a very small minor thing. And I'm going to tell you straight up, in my mind if I had the power I would take all the people it would take to do that job and do whatever I had to do with them in order to do that job.

V

A CONCRETE CAGE

I'd been sucked into a whirlwind. Over the next few weeks, I talked to Manson several times, although he never actually called me himself. Kenny would dial my number and quickly press the receiver into Manson's hands. I'd believed and continue to believe that Charles Manson is one of the most complex characters that ever lived. And though it could take several lifetimes to understand fully both the depth and distortion of his thoughts, it takes only an instant to become completely immersed in his delivery.

Charles is a natural storyteller and his voice ebbs and flows according to his own unique inventions in rhythm and rhyme. He is lyrical; his words lilt and form both verse and chorus. He snarls and growls. He is often breathless with enthusiasm. He speaks of himself in the third person. During a typical phone call, an occasional howl will escape from the mysterious backdrop of the Corcoran PHU and flood the phone line. But Manson is never fazed.

When we talked, Manson was sometimes engaging, sometimes defiant, sometimes both. He could be funny, candid, even vulnerable. And he could be angry, perverse, and threatening. During our first few conversations, I tried to work up the nerve to request an interview for my book, but I never knew which Manson I might end up talking to from moment to moment. I quickly learned, from talking to other inmates and intuiting from Manson himself, that the two most important rules for having any kind of relationship with him are: (1) Never ask him for anything, and (2) Never allow yourself to be dependent on him. Manson explained to me that at least ninety percent of the letters he receives are from people wanting something. People all over the world want his autograph and his art; almost daily he receives requests to fill out and sign questionnaires from students writing various papers. He gets a lot of mail from musicians. There is so much mail that one man could not possibly read half of it. Kenny told me Manson sometimes opens an envelope just to see if there are stamps inside; he couldn't care less about its other contents. He once covered an entire wall of his cell with postage stamps.

Those early phone calls were amazing. I feel as if we both went through a feeling-out process, Charles testing me all the way. My challenge was getting past the fixed idea of Manson with which I'd grown up: the famous, legendary face of evil. Manson, on the other hand, was struggling to determine my intentions. It became clear that the man isn't capable of trusting anyone. He inquired over and over again what my "real motives" were and had trouble accepting the truth: that I was interested only in communicating with someone I found fascinating.

When I finally found the nerve to ask Manson if he'd do an interview, he seemed surprised I hadn't already tried to take his words for my own purposes. "What, you're not recording this?" he asked. I assured him I wasn't and then, once he seemed willing to listen, I explained the concept of my book and what I wanted it to accomplish. Charles thought the idea was cool. He liked philosophizing about non-duality, oneness, the deeper truths. He gave me permission to record everything and said our conversations could constitute my interview. I realized then that

Manson couldn't call on a whim whenever he wanted to talk to me. I hadn't given him my phone number, hadn't even written him a letter. Kenny had been mediating every aspect of our relationship, because I was "technically" Kenny's friend. He had found me. There was no way he was ever going to "give up" my phone number. So I wrote Manson for the first time and gave him my number, to call whenever he liked. And he wrote back on a sheet of his own stationary, personalized with a header typed in a wobbly rainbow-colored font. "MARLIN," the message began in large, carefully constructed capital letters, each traced upon itself over and over with what appeared to be a curious combination of doubt and certainty.

"As soon as I catch up with nothing – I can be myself and relax and be, being, be, free to relax the inside of just being becomes itself in always of all and everything just becomes music."

I wouldn't receive many more letters. He would often send signed pieces of paper or postcards, but rarely did he ever write. When I asked him why he'd lost interest in writing letters, he said he didn't have the time anymore. And he claimed that, by simply sending postcards and putting his name to a piece of paper, he was "keeping the lines of communication open." But communication with Manson was sporadic at best. Sometimes he would call two or three times a day. And then, without warning, his calls would stop, and I wouldn't hear from him for a couple of weeks.

In the interim, I continued to talk to Kenny almost daily. He routinely asked for stamps and envelopes. He wanted to be taken care of and felt he needed some sort of outside advocate. Kenny always had a problem—his mail was held up or his property was confiscated—and he'd constantly request that I call or write the warden or property clerk on his behalf. I'd usually give in and do what he requested; Kenny could be relentless.

I'd begun talking to Manson, learning his personality, acquainting myself with the way he spoke and thought. But I was craving to learn more about the deepest, innermost level of Corcoran, the dark black hole of the PHU from which Manson thought and wrote and served his time. My Internet research yielded not one single photograph of Corcoran's PHU. It's fairly easy to obtain picture of cells in other units of other California state prisons, but the nature of Charles Manson's unit seems an intentionally well kept secret. My conversations with Manson were infrequent and intermittent; they were on his terms and therefore dealt mostly in the abstract, the philosophical, the ideological. When I tried to talk about what it was like in prison he would sometimes deny he was even there: "There is no prison. That's all in your mind." Other times, he could only vent his frustrations about being incarcerated. I was never really able to get a feel for his environment. I wanted to commission someone to paint a picture in my brain of Manson's habitat, the tiny eight-by-twelve concrete cell he'd occupied for twenty-one years. Kenny tried to help me understand, but he wasn't particularly insightful; similarly, the other PHU inmates I talked to were pretty easy going, simple, not very forthcoming or able to describe their surroundings in any consistent, meaningful way.

I knew quite a bit about Corcoran's general history. Corcoran is a small city of 25,000 people, initially built on agriculture in rural California. Today, it is world renowned for its prison. Corcoran Prison was built in 1988, as a state-of-the-art facility designed to house some of America's most dangerous and troublesome inmates. The prison was initially intended to hold 2,916 inmates; today more than 5,000 inmates, or one-fifth of the entire city's entire population, call Corcoran Prison their home. More than half of these inmates don't stand a chance at getting parole. They live out their lives in a quiet, often desperate solitude, a most primal existence. Their every move is heavily monitored and controlled. The Protective Housing Unit is where the most "famous" of these inmates are kept. At its inception, PHU housed forty-four inmates, but today its numbers have dwindled to just fifteen. These inmates are known informants, "celebrity" criminals, or prisoners charged with offenses so serious and disturbing that they need to be protected from the general prison inmate population.

Corcoran has been credited, shamefully, as the most dangerous and dysfunctional of California's thirty-two state prisons. Just eight years after Corcoran opened its doors, it had already lost more inmates to fatal guard shootings than had any other prison in the country. Based on analysis of interviews and documents surrounding these deadly incidents, some have concluded that many of those shootings were unwarranted and resulted in the deaths of inmates who were "innocent" in the pursuit of those who were unruly. Corcoran is notorious for its "gladiator days," a period of time during the late '80s and early '90s in which prison officers actually staged fights between inmates. When a major news network broadcast footage from such a fight in 1996, the California Department of Corrections launched an investigation of the prison, which ultimately found no evidence of a conspiracy to intentionally kill prisoners.

This is all I knew of Corcoran, until I started talking to David Hooker. David was different from all of the other inmates on PHU. He was able to describe the unit to me in a way I could understand, and with an honesty that was, at times, brutal. He had a determination about him that was inspiring, especially since, unlike the overwhelming majority of PHU inmates, David will come up for parole. David's insights into Corcoran Prison were especially interesting to me, because he and Charles Manson consider themselves brothers.

David was serving twenty-five years to life for the "murder" of his father, Thomas Warren Hooker, a highly respected and heavily decorated retired LAPD cop. In April 1993, an early morning fire broke out in the Hooker's Los Angeles three-bedroom home, and while Hooker's adopted son David and his third wife Joy were able to escape uninjured, Thomas Hooker, blind and deteriorating from diabetes, wasn't so lucky. He died from smoke inhalation in his bed. Out of respect for David, and the fact that he is preparing for his parole hearing in 2012, I won't go into any of the details of his case.

The first time I talked to David, he was very upset. Of course, Kenny had initiated the conversation. He'd called me and said, "Hey, Marlin, you're pretty good at talking to people; could you help this guy out?" When David got on the phone, he told me that he'd planned a visit with a friend that day and the visit had fallen through. He was devastated because he'd looked forward to the visit for a long time. Visitors are infrequent at Corcoran PHU.

As I talked to David, I was impressed by how polite and articulate he is, even when upset. He is extremely respectful at the same time that he is open and honest. David has an easy nature about him; he sounds like an older biker, laid back and casual, yet he speaks carefully, considerately.

David would call me again, and I really enjoyed our conversations. It became apparent that he was not like most of the other inmates on PHU. He is at peace with the solitude and is generally optimistic. He is an avid reader and learner. And, even though he deals with chronic, debilitating back pain, he never complains. Unlike Kenny, David would call me only every few weeks. He made it clear that he valued our relationship too much to risk becoming an inconvenience. But David never felt like a burden to me. Getting a feel for Manson's home, through David's eyes, was a revealing and fascinating experience.

David told me it would be difficult to reproduce artificially, outside of a prison, that feeling of "I am absolutely stuck. Changing my situation is completely hopeless, This is it, so I've got to deal with this." It's something you have simply to accept and move on. Most people cannot imagine existing in an environment such as PHU without going completely insane, but there are circumstances (an egregious disability, a terminal illness) even a complacent prisoner couldn't imagine enduring. Yet, for anyone living through anything undesirable, reality eventually becomes normalcy to such a degree that it can be painful to return to the "real world." David, who will be eligible for parole in two years, maintains that release from prison can be just as traumatic as entry. "When I got out the last time I had to wait for somebody at a mall, and looking at all those people, it was like 'holy shit, it's like the bar scene in *Star Wars*; where the fuck am I?'"

David explained, "You have to kind of adjust your frame of mind to 'Okay, I'm here, I live in a box now and I'm going to have to figure out a way to remain sane and have some kind of life that isn't completely empty.'" But that's difficult to do in a unit in which creative and intellectual outlets and opportunities are dwindling by the day, and those who succeed at maintaining their sanity are the exception and not the rule. Inmates on PHU escape the usual prison pitfalls; there is no overcrowding, no gangs, no drug wars, no sexual predation. But there are also no self-help group, no AA, and no educational program. David was taking college courses before the prison completely cut the curriculum.

David told me that most of the other inmates can't deal with being in prison "they are loud, run-around bothering other people, hanging themselves, or doing some other kind of acting out. You have to learn how to deal with mental pain, without letting it drive you crazy. Charlie does that and I think I do that too, for the most part. It's weird, I mean especially a place like this where most of the people are here because you know they're just scumbags, they are, they don't care basically. If they're not sociopaths, they got serious psychopathy going one way or another. They couldn't live anywhere else so they end up here, so Charlie deals with that too. Signs of serious depression abound; most inmates grossly oversleep and have trouble maintaining rational thought and reasonable temperament. Well, you see the different signs of depression all the time, people sleeping, over sleeping, people being real testy and just ill tempered, when normally they're kind of rational. We've had a couple of people kill themselves since I've been here....both manual and mechanical strangulations."

I asked David to describe PHU, and he did so completely that I no longer could only envision Charles clanging in an otherwise empty metal cage. The unit consists of two tiers and twenty-four cells. The bottom tier contains cell numbers forty-one through fifty-two and the upper tier houses cell numbers fifty-three through sixty-four. Each cell is designed to hold two inmates, except for one wheelchair-accessible cell designed for an inmate protected under the ADA. The beds are big slabs of concrete equipped with thin mattresses and hollowed in two places each to allow storage of personal possessions. The head of each bed is attached to the back wall, just below a small slit of window about four inches wide and two and a half feet high. Between the two beds and two windows is another concrete block attached perpendicularly to the wall and extending about two and a half feet, parallel to the floor. It's supposed to be a writing desk, but David asserts it's more of a coffee stand or a countertop than a writing surface. A few shelves are mounted on the cell walls and there is a "toilet and sink combination." As a whole, according to David, a Corcoran PHU cell can be described as "basically bedrock."

to be true?

Case Worker

So when I got out I went to the case worker in LA, and I said, "You know what, man, I don't wanna be out here. I don't have a job, I'm out here, I don't know anybody, I don't know what I'm doing out here, whatever 'out here' is." ...[O]ut here was another planet. I got out and I was supposed to meet some guy's wife, and she wasn't there, you know. I had been lied to all the way down the line, but I didn't know the difference. When you're in there and everybody lies to you, you don't know they're lying. You get out and you find out they were lying all those years. I met the preacher in the parking lot, and I said could I get a ride to the bus stop. No, he was in a hurry, he had a committee meeting. I thought the preacher was real, I thought he was love and Jesus. I didn't realize he was just another case worker doing a job, and playing preacher for a pay check. He wasn't a man of God.

Witness Program

So then I'm in the witness program, and they put in the paper, "Charlie Manson was shot and killed at a party." That was in the Frisco paper in 1967. You could probably find it if you looked in the paper long enough, where I died over there. The reason is the federal government does it like that because they don't want people in the prisons to gain strength by watching you make it on the outside, 'cause if you make it, all the convicts in prison will try to make it. They don't want that. They try to put that to rest, try to keep that down, so they say I died. That's when I appeared with the Grateful Dead. At that time I didn't understand what I understand now. I never realized they had me on the program, played on my program. I thought that only happened inside prison. It happens outside too.

Bottom Lines

I see the bottom lines on everything. I see the bottom of it. Richard Nixon had the top of me. Richard Nixon is my divorce court. He's my Elvis Presley's testicles. I go to court and I'm standing in court. Court wouldn't be there had I not been standing there. So the court rides on what I'm doing. The judge gives somebody a position to represent me. The district attorney takes a position to represent me. That goes off into the sheriff, goes off into the psychiatrist and the doctors and the cops and the sheriffs, and the highway patrol. Probably when I'm standing in that courtroom for stealing a car there's probably 150,000 people representing me. The National Guard is representing me. The park rangers are representing me. All the prisons are representing me. The boys' schools and reform schools are representing me. I'm the king of crime. I'm the criminal. I'm the juvenile delinquent, the rebel, the outcast, the unwanted. I'm everything that everybody looks down on and is standing on, spitting on, cursing and calling names, and hating, buying and selling all the different things.

Pretty soon it just gets to be a part of my mind and my life, get everybody working me and doing whatever they can get away with and whatever they can get from me. So then I call that "my me," and I get outside and I look at everything you guys are doing in your life out there. See, I got a life in here and everybody that comes in here is feeding on my life. The psychiatrist wants to come in like he's helping me, and the sociologist and the penologist and the criminologist and all the "ologists," and make rules. They're going to make rules and wait for me to do something crazy and then they can come in and playact like they're sane. Then they want to handcuff me because they need my hands for something so they're representing my hands with it. They're representing my heart for that and they're representing my head for those things. They're cutting my hair and selling it for something and making pictures and books and changing my name and saying they're me in another perspective. They're my divorce court. Pretty soon I see where everything's going and it's all in my life, man. Have you ever considered what it would be like for a human being to be kept in cages and prisons for sixty-three years?

Krishna

They did a training class over here and most people don't realize why they did the training class. They think it was because of something that they were told. But actually what it is...all the microphones are over here. You got the whole world hearing but they won't admit it. You know, that's why as soon as I got a cell phone, they went right to it, got it quick as they could because they knew that a cell phone is a threat to all these microphones, because they got their own private lines on what's going on. Because the whole world is right here. But you don't see that because it's been coming for years and years and years. It started... when Krishna Venta blew himself up in the fountain of the world in Box Canyon, California. Krishna had a cult and they were based on the water and there was the Feather River project that just started. Land was fifty cents an acre at that particular time.

Now the same land is 50,000 dollars an acre because what they did, they went out and they took the water holes and put them in a tank and put them in a pipe and brought them down in a river and brought the river down and sold the water to the city. And all the animals died. They didn't care about that, you know. They didn't care about the wildlife and whatever, the snakes, they just took all the water off the land and put it in these artificial rivers and it dried the land up, man. And Krishna seen it because he had a big fountain in his cult area and when it dried up it stopped, and he said, well, you can't buy and sell the water. The water's for everyone. If you start buying and selling the water, man, you're taking the animals off the earth. There will be no animals left. 'Cause the animals can't afford to buy a drink.

People wanted to send Patty Hearst to the graveyard and it came to me, like what should we do. And I said we've had enough trouble. No, yeah, she was right on but she was not right on. She was there and she just got involved with some bad people, you know, and in other words they had her. See, what should have happened is Patricia Hearst should have been with me to start with. If she had been with me to start with, she wouldn't have had to go and prove the things she went through, and we could have had some say with the water at this particular point. See, because what happened is, the thought I'm here in, right now, at the end right now, was started on this level in the State of California by Krishna Venta when he sacrificed his life and the life of nine women. I think it was nine, maybe it was fifteen, but what he did when his fountain turned off, he put dynamite under his house and blew everybody up. But the thing, he didn't know that what we learned from that was the people that pick up the mess they don't tell the truth. In other words they lie. Them guys didn't die the way they said they did.

No way in hell are you going to convince me that those people laid in that fire and they didn't jump up and say ouch or run or do anything. That's bullshit. That was all put up. Yeah, that was the FBI, that was the system trying to get around for what we'd already done. I was in reform school when Krishna came on TV, that he had blown himself up with all his women, but you know as a child, I wasn't impressed. That was just another movie. So when I ended up over there at that area, with all his women thinking what the hell am I doing here? You know it's like the spirit of everything had brought me there, you know, and there was just, like, the spirit of my life is what brought you here. And the spirit of your life will bring somebody to your book. Yeah, just follow. You know now I'm taking credit for something that's really not my play, but you know it was in the spirit of what I was doing.

My Fans

Want to hear another perspective? The people that did all this stuff, you know, they were my fans. They weren't my family, they were fans and they wanted to get me over and that's why they did it. That's what the whole thing was created for. Susie came to me with a butcher knife and blood up to her elbows saying, "I love you so much and I love your music so much and I just killed myself for you. I give you my life." I told her, "All you've done, witch, is put me back in the penitentiary for the rest of my life. You haven't done me no favors." All that was supposed to be for me. You know, they did all those murders for the love of me. It wasn't love of me, it was love of their own life that they seen in ATWA. When I seen what I seen and I woke up to what I woke up to, I communicated that to them and they seen that, and when they seen that they said wow. This is our life, where, you know, Charlie can save us.

The Beatles ain't going to save us. They looked at the Beatles. The Beatles wasn't our heroes. The Beatles were punks, poobutts, rumpkins. They were doodads. They wasn't saying anything. The music was good but what they were saying was nothing. It was just Rocky Raccoon and a Bible set against a Bible and all that shit. I mean it was nice but when you're talking music to God, man we're not talking... Marilyn Manson, we're talking Moses, we're talking angels, we're talking zodiacs, we're talking universal love. When I got arrested, and I got busted, all the people there were going to start an E.L.F: earth, love, and family. That's what I got convicted for, being the earth, love, and the family. Fucking Susie gave her whole life for those people, man. They didn't show her one minute of mercy. They played on that girl. That was their little playground, Susie. Like it doesn't bother me. I never lived in that society anyway. I've always lived over here in the basement. At the bottom, wherever that is. Does that make sense? Susie gave her own life, man, for ATWA. She may have snuck out the side door, I don't know. I don't believe nothing they say, you know that.

VI

FROM THE INSIDE

Prisoners on Corcoran's PHU are issued two sheets, a pillow, and either a cotton or a woven wool blanket, the former usually preferred over the latter, which itches and sheds and "gets crap all over the cells." TVs are allowed, and so are three main appliances, an appliance being a radio, musical instrument, lamp, hot pot, or typewriter. What flies in terms of accessory appliances depends solely on how strict the guards are at any given time. Prisoners are technically allowed either ten or twelve books each, but the few who read as avidly as David are usually given leeway to store more. An inmate's total accumulation of personal property, everything from tennis shoes to clothes to chess sets and decks of cards, should occupy no more than six cubic feet of cell space.

David believes you can tell what sort of man a prisoner is by the way he keeps his cell. An unstable and insecure person is likely to stack and hoard property in his space, as though his belongings anchor him to his sanity. Others, like David, accumulate very little. "Other than a couple of personal photographs and letters, you could set fire to my cell and I wouldn't care." Other guys are less attached to stuff. They have almost nothing in there purposely. Those are the guys that live with a lot of deprivation, been through different prisons, they just don't want to have all their stuff taken away from them, they're not leaving themselves open to being ripped off. Or suffer any kind of loss that they don't have any control over. You can do a lot of things to maintain privacy and control over your immediate environment and what's going on around you. There are inmates who possess almost nothing, seemingly on purpose as a means of control. Because what you don't own can't be taken from you. Although, prisoners on PHU are subject to a lot less theft and are required to hand a lot less contraband over to authorities. There are punitive cell searches, during which "they tear your crap up," but far fewer than on other units. David told me, "This unit is sort of like a stupid step child, tolerated by an apathetic step parent. They will come in and do a spanking but usually they just prefer you to not be their problem, so they'd just as soon ignore you if they can."

I asked David what Manson's cell looked like. "Lived in," David said. Fortunately, he was willing to clarify further his assessment and described Manson's space as "cluttered" but organized, in that there is a home for every possession. "He's not fastidious, but he's not a slob either." All in all, David sees Manson's living space as a reflection of Manson's (relatively) active lifestyle; on any given day, the things that are out of place are those he's used for that day's projects and activities.

The area outside the cells is filled with tables and chairs for the inmates to eat, play cards, and just hang out. There are a TV and a few large fans, a table at which the overseer sits, a bookcase and two showers (one on the bottom tier and one on the top). David cites a main difference between PHU and any other prison unit: "Unlike mainline, where it's 'five minutes in the shower and then get the hell out,' these guys [PHU inmates] seem seriously inconvenienced if you ask them to get out within twenty minutes."

Getting along with the guards in PHU is about knowing the patterns and tendencies associated with an officer's specific background. Those that start off or have spent a lot of time on PHU generally have good relationships with the prisoners; they are quite familiar with each man and treat him accordingly. But those guards that have consistently worked in crowded and violent units, those that have had to worry about, as David says, "somebody trying to spear them through the door, throw shit and piss on them, spit on them, or scream at them –'You did this!' or 'Where's my fucking mail?' or 'I know you stole my stuff!' –" generally approach work on PHU with a lot of hostility. It is a gradual process, getting to know the inmates and the system, to realize that PHU isn't an ordinary unit filled with ordinary prisoners. At any given time though, David says, he deals with three types of authority: the cops that "start out as assholes and stay true to those colors," those "who are fair and even handed" from the first minute they step onto the unit, and those who "will smile at a man on Tuesday and then look at him on Wednesday like 'who the hell are you?'" The latter, according to David, is the most difficult type to get used to.

For David, the most difficult relationships to navigate on PHU are those he may or may not form with other inmates. For starters, even though most of the inmates are serving life sentences, the atmosphere in PHU remains transitory. Inmates can be transferred on the spur of the moment. Even Sirhan Sirhan, who seemed to be a permanent resident of PHU after serving almost two decades behind its walls, was transferred to another prison suddenly in 2009. Says David, "You get real close to somebody and then they're gone. That's a reason why you don't bother to get to know somebody: because you're probably not going to know them more than a few years."

There's another, more sinister reason to be careful with the bonds you forge in PHU. Letting a person get close to you and exposing too much of your personal thoughts or feelings is dangerous because that person is highly likely to use that information against you. So most of the unit's inmates are rightfully reserved, closed off to most any personal connections in order to keep themselves from becoming vulnerable.

In prison, you could keep completely to yourself and still end up accidentally acquiring or dispensing enough information seriously to endanger your life. That's how David ended up on PHU in the first place. Once, in federal prison, he unwittingly became a walking target. One day, he was in line for the phone on the second tier of his unit, waiting at a distance for the man in front of him to finish his conversation. David was leaning on the railing overlooking the unit's first tier when, from a full bird's eye view, he witnessed two men in army jackets enter another man's cell and strangle him to death. David knew all parties involved, the victim and the men that killed him, and he was aware of how easily his life could be threatened if he so much as batted an eye. So he kept his mouth shut, even through a complete FBI interrogation. "No," he said. "I didn't see anything; I don't know anything; I was probably sleeping; I didn't hear any noises." He played it cool and kept a straight face, hoping the incident would remain unresolved and he could feel somewhat safe again. But the two murderers were arrested the next morning and thrown into the hole. Someone had squealed. A few days later, another inmate interrogated David. The inmate said he knew David had seen everything and asked if David "had a problem" with what had happened. David assured the man that everything was fine. But a few days later, on his way out to racquetball, two men tried to stab him from a blind spot in a dark corridor. If he hadn't been carrying a racket, he most likely wouldn't be talking to me today.

Most likely, if an inmate isn't trying to pull you down, he's trying to use you to pull himself up, according to David, who spoke to me extensively about "a certain inmate" we both knew who would schmooze and scheme to work his association with Manson for all it could possibly be worth. This inmate would tear a page from the PHU rulebook and threaten to point out another inmate's misbehavior if he didn't respond to bribery and blackmail. "It's jealousy, insanity," David said. "He's not getting anything from Charlie, so he goes over and threatens and threatens and threatens. Charlie is seventy-six years old. You don't threaten somebody who's that old because stress is the number one thing that kills people that age."

Once, Manson asked David to interpret a postcard he'd received that had supposedly been "returned to sender." The front was embellished with a Warhol-esque collage of four pictures in four different color filters plus a forged Charles Manson signature. When David flipped the post card around, he saw Manson's name and address written in a loose, scrawled handwriting similar to Manson's own. David asked, "Did you send this?" Manson shook his head. "Naw, I didn't write that." And then David noticed a small message intended for someone on the outside, instructing him or her to "take care of" a certain inmate on the unit. "It would be pretty altruistic of Charles Manson," David laughed, "to send postcards with only the concern of protecting someone else."

All systems operate under a specific set of codes. Prison is no different. As I talked to David, and then to Manson, I realized the great level of mutual respect they have for one another. They both know how to do time. Their cells are right beside each other, but both seem aware of each other's need for space. They both appreciate art and will sometimes work on projects together. And there is a certain degree of give and take. I learned Manson is teaching David how to play guitar. And David, who studies law, helps Manson negotiate the barrage of legal issues that crop up almost daily on a prison unit that seems to run on paperwork. I got a strong sense that David is not one for name-dropping, and that the fact that he's never tried to cash in on Manson's fame is the cement of their bond.

Too, David and Charles have similar, broken backgrounds. Manson's childhood was so dysfunctional it's become the material of legend and lore. It's been said that Manson's mother, just sixteen when she delivered her baby boy, once tried to sell her child to a waitress for a pitcher of beer. Manson never knew or was able to identify his father, and was ultimately rejected by his mother and placed in a court-appointed school for boys. David tells a similar story of childhood abandonment before Hooker adopted him. David claims that his mother allowed his father to leave her only as long as he "took the little fucker with him," the father was an apathetic parent. Like Manson, imprisoned in juvenile facilities most of his adolescence for a string of burglaries, David resorted to petty crime and spent a lot of his early life "locked up."

David described himself as a member of the "suspect class." He grew up hanging out with bikers and belonging to the outcast crowd, which made him an easy target to the sort of people who are always looking for someone to label. Living on the fringe, a person experiences all sorts of underground cultures. "I've seen all kinds of stuff, well, Satanist stuff," David explained, "but someone who calls himself a Satanist is not necessarily anti-Christian; Satanism is an aspect of Christianity. Those kids are just going for shock value or trying to express a darker feeling of exclusion." David explained that society frowns upon the expression of darkness inherent to Satanism or other alternative cultures because "someone from 'regular' society sees that and he sees it as completely different from himself. Most people living a 'normal' life are denying their darker thoughts and urges, but they're human—and they've got them."

I could immediately identify with what David was saying. I've always belonged to various subcultures on the outskirts of society. Music was usually the only thing that brought the kind of kids I knew together. Within the music community, a person can find an understanding, a sense of belonging, the kind that's so important to adolescents trying to figure themselves out. In the '80s, if you wore an SNFU shirt and you came across another kid wearing the same shirt, there was an immediate connection, and you had found an instant friend. It felt as if you already knew one another, because you had already been introduced to the same ideals, ethics, beliefs, whatever. Outside of the music world, inside the walls of what are all too often overly conservative high schools, you could expect the complete opposite reaction to your long hair and rock music and dark clothes. I never acted out in high school, never gave anyone any reason to believe I was a danger or a threat, but I can remember the intensity of students' and teachers' reactions to me. Once, a bunch of worried parents even held a meeting to discuss how to deal with my influence on their kids. They believed I could introduce them to drugs.

Of course, not one of those parents ever approached or talked to me. People fear what they don't understand. Had any of those men and women bothered to get to know the kid they intended to vilify, they'd have been shocked to discover I'd never done a drug in my life.

David told me that you could see the extent to which people project their fears onto a single person, and the effects of this phenomenon, in the case of Charles Manson. "Look how they vilified Charlie by putting all that crap on him. I'm sure it's changed the way he projects himself outwardly, especially during major media interviews. In the past, you would see him on TV and he'd act like he was thinking, 'I know you expect me to be this, so I'll show you this; I'll show you all about what you've got going on in your own stupid head about what you think I am.' But he sure is not going to go ahead and unburden himself of his darkest thoughts and deepest beliefs in that kind of venue. Some people end up getting very much the wrong idea." One clip from a Manson interview has gone viral on the Internet, racking up millions upon millions of views on YouTube alone. It shows Manson, dressed in an orange jumpsuit and sitting in front of an American flag, responding to the prompt, "Tell me, in a sentence, who you are." Manson literally leaps at the chance to answer, lurching forward into a series of erratic facial expressions and gesticulations. He shrugs his shoulders, cocks and contorts his brows, rolls his eyes, and sticks out his tongue. After almost ten seconds of this, his shoulders rise futilely one last time and he shakes his head as he replies with all conceivable sincerity, "Nobody."

"The public persona is something created outside of him. He

wasn't any of that. That was the newspapers and magazines and news broadcasts trying to sensationalize the story; they made the Manson Family sound like they were all a bunch of rabid dogs feasting on babies." Because of this, David said, people are all too eager to jump to the conclusion that Charles Manson is a master mind, a mind reader, a manipulator capable of directing the masses to do his dirty work. "The last thing he's trying to do is control somebody or get somebody else to do things." The man David calls his friend is an "unassuming" inmate who's been in prison the majority of his life and is, therefore, expert at doing time. And part of doing prison time is knowing how to keep most people at arm's length. "So many people have tried to fuck him over, and rip him off, and use *him* for one thing or another."

Hearing this, I had to ask David if he felt Manson was at all accountable for the Tate/LaBianca murders. And he answered me confidently, "Whatever they were doing, I don't think Charlie gave them guidance; I don't think he said, 'Go to this address, and perform these specific acts.'" He qualified his answer further when I pressed him. "At the time, there were all these radical things going on. I could see that he could get paranoid and say, 'Hey, look, do what you need to do,' but, beyond that, I don't think he sent anybody anywhere with instructions to do any specific thing, including not murdering anyone." David attributed the murders to "happenstance" on the part of all people involved. And he vehemently denied the possibility that Manson brainwashed his family members. "You can't make someone do something they don't want to do," David said. "That's absolute bullshit."

I asked David how he and Charles met, the series of events leading to their eventual friendship. In fact, before he was transferred to PHU, David didn't know much about Charles Manson. "I was born in '62, so I was pretty young [during the Mason Family murder spree]. I remember hearing his name a lot as a kid, but I didn't really pay a whole lot of attention." Charles was in the hole when David arrived on the unit in the late '90s, and so David's initial introduction to the notorious inmate was though the incessant rumors he heard circulating in different parts of the prison system. "They'd say that if someone got transferred to PHU, they could end up making millions of dollars from the Kennedys for killing Sirhan or from the Folgers for killing Manson." David, who'd been transferred to PHU in the first place for "knowing too much," was simultaneously reluctant to hear this gossip and intrigued by the thought of how a man with such a large price tag over his head survived in such a system.

"When Manson got out of the hole, he'd been here for a while so he knew everybody. He came in real comfortable with his environment and we were talking to the same people, so we ended up meeting each other pretty quickly." David said the two started "slowly getting to know each other." Though neither was particularly interested in making new friends, the two began "bouncing off each other," sharing life experiences and ideas about music, literature, and art. David said that the two felt like kindred, creative spirits in a place filled with the ill tempered and uninspired. "You kind of gravitate toward people; if you're not full of shit you kind of gravitate toward people who aren't full of shit." Ultimately, though, David claims their friendship is really founded on trust. "Like I said, the guy does his time; he kind of stays to himself, partway for privacy, partway because a lot of these guys are snakes and try to burn anything that they can because he has resources on the outside through all the people that contact him. Rather than being one of the flies trying to suck blood out of his ear, I'm just another cow in the field. I'm trying not to be too involved, trying to just kind of do my own thing. He influences other people by his thinking, his philosophy on certain things. Charlie has a "let it be" kind of an attitude. Other people's interactions with him, don't impact the way he thinks, the way he acts, or the way he believes things. They end up by their demands, and wants placing pressure, intentional or not, on him. That's how they impact him most, the outside forces, but it's not so much outside thought. He is pretty much locked into his thoughts and beliefs, and the way he sees them."

Knowing more now than I ever thought I'd know about his home, it intrigued me to imagine the kind of art Charles Manson produced in prison. I'd learn from David that Manson deals mainly in the abstract: lots of squiggles, circles, and color. He will get to work on a new piece whenever he can get his hands on new pencils, crayons, markers, or colored pens. Art supplies are pretty difficult to get a hold of in PHU. Manson rarely finishes his projects and he will often start something, move on to something new, only to return to work on something he began long before; he sees everything as a "work in progress." Though somewhat dissipated, distracted, he evidently puts a lot of time and effort into his work.

Because of the extensive time he'd spent in the hole, it had been years since Manson had produced any art. One day, unexpectedly, I received a drawing he'd created for me of a coy fish. Manson had started calling me "Fish," because of my first name, and so I assumed my new nickname inspired his subject. The piece arrived in a package made of two envelopes crudely taped together. It was an extremely abstract composition made from red and blue colored pencils; initially I had no idea what the piece depicted. I was more struck by the fairly large spider that fell from the envelope and onto my floor before quickly scurrying under my couch, never to be seen again. When I told Manson about the spider, he found it quite amusing. He didn't attempt to explain the incident. He merely laughed.

My Inmate Friends

Let the dead bury the dead, you know what I mean? I've got my partners; I've got some dudes in here that are really straight up, man. They've been through a lot of hell. You say you've had a bad day, and that's a joke 'cause your worst day in your miserable life couldn't be half as miserable as two seconds of these guys' lives in here. They're all busted up, they got bones broken, and scars all over them, half their faces are missing. These guys have been through it, man. Even Kenny, he's been kicked in the head, he's been stomped on, he's been through a whole lot of stuff, man. Even though he lies all the time, he's still a character. I love him, I respect him, I look out for him, you know, but I have to be careful, very careful.

There are a few that don't exist that exist, and, in other words, they know that they don't exist. So they exist in that. Kenny don't exist. You know you can't just lie every word and exist, man, because lies don't exist. It's like an artificial apple, man. It looks good but it's made of rubber. There's no life in it. No, see, like the way things are protected, it's really the older you get you figure out how protection works, you know, like you're protected by things that happen. If you have enemies and somebody destroys your enemy and, then, your enemy sees you walking with them, then they won't bother you. You learn from chickens. You learn from dogs and animals, how that alpha wolf, the alpha male, he controls the protection. So it's, like, they come to me and say do you want this done or this done, you dig? And by what I say will be a mound of protection. I'm the king of the underworld, or the queen of the underworld. Any way you want to put it.

You see it from your perspective, but you don't see it from the point of view of somebody that everybody hates and, you know, everybody fears you, so they want to destroy their fear. And the more bad they do you, the worse they hate you. When they do you some wrong then it's all your fault. You're no good and somebody should do you in. Tomorrow I got the paint shop coming over, and they've been taking all the windows out of certain cells and they want you to move everything around, so I can see they're all setting me up for something. All my friends that are supposed to be my friends, they've become aware of it and they get to moving off and acting like they don't know me. You know, when you're in jail with a whole bunch of people who think they did bad and think they got wrong coming, they think they got bad coming and they wish bad on everything, because they feel guilty about all the stuff they've done. It's difficult to live in an area like that because you got to be on the defensive with everybody and you can't trust anybody about anything because they are all lying to you, cheating you, getting you every way they can. And you've really got no such thing as a friend and brother, and honor seems to be a joke that died in some foreign war before you were born, and there's nobody here.

Pincushion

There's a difference [in] the inmates that don't kill. I don't know whether you've met any of those. Those are the hard cores. Like this friend of mine who shoveled dirt in the captain's face. Captain rode the horse over him, broke his leg, and then stomped on his neck. Broke his jaw, knocked out his teeth, kicked one of his eyes out, stomped his ear off. And he looked up at his teeth falling out of his mouth and he said, "You ain't going to kill me, are you captain?" And the captain said, "No, I ain't going to kill you." He said, "I knew you didn't have no balls, you punk son of a bitch." That's the kind of mentality that you're dealing with when you're dealing with Manson. I can't judge anyone, but I can judge everyone. Here is the way it works. Sixty-three years in prison. I've been in here with everything you can think of. My cell partner killed his last cell partner, they called him Pincushion, who got stabbed about three hundred times. Every vital organ in his body was stabbed. He's a hell of a dude, man. He'd get up on a chair and say there's no knife made that can kill me, and he'd defy everybody.

Everybody but one guy. Killed his cell partner and he used to hold him up for count and tie him with string and hold him up to the bars. He cut parts of his legs off and made sandwiches, cooked him. The judge asked him, "Why did you keep that body, after rigor mortis had set in, in your cell?" He said, "Because that asshole was still good." He liked sticking his dick up somebody's asshole and if you wouldn't let him stick his dick up your ass, he would beat you up, knock you down, then he'd pull your pants down, then he'd get up your ass and fuck you up the butt. He'd come to me with that and I'd knock him out, then I'd throw water on him, and I'd tell him, "You might have done that to other people but you fuck around here and you're going to lose whatever you got, 'cause I'm going to take everything you got if you do that again!" He knew I wouldn't stand for that shit. Had the other guy done the same thing he could of still been alive that's what prison is. Prison is, you don't judge people, you accept them. If they get out of line you knock them out. When in doubt, you punch them, you punch them as quick as you can, and as fast as you can, and you knock them out.

Time Zones

You notice that retarded people are always truthful, and people that live in wheelchairs, they got a different frequency, they move kinda slow because they can't go fast like us so they're more attentive towards things. Slower. I've found they're smarter actually. They've got that guy in England in a wheelchair that's all gimped up, Stephen Hawking. I met a guy like that, in Vacaville, at midnight in a hallway, in an isolated room all by himself and he thought he was running the world. He had a computer there and he was on life support systems and couldn't get outside because nobody cared. Nobody liked him, nobody cared about him, no one would help him. It was him that was taking care of everybody and I told him, "I'll come up and get you and take you out to the chapel garden." So every weekend I'd come from the chapel and get him and take him out, and he had a wheelchair with a life support system on it and he gave me a silver cigarette lighter with a turquoise guitar on it and we were real good friends. But we wasn't on the same frequency because I was moving real fast and I couldn't get involved in what he was doing, because I would have to give up a big percentage of what I was doing to slow down with what he was doing.

I noticed a difference, time zones. I called it time zones. I mean, he was actually really running the world and he'd been like this all his life, and all his life he's lived in that sort of reality. He only had one finger he could use, both of his legs were all gimped up and his arms were all gimped up and he had a thing on his neck... that had hoses hooked into it. He had to hook this hose into his neck so he could breathe and then whenever he took the hose off, the only way he could talk is he had to put his finger over the hole. And when he talked there was no slack in his talk. All his talk was direct, and precise. Everything he did was just perfect because he couldn't make a mistake, 'cause if he made a mistake he'd be in bigger trouble than he was already in. I asked him, "What are you in prison for?" He said, "Rape." Ha, ha, ha. I said, "How the hell did you possibly rape somebody?" He said, "In my mind." I lost track of him because he was too powerful for me. My ego was too big and somebody else started bringing him down, and as soon as I got him on the ground he got two or three other dudes working for him, dig? He was running it, man. He was up there on his machine and I didn't have enough sense to keep hold of him, you dig? So he was, just, he was the boss man, he was a leader. He was more powerful than that guy they had on TV from England. That guy's pretty powerful.

VII

HOLLYWOOD

*O*ne evening, Kenny called on an urgent matter. He said it was a good thing I was home, that the "old man" was "freaking out" because an interview he'd been organizing with BBC had fallen through. Once he had my attention, Kenny put the phone down and went to retrieve Manson. When he got on the line, Charles told me that "this shit always happened," that he hated the mainstream media, that they always promised him everything and delivered nothing. He assured me that when they did provide him the opportunity to give an interview, they purposefully twisted his words around to make him look like "an idiot." Manson sounded determined to salvage the situation. "You're in Canada, right? They can't stop the world press from coming in here and doing an interview." I told him I had a few friends involved with film and promised him I would try to figure out how to get him his interview. Manson was still venting about his rights and freedoms being taken away when the call ended.

A few hours later, I received a call from a man who identified himself as "Graywolf." He was not in prison, but he was one of Manson's closest friends and confidantes.

"Do you know Charlie?"

"Yeah."

"Do you know Kenny?"

"Yeah."

"Good, good, okay."

Graywolf told me he'd called because Charles wanted to get a camera into the prison in order to film what was to be his "final address." I learned that, for the previous fifteen years, except for the BBC interview that came to nothing, Manson had refused all offers from mainstream media. He was tired of what he felt was biased editing, a process by which his words were torn apart and pieced back together in ways intended to make him appear insane and unintelligent. Manson now wanted to take the reins into his own hands and find a way to produce an authentic self-presentation. He sought a one-shot deal, a single opportunity to be able to express his thoughts and ideas, uncensored, unedited. And because the State of California has banned all face-to-face interviews with specific high-profile inmates since 1996, desperate and secretive measures were required to fulfill Manson's plan. Manson insisted that this address be visual; he envisioned it as a global media event that was truly worthy of the world's attention. It was crucial that his message reach as many people as possible.

Graywolf and I talked about the logistics involved in accomplishing this. Manson wanted the opportunity to address the world, to convince everyone to unite under one common goal, which was "to turn from war on each other to war on pollution." This war on pollution, out of all the ideas attributed to Manson, even out of all the ideas he has attributed to himself, is today his single, solitary focus. By now, I was well informed about Manson's fervent dedication to his personal philosophy: ATWA, the acronym for Air, Trees, Water, and Animals. Manson coined the term in the early '70s to express his prescription for the planet's survival. The four components are dependent on each other; and humans, in turn, are dependent on the sum of the four parts. Manson had explained to me that if people would just make ATWA a priority in their lives, most of the world's problems could be immediately solved. "That sounds like good common sense," I'd told him. But he insisted the logic inherent in his ideas made no difference in how people perceived those ideas. "Most people lack common sense," he growled.

Manson would interrupt completely unrelated discussions to tell me, "Air is the first order." It usually didn't matter what we'd been talking about; inevitably, each conversation culminated in one of Manson's passionate soliloquies centered on saving the air, the environment. Manson's level of environmental awareness initially surprised me; it seemed so at odds with whom I'd expected him to be. I couldn't believe that a man who hadn't touched a tree or walked on grass for more than forty years could have these beliefs. But, as I listened to how determinedly he spoke of the subject, I began to see his desire for a pure planet as a natural extension of himself. This was the truth he valued above all else.

I was also surprised to discover the level of respect Manson has for the military, the uniform. I had always assumed Manson hated authority, and all that goes with it. As we talked about the military, I discovered Manson's respect was actually admiration; he expressed a very high opinion of all soldiers, from all countries and in all wars. Manson seems like the quintessence of chaos, so his praise for the order that holds everything together almost sounded to me like a contradiction.

I already knew the strength of his beliefs, the gravity with which he spoke, the passion that infused his ideologies. And so I agreed that a uniform would be fitting. Manson informed me that I would have to be in uniform as well, that absolutely everyone on the production team would have to dress up. He was excited about this project and wanted me to help direct and organize the effort. I was immediately engaged: Charles Manson, the man whose insight and insanity had intrigued me for so long, wanted me to organize his final public appearance and prompt his departing words. I could do that. I began referring to him as "General." I also started to call him Charlie.

To me, Charlie is simply a man. I don't believe he has any superpowers; I don't think he is any more capable than anyone else. I don't begrudge him his unconventional way of thinking. I suppose this is because in my work I spend so much time with people just teeming with intense and extreme thoughts and beliefs. For more than forty years, Manson has tirelessly insisted that the planet is dying and the future of humanity is in bad shape. His stance is radical, partly because it is grandiose to believe one man can single-handedly command the entire planet. But what interests me is that Charles began cultivating these ideas long before the age of Al Gore. And what's more remarkable is that Manson came to these conclusions in a cage.

To Charlie, I was a loyal friend. He told me one day that he spends a great deal of time watching the way people interact with one another and has honed the ability to tell when people are being real and honest and when they are being false and deceptive. He'd decided I was trustworthy. When I asked him how he knew this, he said, "Easy: the way you are with Kenny." According to Charlie, most people would have "dropped" Kenny after he facilitated a connection to Manson, his famous friend. I hadn't. Manson has cultivated many ways to gauge and test a person's loyalty. The assumptions he'd made about me from studying my relationship with Kenny made sense. Some other observations about honor and devotion were less clear.

For example, Manson told me about a character he'd met on death row in the early seventies. "Pincushion" was famous for being the most-stabbed inmate in the history of the American prison system. Pincushion's real name was Roger Dale Smith, and he'd originally gone to prison in 1964, for stealing a wallet from JCPenney. Throughout his time in prison, members of groups such as the Aryan Brotherhood and the Mexican Mafia stabbed Pincushion numerous times during conflicts that Pincushion claims he alone provoked. Eventually, Pincushion attacked and killed his cellmate. He was sent to death row for the murder, transferred after California *v.* Anderson abolished California's death penalty, and eventually moved to Corcoran's PHU in the mid-nineties. He's since died, according to the men on the unit, from cancer.

After they'd met, Manson "hooked up" Pincushion with Graywolf and sat back over the next few years to see how the relationship developed. Manson said he'd been impressed with Graywolf's patience and fortitude in sustaining the relationship, because "Pincushion could be a mean son of a bitch." After spending considerable time watching the two interact, Manson concluded that Graywolf had all the characteristics of being an "honorable" man and that Graywolf was truthful, loyal, and righteous. Manson said he learned a lot from Pincushion, who he deemed the "best of the worst."

I began talking to Graywolf almost daily. He told me he met

Manson in 1969, after Graywolf found himself out in California. He'd arrived just as everything Manson created was starting to fall apart. Intrigued by Manson's environmentalist philosophy, Graywolf met most of the remaining Manson family members and even visited Manson himself in prison. And throughout the following forty years, Graywolf has upheld the highest level of loyalty to Manson, and to ATWA, which to Graywolf isn't just a message or an idea, but a way of life. He's worked tirelessly to promote ATWA through the creation of newsletters and other media, coupled with a nonstop approach to networking. But though Graywolf is unrelenting in his commitment to Manson's words, thoughts, and ideas, he does not ascribe himself any level of importance higher than that of a true friend. Graywolf feels that he is in no way Manson's right-hand man. But he is capable of contributing a great deal to Manson's effort, considering the limitations surrounding a man who's been incarcerated, often in solitary confinement, for more than the last forty years. Charles has never even experienced the Internet; he exists as a relic of another era, frozen in future time.

In the midst of planning Manson's final address, I unexpectedly received Corcoran visiting papers from Charlie and Kenny. And so I quickly became acquainted with PHU's visitation policies. If an inmate wishes to receive a visitor, he must send out a visiting form, signed, to the visitor. The visitor fills it out and mails it back to the prison to be processed. The approval procedure can take anywhere between four to six weeks, after which time the inmate learns whether or not his visitor has been cleared. I was more than a little surprised to receive the forms from Manson; it was common knowledge that he'd recently obliterated his entire visiting list (something he routinely does according to whim) and had refused to see anyone. When I spoke to Kenny about the possibility of visiting Manson, he asked me to keep quiet on the issue, especially when talking to Manson himself. Kenny told me the old man didn't like to talk on the phone about visiting. I'd have to wait for Kenny to suggest a good time to make the journey south to Corcoran, assuming I'd obtain clearance.

It started to look as if I wouldn't. Weeks went by, then months, and after six months of waiting, I began asking Manson if he'd heard any news regarding my visit Each time I mentioned the matter, he acted as if he had no idea what I was saying. So I called the prison to inquire about the status of my application. I was told that I was "approved but pending," and that everything should work out in my favor within three weeks. But when I called back after three weeks, I was informed that, due to matters of confidentiality, the prison officials could not share any information with me. Graywolf suggested I work out the issue exclusively with Manson and wait for him to tell me what I should do. Eventually, I got Charlie to listen to me. And he revealed, cryptically, that his door was always open to me; I just had to find a way in.

I decided to go to California. Of course, I wanted to meet Manson, but when it comes to Charles Manson, nothing is ever what it seems, and our relationship rarely ever worked out as I expected. So I planned the road trip as an adventure. I had accumulated a few weeks of vacation time from work and I could think of no better place to enjoy my freedom than on the open road, gazing at the beautiful western scenery, listening to great music, contemplating the complexity of my new friendship with a man who'd intrigued me my entire life. I planned to keep a loose itinerary, and devote myself to visiting a few old friends along the way. I would go to Hollywood because, for as long as I can remember, I've felt drawn there.

To me, Hollywood feels like home and I've been its frequent visitor for the last twenty years. Sadly, Hollywood is not what it used to be; its history seems to be fading, fleeting, so much so that I wish I could have lived during its glory years. Still, I feel as if I can relive history just by walking around the famous monuments, the theaters, the restaurants, the Roosevelt hotel. It's always fun to find Houdini's star on the walk of fame, though for some reason I can never seem to remember where it is. I make a point to stop by Grauman's Chinese Theatre, to see the celebrity signatures, handprints, and footprints forever preserved in concrete. When I find them, I always rest my hands over Marilyn Monroe's delicate impressions. I love the clubs on the Sunset Strip, where rock 'n' roll made its debut and still echoes from such legendary establishments as Whiskey a Go Go, The Troubadour, and The Rainbow room.

This visit, Hollywood took on a whole new meaning. As I visited the familiar landmarks, I thought of Charles roaming the streets, hanging out. He had once lived just off Hollywood Boulevard. I remembered a story he told me before I left, about his days dancing at the Whiskey a Go Go. One night, he'd danced so crazily that sparks flew; he cleared the dance floor and when he had everyone's attention he summoned the ten most beautiful girls at the bar to dance with him. Not one declined. "No one could believe how I could move," he'd laughed over the phone. Walking down Hollywood Boulevard, I was overwhelmed by the thought that I was somehow participating in history. If those streets could talk.

My friend Mark Hollywood Hatten grew up nearby, and his father is the groundskeeper of the former Houdini estate. Mark once gave me several old keys he'd found while exploring the property as a child. He believed they once belonged to Houdini; I do too. When he heard I would be in California, Mark encouraged me to meet his father, a man everyone called "Robin Hood," a legendary percussionist who'd once been a member of The Doors. Robin Hood was a fixture at the old Tom Mix cabin, the "hippie cabin" as it was popularly known, in Laurel Canyon. Right off the Sunset Strip, the cabin was the hot spot for all the "freaks" once the bars let out. Frank Zappa, The Byrds, The Stones, Buffalo Springfield, Joni Mitchell, Charles Manson, pretty much everyone involved in the '60s rock scene would hang there. Even Houdini was into the scene; he had constructed an elaborate network of underground tunnels that traversed the distance between his home and his favorite hang-out. Houdini also hollowed out parts of the Hollywood Hills to create concrete cabins for parties and get-togethers. These secluded spots were some of the Manson Family's favorite places to gather.

I met Robin Hood for breakfast at a small diner on the Sunset Strip. He looks exactly like an older version of his son Mark. He has a Nordic, Viking type style; I could see him being a tough, strapping man in the day and, by all accounts, he was. He wore a blue bandana in his long white hair and he was draped in at least fifty necklaces and probably one hundred bracelets. When I commented on his jewelry he told me, "This is nothing. You should have seen what I wore in the '70s." I got the impression that he'd always had this look and was currently just an older version of his former self. We talked about his life, my friendship with his son, and his days working as the groundskeeper of the Houdini estate. When he offered to take me on a tour of the property, I jumped at the chance.

While we strolled around the estate, Robin Hood shared stories of his glory days and pointed out the notable aspects of the area. Eventually stopped in front of a wide-open space. "This is where the cabin was," Robin Hood said, sadly. He explained that the cabin had burned to the ground in a fire that hadn't been the cabin's first.

We talked about Houdini, who died under mysterious circumstances on Halloween, October 31, 1926, at the age of fifty-two. One of his last requests was that all of his personal effects be destroyed so his secrets could be buried with him. This request was never taken seriously, and, as possible consequence, there subsequently have been several mysterious fires related to Houdini. Robin Hood pointed out that on October 31, 1959, Houdini's Laurel Canyon mansion burned to the ground. Exactly twenty-two years later, on October 31, 1981, the legendary hippie cabin was finally finished off after several previous fires. "The last time, the fire department just let it burn." Robin Hood looked as if he could cry as he said this. He hadn't been out to the site in more than ten years, and I got the sense that he wanted our visit to bring him some sort of closure. We stood in silence, looking over the few scarce pieces of foundation that remained. Robin sighed and I knew it was time I leave.

As we made our way back to my car, a beaded turquoise necklace fell from Robin Hood's neck. He scooped it up and immediately handed it to me. "What's this for?" I asked. "It's an old hippie thing," said Robin Hood. "When you lose a piece of jewelry, you have to give it to someone else." I accepted the necklace and hung it on my review mirror before we drove off to Sunset Boulevard. On the way, I asked Robin Hood what he thought of Charles Manson. He shook his head. "I didn't like him; he once took an ax and chopped up my drums. I had no money to get them fixed." Robin Hood believes Manson wanted to be like him. Robin Hood was a highly respected musician. Everyone wanted to be in a band with him. And so, Robin says, Manson saw him as a rival. "I think he was jealous of me." Later, I would ask Charlie about Robin Hood. "He's alright," Charlie remarked, before denying his involvement in the drum incident. He could have sworn he remembered "some girl" breaking Robin Hood's drums.

Eventually, I set off to meet Manson. The correctional facility is roughly a four-hour drive from Los Angeles, so I was able to leave one Saturday morning and drive directly to my destination, the forbidden fortress known as California State Prison, Corcoran. There are two major prisons in Corcoran: one is a substance abuse treatment center and the other is the state prison. Corcoran basically sits in the middle of the desert. It is extremely secure and eerily quiet. Everything is gray, including the gun towers that loom overhead and the buildings are large and spread out, so as to consume a massive amount of space. Thinking about how many prisoners have lived and died inside, you would expect to see at least a few people walking around, but there is no one. Instead, there are giant expanses of gravel surrounding structures built from solid rock. The prison's seal, which depicts the state of

California and a few of the jail's building and towers, is stamped on a stone wall surrounding the metal gates.

I made it past the first guard, who was standing in a small booth, almost like the kind you'd find in any paid parking lot. He approved my passport, but when I told him which inmate I was planning to visit, he told me not to get my hopes up: Manson wasn't seeing anyone. I parked my car in a gray, graveled parking lot and once I was past the gates, I was surprised to see so many families inside, so many children. As I made my way into the processing area, I rehearsed everything Graywolf had said to prepare me: be confident, tell the guards, "I am on the list," ask for a visiting form. When I completed the form and submitted it to the guard, he immediately turned me down: "Manson does not accept visitors; there is no one on his visiting list." I insisted that I had been cleared, that Manson was expecting me, and for the following five minutes, I watched four guards hover around a computer, trying to figure out if they should let me through. They eventually decided that even though I'd been cleared, the "pending" part of my application still had to be handled by someone higher up. And since it was the weekend, there was no one around who could help me. I was denied and instructed to contact the warden on Monday.

I was disappointed, but not surprised. And I had yet to meet Graywolf, so I regrouped and organized the next leg of my trip. I called Graywolf to fill him in on what happened at the prison. He wasn't surprised that my visit had been declined either: "This sort of thing happens all the time," he remarked. I asked Graywolf for directions to his home, but he gave me directions to a public park instead. Driving to our meeting place, I felt a little apprehensive. I had spoken to Graywolf on the phone, grown accustomed to his North Carolina accent and his deliberate, confident, articulate style of speaking. But I had no idea what he looked like, and as I approached my destination it seemed increasingly strange that he had asked me to meet in a park.

I arrived first. As I stood there, waiting, Graywolf pulled up in a small, blue four-door sedan and parked beside me. It put me at ease to see that Graywolf looked the part of the man he'd seemed on the phone: a healthy fusion of southern gentleman and mountain man. We introduced ourselves and, before I could say anything else, Graywolf urged me, "Come on, let's go this way." He seemed alert, overly cautious. Eventually, he explained to me why he had to be so vigilant: Manson attracts an unbelievable number of unstable people. All kinds of men and women from all walks of life want to be associated with him, for all kinds of reasons. And it's often impossible to determine precisely what those reasons are. People actually think they can just walk up to Corcoran and visit him, as if he were that accessible. And though there is a tremendous number of people who want to be near Manson, there are just as many, if not more, who wouldn't mind seeing him dead. He is one of the most hated men in America, often held to the same level of notoriety as Adolf Hitler. A bit into our walk, I began to appreciate the serene privacy the park provided. I wanted to understand Graywolf and the complex history he shares with Manson as completely as possible.

Graywolf is now sixty years old. At age twenty, he met Charles Manson in Los Angeles. It all began one day, while hitchhiking in the San Fernando Valley, when he happened to score a ride with Manson family members Lynette "Squeaky" Fromme, who was later convicted of attempting to assassinate President Gerald Ford, and Sandra Good. Once inside their car, Graywolf noticed a large book on the front dash and asked, "Is that a *Bible*?" They replied, "Yeah, that's a *Bible*," without looking back. "It's a good book," Graywolf affirmed. At which point they turned around and the three made an instant connection. They started talking about the Bible and how it related to the plight of the modern world. Graywolf hit it off with Lynette and Sandra so well that they told him about their community dwelling at a ranch in Chatsworth, and encouraged him to visit. "Bring candles if you ever come," they insisted. It took only three days for Graywolf to respond to the invitation, and once there, he stayed for six months. I asked him to describe the community:

> "It was a group of people living together in sort of a mutual agreement of peacefulness, and harmony, and non-ego-type living. Everyone was responsible for himself or herself. No one there was telling anyone what to do. No one was pushing you to be something or not be something. And yet if you could handle that, and grow in that self-awareness within the group, you would begin naturally to take more responsibility for the world around you. Like by helping to make sure the horses were always cared for. There were group meals too, every evening by lamplight, and singing together afterwards. It was an exciting and joyful place to just BE."

By the time Graywolf arrived at the commune, Charles Manson was already in prison. One day, Lynette and Sandra summoned Graywolf. They were on one of their frequent trips to the jail to see Charlie. "We think you'll probably like Charlie," they'd said, and so he went and met Manson for the first time, from behind a screen window.

I asked Graywolf to describe his first impression of Manson and he told me, simply, that Charles was a person who was "basically illuminated, a man with an immense presence, an undeniable energy about him." Graywolf attended some of Manson's trial and has kept up with Manson ever since. A decade ago, Graywolf decided to reconnect and write Manson a letter, and the two forged a friendship they've maintained through the mail and over the phone. Graywolf's visits to Corcoran prison began just a year and a half before I attempted to visit Charlie, but they are frequent: once, twice, sometimes three times a week. And through all this time, from his introduction to Manson in the aftermath of the Tate/Labianca murders, to his continued communication with him behind the foreboding walls of Corcoran State Prison, Graywolf says he's come to fully appreciate Manson's "understanding, energy, and vision for the planet."

Polanski

Hollywood

Well, it's all gotta come to one, and one has to come to one...it's all gotta add up to one. It's going to be one, one way or another, there's no way to get around it. I don't think it could be done any better than through the silver screen.

Here's what they do. People come in and they say, "Hi, we want to be your friend. We like you. We think you're really cool. You did nice things, blah, blah, blah, you know. We'd like to get this and we want to help you. We got a website and our website is really doing good." And then they say, "Charlie and our website, Charlie and our website, website, website, website." It's always website, website. And pretty soon they say, "I don't have to work now. I got enough money, later. It was nice of you to send us letters. You sure are a fool, we tricked you, we're gone." It's like, man, I did what you asked me to do and I never asked you to do anything, and then when I ask you to do something it's too late because you already got what you wanted and you got your website and you're a movie star now and you're Mel Gibson and you're Tom Selleck and you're Guns n' Roses and it's a whole entourage of all the way back to the Cadillac and heart attacks and saying no slack, no act, your life is over. "Ha, ha, we tricked you, stupid ass, fucking mass murderer."

I raise up on it and I make it happen, and they get me and claim it and say it's theirs. Tom Selleck says he's my Magnum P.I. I stole that from Pasadena in the fifties and took it to Mexico and scared everybody to death down there with something they'd never seen before. They seen that .357 Magnum, they thought I was from outer space. Can you imagine that .357 Magnum coming in a field of .45s and .38s. It's the biggest thing in town and no one's ever seen it before, so what would it do? It would take all of the iron, man, pull that gun out and blow a can apart, one of those big five-gallon cans. So it's, like, I didn't even realize it until thirty, forty years later. I got to thinking about that gun and how it's been following me around. The people from down there have been following me around with that thing. I thought it was just a satellite, a Russian satellite. It's the Sputnik. Remember the Sputnik? Well, it just so happens that the penitentiary I was in had a yard about as big as a football field and that Sputnik used to go over it every night and I would think how in the hell could that happen? Of all the world, why would that Sputnik come over my prison.

David Carradine was my cousin; he was a sorry old thing. Yeah. Well, he could have helped me a little bit. All he had to do was recognize [me]and say hello and send me a letter or come and visit or something. That would have took four or five cops off my ass, but he wouldn't show like he was anything that belonged to what we were doing, but he made a couple of movies off of what I was, him and Tom Selleck too. There's a whole bunch of fucking assholes that have been riding on my life man. Bruce Willis, Tom Selleck, Mel Gibson. You know how those dudes are. The only one that reached out was that guy that did Easy Rider, what the hell was his name, Dennis Hopper. Angela Lansbury's daughter is a good friend. Nancy Sinatra, I made her mad at me. A lot of them were mad at me because I never... was impressed by them, you know. Neil Young and I got along good because he wasn't... a show off and he wasn't trying to bully people around, he was pretty good too....James Taylor, he came off of England. Like his daddy got him over, you know. When you got parents, your parents can get you in and out of things that you can't get in and out yourself because you're not in that generation.

I got a new pair of shoes, and the shoes I [loaned]to somebody in 1957, I loaned him a pair of shoes, and I told him, "You can't wear those shoes, they're too big for you." He said, "I'll put toilet paper in the toes," and he took my shoes and he said, "Let me borrow your gray suit." So he borrowed my gray suit, and he said, "Do you got fifty dollars?" So I gave him fifty dollars. He said, "And if I score this broad from the beauty parlor, I'll give you half of everything I get." I told him alright, 'cause I was young and I didn't know. And he married Cher. His name was Sonny Bono.

Fantasy

I was thinking about how to communicate reality to a fantasy land where people are actors and movie stars, put up shows and overall bullshit. How can we get back to reality? I was thinking that if we play act, like we're not acting, and everybody that knows that we're not acting knows that it's a reality to do it that way. If we was to do an interview that was a reality to get through to the minds of the people that this was not an act, that it was not an interview for money. It wasn't done for entertainment. It wasn't done to try and get a vote or to win approval or to get attention or to enhance some particular political view towards whatever. Is there any way we can communicate a reality? Charlton Heston said that very, very strongly, and he convinced thousands of people. He had people that thought he was God; he was so intense with his acting. But how do you know the difference between an act and what is not an act?

I mean if you come to interview me and I cut your throat and *throw blood all over the camera and they see your body lying there, they might think you're just another cowboy act, man. And then they see you in a toothpaste commercial the next five minutes, selling toilet paper. You know, so how can you get through to that kind of mind that has already been impressed with so much fear and locked to so much insanity. You've got a high spiritual level of existence where the altar is the sacrifice of a human life. They cut the heart out of a young girl and hold the heart up and eat it in front of everybody and say, "This is the reality of everyone gives this much love to their priest and their God, and everybody must work in the field and grow cotton and do what the master says." You know, you've got all these servants doing all this stuff 'cause they want to give the best love, as this girl gave by giving her heart.*

But, actually, she didn't give her heart. They just had a bunch of guys in the back taking it and telling everybody on the backside that if you don't do what we tell you this is what we're going to do to you. They send soldiers to die in war because they can't face the reality out the back door. The trash can reality of the garbage people. You know they're the ones that have to work it all out and virgins are not sacrificed on the pyramids for good. We could have saved a whole lot of it. The Manson Family changed the whole world. But they won't even accept that, you know. The whole thing is turning out crazy. I just say fuck it, run away, and hide.

There's not that much left of what I'm doing. I boiled up my life down; it took me forty years in the hole. I've never been on the mainline in California. Not in California prisons. I've been mainline in federal prisons in California. But state prisons, I've never got into prison yet. I've always been kept in special quarters with everything they could put on me to push me over the edge because they didn't want to face the truth of what they did. They didn't want to face the truth of how much they owe me for everything they've been stealing, because it's all being run by criminals. Criminals, actors, movie stars and such, you know. Doing everything they say I can't do. No honesty there, man.

VIII

ATWA

*T*hat vision of which Graywolf spoke is, of course, ATWA. I sat with Graywolf for hours, discussing his attraction to Charlie's ideas and his passion for Charlie's philosophy. He explained that ATWA is a concept coined by Charlie and given to the world. But, he says, the world at large is conditioned not to recognize the problems pollution has caused in what Graywolf calls our "life support systems": air, trees, water, and animals.

"With the experiences I've had with Charlie in the last few years, I'm seeing the word ATWA as a tool, a focus. You could say it's a tool to grow understanding. It's an awareness tool. It's like a lens or a mantra. A lot of cultures and traditions have tools like that to focus the mind, and from Charlie helping with this process, I've come to understand that we have to be aware of the problem and the extent of the problem before we can basically focus our lives to solve the problem...to slow ourselves down enough."

Graywolf made it clear that eradicating the pollution has been Charlie's predominant push since the late '60s, when he started the rebirth movement. "There is a balance," said Graywolf, "an equation consisting of water, air, and the ratio of clean recourses verses pollution." Graywolf lamented the condition of the world's oceans and its biggest, most beneficial forests. "Beneficial," he qualified, "from the standpoint of providing medicine, food, cover, and carbon sinks." He spoke of China's industrial revolution, its overwhelming population. "They have so many people. And they have technology with which they can build dams and factories in almost a virtual instant. But they're polluting on such a grand scale, that it's affecting the entire planet."

Graywolf is deeply concerned that the planet is being pushed to its brink, while its people maintain purely materialistic priorities. As he emphasized the destruction of our natural resources–the damming of our rivers, the pollution of our oceans, the failure of our agriculture from the obscene amount of chemicals used to grow genetically engineered crops, devoid of natural diversity– Graywolf asserted that the only way to free ourselves from a bleak and bloody future is by ceasing to entertain ourselves with luxuries like sports, and ending the destructive process by which we fill our lives, our space, with material goods. "None of those things will matter in the near future, because we've gone so long without listening to the truth."

Graywolf believes that a lot of people, especially those his age, have been aware of a pending environmental catastrophe since the '60s. But there are many agents "programming people" to disregard even that which stares them blatantly in the face: parents, schools, and especially the media, which he sees tied to the corporate organizations running the planet. But Graywolf sees Charlie as an exception: "I feel like Charlie, growing up on the other side of the tracks, so to speak, and inside the system of oppression, or at least inside the justice system, 'behind the robes of the courtroom,' as he says, was 'deprogrammed' because he never was programmed."

"We see the shit in the rivers, we see the shit in the oceans, and the only thing we do is add to it for a paycheck. Everybody

Credit: Unknown guard at Corcoran Prison

Charles Manson and I. Just before this photo was taken Manson
remarked "How does it feel to have your photo taken with the most
famous man in the world?" June 2010.

Credit: Marlin Marynick

Taken while going through John Aes-Nihil's archives, slide recovered by the police after the murders, in them the victims appear oblivious to their fate.

Sharon Tate and Jay Sebring posing for Voytek Frykowski on the property at 10050 Cielo Drive during the first week of August 1969. All three of them along with Abigail Folger and Steve Parent would be murdered several days later by members of Charles Manson's so called 'family.' This photo was printed from the original slide owned by John Aes-Nihil.

Self portrait of Charles Manson, based on the famous Life
Magazine cover, arguably the most famous image of Manson.
From the collection of William Harding.

Credit: Unknown guard at Corcoran Prison.

Candid photo of Manson taken during a visit,
photo courtesy of Graywolf.

John Aes-Nihil in the dreaded Mojave desert. He is a filmmaker and photographer, owner of the largest archive of Manson materials and information, recognized in Manson circles as the "authority."

Credit: Marlin Marynick

Unknown guard at Corcoran Prison.

Star, Graywolf, and Manson. Star is a young woman who befriended Manson because of his philosophy on the environment. She lives with Graywolf, one of Manson's close friends and confidantes outside of prison. September 2010.

Matthew Roberts is a DJ in Los Angeles, research on his biological parents indicates he could be the son of Charles Manson. September 30, 2010.

Robin Hood in Laurel Canyon. June 2010.

Credit: Star

Graywolf first met Manson in 1969 after the murders, reconnected with him ten years ago; one of Manson's close friends and confidantes outside of prison.

String spider created by Manson by meticulously tying thousands of knots, made with thread from his clothing. It is the most sought after Manson collectible.

Stanton LaVey is the grandson of Anton LaVey, the founder of *the Church of Satan*. Sacramento. June 2010.

Pentagram necklace made by Charles Manson from toilet paper and string. From the collection of William Harding.

MARLin

Charles Milles Manson - B33920
4A4R-48   PHU
P.O. Box-3476
Corcoran CA.   93212-3476

ATWA

as Soon as I ~~X~~ Catch up with Nothing -
I Can be my self + relax + be, being, be
free to relax the inside of Just being.
becomes its self in always of all +
Everything Just becomes music —

[signature]

The first letter I got from Manson, a lot of our conversations center around music.

Charles Manson. Photo taken during a visit. June 20

Kenny Calihan, an inmate at Corcoran Prison and close friend of
Charles Manson. Corcoran Prison. June 2010.

David Hooker, an inmate of Corcoran Prison and close friend of Charles Manson. Photo taken during a visit. June 2010.

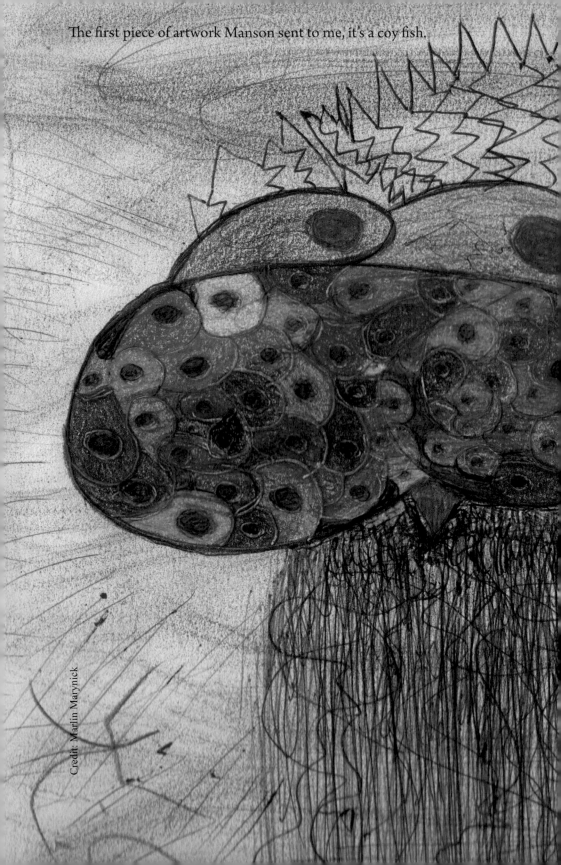

The first piece of artwork Manson sent to me, it's a coy fish.

Credit: Marlin Marynick

Artwork created by Charles Manson, from my collection.

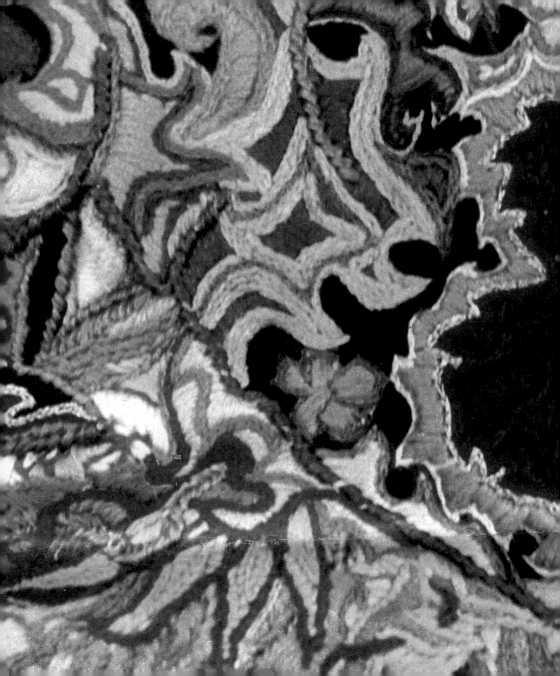

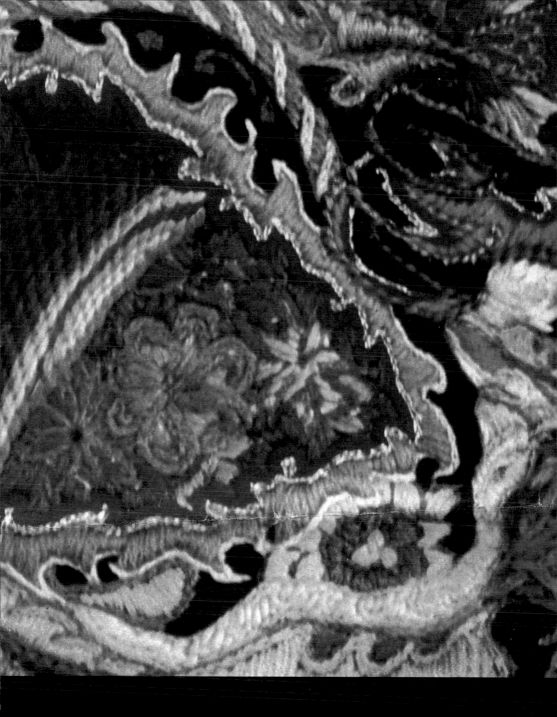

Close up photo of the vest Charlie is wearing in the photo with the crow. Very vibrant and colorful. Once he was arrested, it was cut into pieces, and divided amongst his friends.

Recent artwork by Charles Manson. It is made out of acrylic paint and
pencil on paper. From the collection of Graywolf.

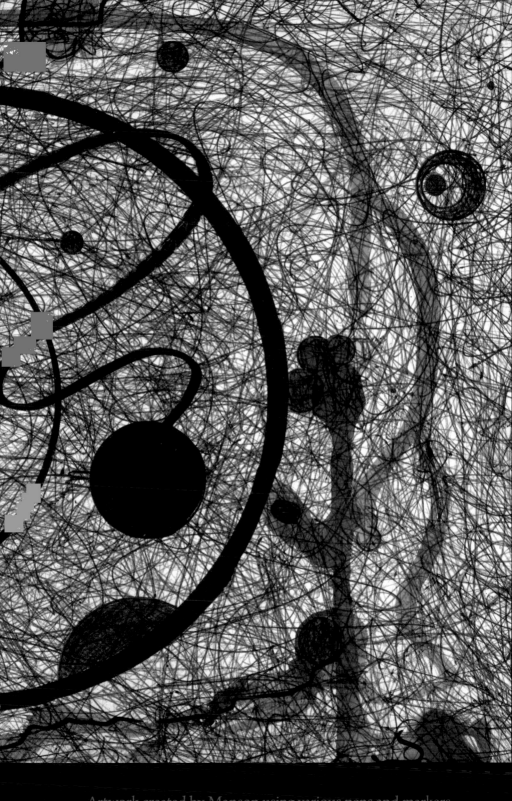

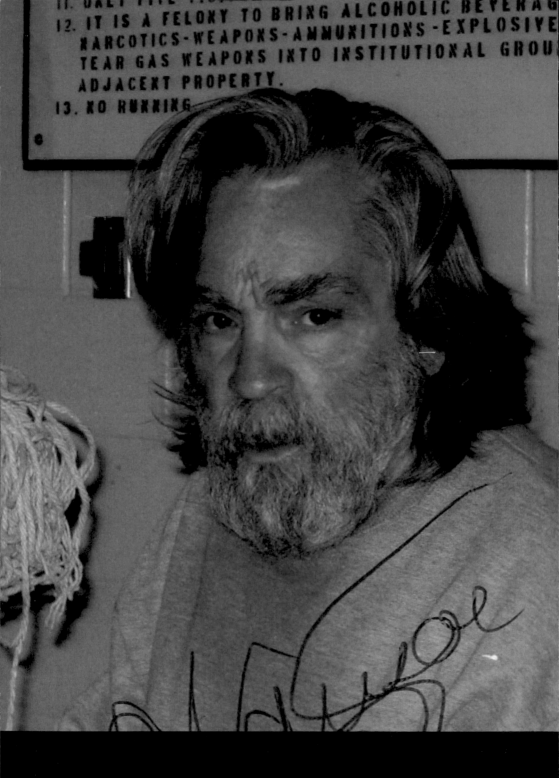

Manson when I started talking with him on the phone, a few months later he would shave his head. From the collection of Graywolf.

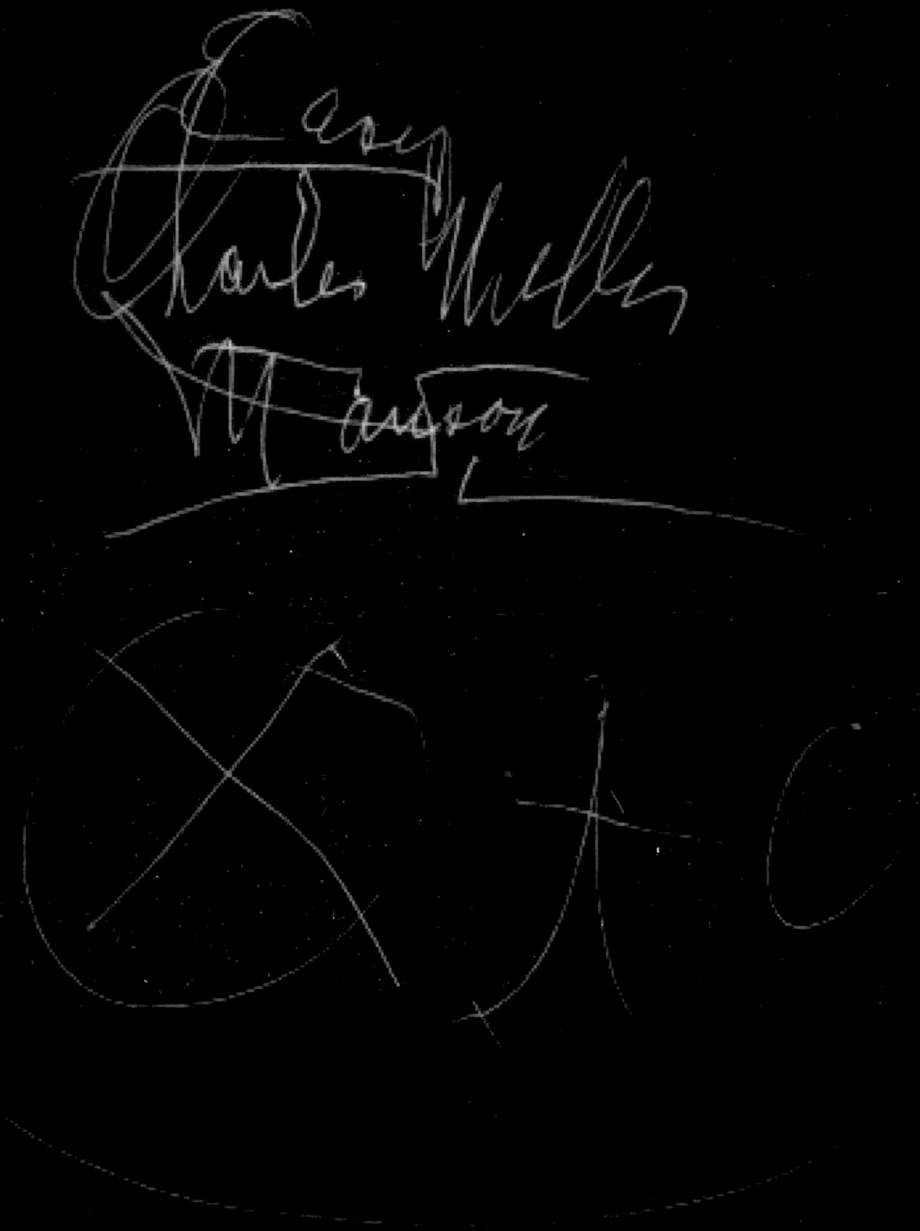
Charles Milles Manson

feels trapped, everybody's confused, everybody's frightened, and the TV just sells more shit right back to us." Graywolf pointed out that over the years the media has deliberately and grossly misrepresented Charlie's essence and turned his ideology on its head. "They've thrown blood at it, they've made it a horror story; they introduce him as a serial killer, which he is not, they introduce him as a mass murderer, which he is not, and then they let things spin out of control from there." This, he says, is because Manson's philosophy requires people to stop spending money on things that don't matter. Manson's solution to pollution is to stop, and start all over again. Graywolf declared, "We have to stop cutting down so many trees everyday and using them for toilet paper and toothpicks. It doesn't make any sense. Unless you happen to be a banker." Graywolf assured me that if we continue as we are, at the pinnacle of the world's wealth the world's people will have nothing left to breathe.

Graywolf believes one of the most egregiously misrepresented and poorly understood of Manson's ideas is a concept called "ego death," which he explained as the process by which a person "ceases to exist, dies in his mind, and thus lives forever." The idea, he says, relates back to Buddhist and other religious texts: "It's a concept, an abstract thought, an ancient thought." To achieve ego death, you must slow down, stop being the person you tried to be for the people you felt you had to please, and, ultimately, be yourself. It amounts to changing your definition of *self*, which others have undoubtedly doled out to you. "This process", Graywolf explained, "is a kind of death, because you die to your old self. You may fast, or meditate, or place yourself into a high-danger, high-fear, high-suffering situation, like a long trip through the desert or a journey to some other place previously unknown to you, perhaps even a back alley in a violent city. You then have to face your fears, what you perceive to be dangerous, threatening, and come out on the other side, reborn." This, says Graywolf, is what the entire planet must do in order to save itself.

"A lot of people have a hard time grasping the concept of ego death, and an even more difficult time accepting Manson's as the only mind free enough of ego to stop the insanity we've organized on this planet." Graywolf fully supports Manson's desire to lead the world under the ideology of ATWA. But until then, Graywolf does his best to respond to people "hungry for a direction, hungry for something that is not tied to money, or just a way to garner attention, but to offer something that represents a long line of people who have given their lives and their energy, their hearts and their souls to changing the direction of what people are doing on this earth." Graywolf went on to say, "It all comes down to one man, his knowledge of the natural order of life, and the truth flowing from that one, egoless soul." To Graywolf, Charlie is like an Oracle, a "Soul" source of valid information supporting a worldwide "green" revolution. Of himself, he says, simply, "I'm just a witness to that."

During my trip, Graywolf invited me to his home, which he shares with a young woman and fellow ATWA devotee called "Star," like "Graywolf," a nickname picked out by Charlie to suit an individual's personality and relationship to him. Charlie gives people nicknames all of the time; often it's one of the first things he'll do when he meets someone worthy of the special attention. Mine, of course, is Fish. Kenny's is "Irish," simply because he is Irish. David Hooker's is "Hook," I suppose in a play off his real name to show he is sharp. But some of Manson's friends, for whatever reason, keep the meaning of their nicknames private. I assume that "Graywolf" is called that because he is cunning and wise. And Star, much like the inspiration for her nickname, is seemingly small, yet extremely bright and in charge of a vast body of knowledge. She has a maturity that makes her seem much older than she could possibly be.

Before my trip, I'd spoken to Star a few times on the phone. She has a lighthearted and laid-back style of conversation. She seems as though she were born forty years too late; her beliefs and values are much more aligned with those of the '60s than with those of the modern world. She is an old soul. Meeting Star in person, I could see that she would have been a classic flower child. She is slight, and wears her brown hair long over loose, relaxed clothing. She smiled a lot as we spoke about her life, her beliefs, her relationship with Charlie. Star is just twenty-two years old, but she exudes a mature ease, a complete comfort with who she is.

Clearly, Charles Manson had magnetism about him during the late '60s in San Francisco, the ultimate hippie hot-spot during the age of the Summer of Love, a time and place set like a stage for a man upholding ancient beliefs on egoless living and environmental harmony. But Manson is still alluring to youth today, forty years later, after being branded America's icon of evil, while serving life behind the bars of the country's most mysterious prison cell. I was eager to hear how Star discovered Manson and, more incredibly, how she became one of his most trusted confidantes.

Star told me about her childhood, which, like all childhoods, contained elements of good and bad. The eldest of four children, Star was brought up in a faith-filled family, with which she attended church every Sunday – whether she liked it or not. Star described a comfortable family environment where there was always enough food, room to run around and play, and an overall feeling of safety and security. But, for a self-described "extremely strong-willed being," conservative family values combined with an overprotective mother caused conflict. "I wouldn't submit," Star explained. "If I wanted to do something or be with certain people, I found a way to do it." Star's mother did not like her daughter's friends and so it took considerable, deceptive means for Star to maintain the friendships she desired. "My entire childhood was spent sneaking around. This ultimately got me locked up in my room for a large portion of my teenage years." Unwilling to run away for fear of trouble with the law, Star stuck things out, and ultimately cultivated a better relationship with her parents and extended family. "I miss them," she told me, "and I try and go back to visit whenever I can."

"Before I ever heard the name Charles Manson, or what it was supposed to mean, I already knew I couldn't believe anything you hear on TV." Star says she's never been influenced by what mainstream media had to say about Manson. Her first encounter with Manson and all he represents didn't come through the television or Internet, but from a piece of paper containing Manson quotes that a friend gave her at school when she was about sixteen. I asked Star to explain what moved her about Manson's words. She told me that most of the ideas on the page were about ATWA. One quote she noted in particular: "Air is God, because without air, we do not exist." Star confessed she sometimes has trouble finding words for the things she thinks, feels, and believes. "I was already hip to what he said, so I felt a real connection. When I read what Charles Manson was saying, it was like reading a lot of my own thoughts, those I'd never really been able to put to words. I read it, and I felt really good. I started writing him right away."

Star doesn't remember much of her end of this initial correspondence, but the gist of her first letter went something like, "Hey, I'm out here, I really have a connection to you, and you're right on. Keep on." Manson responded in no time, with a simple postcard that read, "How far is bunker hill from Chicago?" Star wrote back, "Okay. I got your postcard. It is about a six-hour drive south." From there, their exchange would delve into Manson's in-depth explanation of ATWA. He sent Star a letter stamped with "A T W A," the letters aligned with the numbers "1 2 3 4" and the words "Air Force, Army, Navy, US Marines." Star felt her mind open up. "The people in the government and the military are the people that can get things done. They're the people that can do whatever, because they've got the guns." Star explained that Charlie aspired to designate the four branches of the armed services to preserve the four different components of ATWA. "I really dug that," she said. "I thought, 'Man, this guy is ahead of everybody else.'"

And while Star was happy about her epistolary relationship with her new mentor, her parents were not. "When my parents found out I'd been writing to Charles Manson, they were very, very upset. They were very alarmed." Their reaction to her correspondence with Charlie marked a shift in the kind of information she had to confront. "That's when I really started learning about how evil he has been portrayed to be. Then I knew what the media has said for the past forty years, but, by that point, I didn't care about that stuff at all." Star said she still couldn't believe the extreme opinions people have about a person who's so poorly understood. "They have no idea. What kind of a person can pass a judgment over a man they've never met? Who could pass a judgment on someone just because of what they heard about him on TV? Our world is full of those people; what does that say about us humans? I don't judge anybody unless they've proved their nature to me directly."

Star made the decision to move to Corcoran around the time she began exchanging letters with Manson. She even wrote a song called "Road to Corcoran" about the journey. "It seems like forever ago," she reminisced. "I remember I told my mom, I told everybody, that I was going to move to Corcoran, California, and I was going to help Charlie. Nobody believed me, and when I went, they couldn't believe that either."

Star saved up two thousand dollars from the money she earned working in a kitchen at a retirement home. And in 2007, she made the move to Corcoran. When she got off the train, it was a sweltering 115 degrees, but all she could think was, "Ah, so this is my town." The only employment the teenager could find was a job at a fast food restaurant. Eventually, she found an apartment. At around the same time, she met Graywolf while he was visiting Charlie. He made successive trips, until finally, Graywolf moved to Corcoran too.

Learning more about Manson's life in prison, Star became

acquainted with the unprovoked, routine hostility Charlie receives from prison officials and fellow inmates alike. She got to know the other prisoners in PHU, and even visited one of Manson's inmate friends. "One inmate I was visiting became very jealous of Charlie. A lot of problems arose; fortunately he was moved to a different prison and I cut off association with that person." Star explained that there still exist masses of people who want to keep Charlie down, so-called "professionals" inside of Corcoran prison, and on the outside, "an entire world of people that believe what they see on TV." I asked Star why. She explained that Manson is met with a lot of jealousy from people who are either inadequate, or unhappy with themselves, or both. And she described the existence of an unending chain of people, under pressure from other people, under pressure from someone in charge who is threatened by what Charles Manson has to say. "It's the reason we're having such a hard time getting cameras in to Charlie. They don't want people to rise up. They want people to keep popping pills and drinking beer and sitting in front of their TVs all day long, getting up and going to work so they can buy more of their stuff while they continue doing whatever the fuck they want to do to our planet. They're going to keep doing it as long as they can get away with it. They don't want someone like Charlie saying what Charlie says."

I asked Star what she hears Charlie saying. She defined ATWA for me:

"Air, Trees, Water, and Animals. It is the life that is growing and living on this planet, that is orbiting around a star, that is orbiting around the Milky Way Galaxy. ATWA is our life on the planet Earth. Scientists would probably call it the biosphere. ATWA is a movement and intelligent life forms, against the things that are destroying life on Earth."

Star expressed that her lifestyle works to promote ATWA and reject pollution of our natural resources, but she lamented, "It's hard to do that, with the way our civilization is set up." Star told me she used to want to run away to the mountains and live like a Native American, but Charlie compelled her ultimately to reject this idea. "I wasn't going to change anything by running off into the mountains, or into the wilderness somewhere. That wouldn't stop the people from cutting down trees in Madagascar or killing whales off the coast of Japan." Star knows she's just one person, but she envisions herself as a single ant in a giant colony. "I feel the need to take action. If humans were ants, a lot of them would be fucking around the anthill, doing nothing, and some of them would be completely destroying the nest. I'm going to try and rally all the other ants to stop this self-destructive behavior."

Star noted a few of the plans Manson has proposed to end the world's environmental woes. "First of all, we have got to get back to the horse; that's what Charlie said forty years ago. He's been saying it all this time but nobody wants to listen to him because of what they've heard on TV." Star acknowledged that a global regression in transportation would be part of an extreme approach to saving the planet, but, "The only solutions we have are extreme solutions because we're in an extreme situation." She suggested that a dense wall of denial prevents people from accepting the immensity of what has to be accomplished, what has to be changed for humanity to see its future. "We have to stop making plastic. Just stop. We need to stop making all those stupid little fucking toys; we have enough already." Star further clarified her stance. "I do believe, though, that we should keep and use the technology we need to help solve our problem."

Then, Star proclaimed, there is the issue of the world's population. "There cannot be six or seven billion humans on the earth. It's not going to last. The earth cannot sustain six billion people, especially with what we're doing to the earth now." Star was most upset with the way humanity's exponentially growing numbers affect the purity of its food supply. She was greatly concerned with recent trends in agriculture, the extreme amount of pesticides required to grow the planet's produce, the hoards of animals butchered for their meat. "We need to stop having babies. We have to stop using all these soaps with chemicals and antibacterial bullshit in them. Germs are here for a reason!" The reason for germs, Star said, is natural population reduction. It's the fact that we have eliminated so much of what ails us that so many people live long enough to produce so many more people. And though the thought of allowing disease to control the planet seems grim, it isn't as dismal as what Star sees as the alternative. "Either we start implementing these changes now, or it's going to be a really, really big disaster and there's going to be a lot of blood, guts and horror, all the things people want to see on TV. It's going to be real."

I asked Star about being a young woman and simultaneously being a friend of Charles Manson, a man accused of pimping young, impressionable women, brainwashing them, encouraging them to do his dirty work. In televised interviews, Manson seems to espouse distinct, double standards with regards to gender, stating that women are "nice" as long as "they keep their mouths shut." Star told me that the media is guilty of twisting Charlie's words around and arranging the interviews specifically to show him in a bad light. "Charlie doesn't hate women; that's crazy. He says that woman is the Earth, and Love. Man is the Sky, and Honor." In their relationship, Star asserts that Manson displays "the utmost care and respect at all times," is "honest, truthful, and forthright," and would "never try to break the will of anyone whatsoever, be it a man or a woman."

Because the overwhelming majority of the Manson family members were women, I asked Star to explain Manson's masculine appeal. "He's a patriarch," said Star. "A real man, not a momma's boy." She further explained that Charlie is absent of ego at the same time he is fully responsible for his own unique character. "He didn't really have parents the way most people do. He kind of raised himself, learning from a lot of different people, a lot of different kinds of people. He's his own person; he's unique." Star attributed some of Charlie's charm to his talent and good looks. "I know that, if nothing else, the other girls simply enjoyed watching him move, like I do. He's got his own motions."

I enjoyed my time with Graywolf and Star in the comfort and simplicity of their home. Their space is a testament to their values: small and efficient, absent of frivolities like television. Framed photographs of friends and family members hang about the walls. Star and Graywolf have ATWA friends all over the world, and so there is a small computer set up in the living room. Propped up against the couch are a guitar and a violin. Star and Graywolf are both passionate and accomplished musicians and they specialize in traditional mountain music. They are vegetarian and Star is a great cook. They spend as much time as possible out of doors.

We spent the rest of my visit going through old photos of Charlie, and I listened, rapt, to the many Charlie stories Star and Graywolf had to tell. Most of the photos were from their visits to Corcoran Prison. These shots depicted Manson in various roles and poses, almost as if he were an actor. There were photos of Manson wearing dark sunglasses, Manson with a Bible, preaching, Manson playing chess, and Manson acting like a goof. The collection is a candid look at Manson, unlike anything I'd ever seen. In a few other pictures he is looking directly into the camera and, though he has aged, he still showed the same intensity, inherent in all of the infamous photographs taken of him in his younger years.

In one photograph, I noticed Star was wearing a string of beads that now were hanging nearby, on a wall by a calendar. Curious, I asked her if the beads had any sentimental value. Star told me that Manson had made them for her out of toilet paper. He'd given the necklace to her the first time they met in person. "He turns the paper back into wood," she explained. She removed them from the wall and handed them to me to examine. The beads were large, yet light, pretty and purplish in color. It was clear that a lot of care had gone into making them. Already aware of how difficult it can be to obtain art supplies in prison, I asked Star how Charlie had managed to paint his creation. She told me Manson used whatever he could get his hands on: ink pens used for letter-writing, mustard left over from lunch, even his own urine if nothing else were available.

We talked about collecting, some of the other creations

Charlie works on in his cell. Graywolf sat beside me on the couch and presented a small black box. He carefully removed the lid, revealing an object obscured by thin tissue paper wrapping. Graywolf gently uncovered a miniature string-art spider, the most rare of all Manson collectibles, handmade in secret from thousands of knots formed in the thread Charlie unravels from his underwear. Graywolf explained the tenderness with which Charlie forms his art-animals. He talks to them, even sings to them while he shapes their rounded bodies and spindly legs, as if to infuse them with life. They take months to make and are extremely rare, so, though I had heard about them, I had never actually seen one.

I'd spent a full day with Graywolf and Star. It was getting late, and I was getting ready to leave. Graywolf asked me what my plans were for the next day. I explained that I was going to meet and visit with William Harding, another friend of Manson's, a collector of true crime memorabilia who visits numerous convicted killers across the country. William had amassed one of the largest collections of true crime artwork and artifacts in the world.

Graywolf and Star said they wanted to send me off with some music. Graywolf got his guitar, Star picked up her violin, and they proceeded to play some of the finest traditional music I have ever heard. I was completely taken aback. They played three or four songs for me, we said our goodbyes, and made plans to get together in a few days. As I walked to the door, Graywolf called after me, "Aren't you forgetting something?" I was confused until he handed me the small black box with the string spider inside. "Serious?" I asked. Graywolf smiled and said, "Yah, just make sure you give him a good home." The door closed behind me. I could hear Graywolf and Star resume playing, the music slowly fading as I walked to my car.

Manson called later that evening. He said he'd been ready to visit that day, but hadn't gotten called down to the visiting room. I explained what happened, and assured him I would contact the warden as soon as possible. I told Manson about the rest of my trip. He seemed pleased I'd connected with Graywolf and Star.

PAST Commitments

The News

Prison is something that was invented hundreds of years ago that had a reason, but there's no reason for that anymore. They're still living in the shadows of forcing people to be in cages and they don't realize what's really going on, that everybody that's doing that is going to be killed. What are you doing? What are you doing with all these kids locked up in cages? What is it doing? It's not doing anything. It's just making it worse. What is crime? They don't care because they don't believe it, they don't know what it is. It's got to be a movie. They're starting it at the border but then the news press won't give it to you. What the news will do is they'll give you a little bit and then they'll take advantage for their news and work it out for what they're doing.

They got the little community, the news community, like, they're not going to tell you that they're running out of water. They're going to go somewhere where they can have water, and if you're running out of water then you won't know it until after it happens because they're not going to give you the news. They're going to give you what they want you to hear. They're dealing you what they want you to know. And unless there's a whole bunch of people getting killed at one time, they're not telling you that there's a war going on around you. You know, they're saying, "Oh well, thirteen people got killed at the border over there, but that was drug related, that's all." There's nothing wrong with drugs. They've got a big problem made out of drugs. Sell them in a drug store. If somebody wants drugs, give them drugs. They want to arrest everybody, put everybody up against the wall, lay them down on the ground and ruin their manhood over nothing. It's still a stupid fucking game left over from old movies.

That's what this state is doing now, man. By the time you get the news it's too late. By the time you find out I mean, and then when people find out they just read it like it's coming from somewhere else, like it's an act, and all you got to do is change the channel, and it's all right. Man, you can't talk to them. They won't listen. You tell them something, and they look at you and say, "Yeah, you're right." They shake their heads and get right back in their cars and drive down the road. You tell them they got to give that automobile up, man. They say, "Yeah, we know." They're not going to give it up, man. They got airplanes that fly over this place and they got contrails that stretch out fifty miles. And then the guy that owns it, he's got his own airplane, he's flying it to Canada.

He thinks that his ranch in Canada will survive because he's using up all the land here for cotton. And he's sucking all the energy up out of the planet over here, thinking that he's got his little biosphere, that he can hide somewhere else and get away because he's got all kinds of money and lawyers doing what they say and all that crap, so there's just no end to it. It's just so big, man.

Butcherman

Butcherman got out of San Quentin and picked up this little hippie chick, and he says, "You know, I just got out of prison, I want some pussy." She says, "No, I don't think so." He says "I'm gonna take it." She says, "You can't take it. I'm protected by Jesus." He says, "I'm Jesus. I'll just take it, and I'll be Jesus." So, he just took it, and said, "See, now I'm Jesus." She said, "No you're not." He says, "I'll just kill you, and I'll be Jesus." She says, "You can't kill me. Jesus protects me."

So, he hit her in the head with a wine bottle, and put her head under the tire. When the highway patrol busted him, he was driving back and forth over her head on the highway, and he had his Bible with him. They got him and put him back in the nut ward, and put him in the cell next to me. He had a single-edged razor blade, and he was using it to make picture frames. This cop came up to him, and said, "You're not bad, you're just a punk." And here's where he got the name Butcherman.

He stood up to the cop and said, "Mister, you don't even have any idea what bad is." The cop said, "I know what bad is." Butcherman took the single-edged razor blade, and grabbed his [own] ear and cut it off, and then he grabbed his other ear and cut it off. He had both his ears in his hand, and he stuck them in his mouth, and he chewed them up, and he spit them in the cop's face. He said, "That's bad, you son of a bitch!" He said, "As soon as I get out of my cell, I'm going after your motherfucking ass. If I did that to myself, you know what I would do to you." He said, "I'm Wilson, you remember that!" And I said, "I christen you Butcherman Wilson."

So, Butcherman would come out on the same exercise yard as me, 'cause everyone was trying to get me pushed over the edge, and they sure wanted someone to take care of Butcherman 'cause they couldn't handle him, no one could handle him. All the doctors turned tail, and ran like rabbits, like they was all runnin' to Canada, trying to get out of the rain. You know how that goes. That place was thriving with insanity, everybody was crazy. You up on Pat Kearney? He was the guy who went and got all those Roscoes. He cut them off and put them in mason jars, the trash bag killer. He was a hell of a dude, man. He had a valid point of view, according to me. He didn't think that fear should be God. People were using fear to get that Roscoe over as God, so he said he had God in a mason jar.

Can You Lie?

Well, an intelligent person realizes you got to have someone to blame so everyone else can get off, you know, find someone that you can put the blame on and you blame them and then you go on about business as usual. I find there's two people you can't lie to: first person or the last person. If you lie to the first person, there ain't nowhere you can go to get away. You can only run in one direction. If you lie to the last person, there's no way to get away. You can only run in one direction. And if you're in the middle and you lie, you can most of the time get away with it for a long time before it catches up with you. But the idea is, like, to give a fuck, really?

IX

MURDER FOR SALE

After I left Graywolf and Star, I found my way back to LA, then to Hollywood. I had driven by a tourist spot, The Museum of Death on Hollywood Boulevard, several times over the previous few years, but I'd never stepped inside. Things were different this time. The next day I would be meeting with William Harding. An expert in true crime and serial killers in general, he is often consulted for various projects, papers, articles, and books. William is unique, not only because he has amassed one of the largest collections of true crime memorabilia in the world, but also because at the same time he has befriended some of the most notorious inmates in the American prison system. As I endured everything on my mind, Hollywood seemed to lose its luster; things began to seem surreal. The Museum of Death looked like the perfect destination.

The Museum is situated about a mile from the tourist area of Hollywood Boulevard. The building itself invokes a curious combination of charm and foreboding. I noticed first the huge, white, wrought-iron gates guarding the exterior, designed to intimidate any would-be thief. Atop the gates grow thick, impenetrable vines, which burst into a halo of red blooms about the cranium of a large cross-hatched rendition of a grinning human skull.

I had seen Manson memorabilia on display before. I'd encountered his art for sale in a New York City gallery and, in Tennessee, I'd visited the Ripley's museum, which boasts a Charles Manson exhibit complete with a set of Charlie's prison clothes. The last time I traveled to Niagara Falls, I found myself face to face with a Charles Manson replica in a wax museum. Manson is a pop culture phenomenon, an icon, and so I felt pretty confident that the Museum of Death would possess some interesting Charles Manson relics.

A soon as I entered, I was greeted by its curators, JD and Cathee. They were incredibly knowledgeable and excited to explain the exhibits. I paid the small admission and ventured inside. One of the first rooms was dedicated to the entire embalming and burial process. There were rows upon rows of equipment beside funeral-home handouts like promotional fans and matchboxes. The size and content of the collection could be overwhelming; there was truly a lot to take in. JD and Cathee told me they'd spent years collecting the macabre treasures and the carefully laid out displays showed how prized each piece was. Taxidermy, specimens suspended in jars, and some of the most disturbing photos I'd ever seen. Suicides, autopsies, murder scenes, the aftermath of a man hit by a truck. There was graphic documentation of just about every way a human being can cease to exist. I saw stuffed remains of animals that had once been the pets of celebrities like Jayne Mansfield and Liberace. A diorama featuring the Heaven's Gate suicides had been constructed; it featured an actual bed seized from the scene and clothing worn by one of the deceased draped over a lifeless, life-sized figure. The purple cape adorned with patches of the cult's logo was mind boggling to behold. I walked through a room dedicated to serial killer artwork, which featured pieces by Richard Ramirez, John Wayne Gacy, and Ottis Toole. I was surprised to find nothing of Manson's on the walls.

I came across the crime scene photos from the Sharon Tate murders in full color, hung like art. It was like looking at a most terrible train wreck, yet I couldn't look away. This event had somehow brought me to the spot in which I was standing. Throughout my stay in Hollywood I had started hearing my inner voice ask, "What the hell are you doing?" Standing here, staring at the young mother, stabbed about her swollen belly and tied from the neck by a rope, that question echoed in my head louder than ever before. I felt as though I were seriously invading someone's privacy; no one deserved to be seen butchered like this. I couldn't help but question what becoming a voyeur to this bloodbath said about me. I was overwhelmed by the thought that whoever did this deserved at least equitable retribution. The idea that Charlie was somehow behind all of this had been ingrained in my mind since childhood. I turned away from the images with this thought: How could you carry the blame for such a horrendous act, whether you were responsible or not?

I rushed out of the Tate murder scene and right into a room dedicated to Charles Manson. The space was filled with a ton of photos, newspaper clippings, odds and ends including a Manson-autographed baseball, and a few of Charlie's paintings. The paintings were a lot larger than the ones Manson had sent me, but I could immediately recognize his technique. Among the quintessential Manson paintings was a piece that depicts a detailed, glow-in-the-dark, underwater scene: a colorful collection of amoebas set starkly against a background of black lines scrawled on white canvas, markings that seemed to stem from careful calibration at the same time invoking a feeling for the artist's compulsion. Some of the sea creatures were detailed down to the cellular level; round, asymmetrical shapes composed of clustered, conjoined circles, each filled with tiny dotted nuclei.

I remember seeing, as I passed through the few remaining rooms, some artwork GG Allin had made with his own blood and hair and some kitchen cabinet doors from which some other rock star (I can't remember whom) hung himself. This completed my tour.

JD met me at the exit, eager to see my reaction. "What did you think?" he asked, as I struggled to find the words to express my astonishment. "That's pretty fucked up," was all I could manage in reply. JD smiled and laughed; I did too. I ended up spending a couple of hours talking with JD and Cathee, who both struck me as wonderful people. JD and I share a deep love and fascination for the bizarre. The three of us chatted about the people that visit the Museum and their various impressions of the treasures inside. "Our favorite reaction," Cathee explained, "is something we like to call 'the falling down ovation.'" Apparently quite a few Museum guests are unable to resist the urge to pass out as well as I was. I was interested to learn how a museum dedicated to death and destruction could originate from such lovely, lively people. I discovered that JD's interest in death stems from his childhood, during which his healthy curiosity about what happens when we die was discouraged and labeled "weird." As a result, he wanted to create a place where death could be explored as a fact of life, where people could learn, ask questions, and confront their worst fears without feeling the taboo. While the images displayed inside the Museum are graphic and unsettling at best, Cathee and JD insisted that just because death isn't pretty doesn't mean it's disrespectful to display it. The couple regards the exhibits and collections as part public service, part artistic expression.

I told Cathee and JD about my relationship to Manson and filled them in on the visits I planned to make throughout the rest of my trip. Through their collecting, they both knew Stanton LaVey, Matthew Roberts, and William Harding. When it comes to circles centered on true crime and serial killers, it truly is a small world. As I prepared to leave, JD told me he had something else to show me. "You'll love this," he laughed. He ducked back into the Museum and returned with a living, conjoined, two-headed turtle. I had never seen a live conjoined animal, and, to me, the turtle was a living miracle, the sight of which totally made my day.

The following afternoon, I met up with William Harding at his home. He was in the process of moving, and most of his collection had already been meticulously packed into crates and boxes. The sheer volume of stuff struck me immediately. William pointed to a large pile of oversized envelopes, artwork, and God knows what else. "That stuff just came in these last couple of weeks," he shrugged. "I just haven't had time to go through it yet." I learned that William is almost constantly sorting and organizing. It goes without saying that the inmates he's befriended throughout the world's prison systems have quite a bit of time and enthusiasm to create things for appreciative prison art connoisseurs.

We went upstairs to the master bedroom, where William showed me his most prized possessions: prison IDs, fingerprint charts, corporal artifacts like hair and teeth. William showed me four teeth, two of which had belonged to cannibal killers, preserved in little plastic containers, almost as if they were rare coins. While he flipped through various boxes, I noticed a lock of Manson's hair. He showed me an authentic Manson fingerprint chart. "How in the hell did you get this stuff?" I asked. William told me that was something he really couldn't talk about. I didn't press him. Instead, I asked him to show me his absolute favorite piece. Without hesitation, he turned to face the wall behind us. "That," he said, and pointed to a black matted frame surrounding a pentagram necklace Charles Manson had made. It was intricate and original in that it was a true piece of prison craft; Charlie had constructed the satanic symbol out of toilet paper and dental floss. I was starting to feel that my trip had really become rich with satanic undertones.

When I'd met William the day before, I immediately decided that I liked him. He has a lot of contained energy, which creates an aura that's more hyper than intense, so he comes across as being very alive. He emits a great deal of confidence and enthusiasm, yet at the same time he seems comfortably average and unassuming. I sometimes try to predict a person's nature before we've met, based on what I know about him or her. For some reason, my idea of what a person is "supposed" to look or act like is almost always completely wrong. Such was the case with William. The more time we spent talking, the more I realized I couldn't find any trace of evil about him. He seemed a complete contradiction to his home, a space filled with the most intimate keepsakes of people held responsible for the world's most heinous crimes.

I asked him how this had started. William explained that his collection had begun as recently as September 2000, when an online search for "Richard Ramirez" yielded fan pages devoted to the "Night Stalker" serial killer's art. William was "instantly amazed." He'd never known art like this was accessible. He said to himself, "I want that." When I asked William what he found appealing about Ramirez's art, he told me he was more transfixed by the rarity of the work than by its quality. William searched for Ramirez's address, wrote to him, and received a letter in reply. Eventually, Ramirez sent William an original drawing. But even then, William's curiosity didn't subside. "So I have met him," he told me. "I still write to him. I've talked to his wife a few times. Once, while visiting another inmate on death row, I saw him just by chance. We waved and exchanged smiley faces; he recognized me pretty quick."

I wanted to understand William's impressions of the serial killers he's befriended, how he feels he can possibly relate to them. He told me, "I could have been hit in the head with a baseball bat when I was eleven, or my mom could have gone through a bad divorce, and my stepfather could have raped me, and these things may have made me so mad that I wouldn't know any way to vent that anger aside from killing people." William said he is a victim of his circumstances just as all other people, including men like Richard Ramirez, are victims of theirs. William further clarified that both experience and character constitute a man's circumstances, and that the former, the latter, or both might drive a man to kill. "A lot of these guys have told me, 'If I could go back, I wouldn't have done it.' Others have said, 'If I got out [of prison], I'd do it again.'" While some men kill in response to trauma, others inherently crave bloodshed. William explained that some serial killers are in love with torture and murder, and in some cases with the people they crush with their desires. William knew some killers who'd spent their lives isolated and without friends. In part, their crimes stemmed from the logic that says if they could just abduct a person, they could keep that person long enough for him or her to fall in love with them. "They have this romantic idea of how it's going to work, then of course it doesn't, and then they have to kill them."

In order to routinely communicate with serial killers and collect their art and artifacts, you have to become desensitized to a certain degree. This doesn't mean, however, that a collector's friends and family will become desensitized as well. William is used to hearing he will go to Hell for writing to serial killers like Ramirez. People think men like William are sick by association. But William insists there is a point at which his rate and level of understanding hits a plateau: "Do I think it's going to desensitize me to the point where I really want a feel, or a taste? No, I don't even eat meat. I have no desire to feel what it's like to hurt a child, a woman, a man; that's not what interests me." It's the fascinating human connection that appeals to William. He described his first impression of Ramirez: "It was behind glass, there was only a small window actually. I was a little nervous, only because the newness of all of it. He was soft spoken, polite. He seemed very shy and was pretty articulate, actually. Meeting him was very laid back."

Richard Ramirez was the youngest child born to working class immigrants in El Paso Texas in 1960. Under the influence of a close cousin who murdered his own wife, Ramirez became a high school dropout and drug user. On June 28, 1984, following a routine drug binge, Ramirez broke into the home of seventy-nine-year-old Jennie Vincow and began stabbing her in her sleep. The act of killing aroused Ramirez sexually, and compelled him to commit acts of necrophilia. The killing kick-started a thirteen-month murder spree, for which Ramirez was eventually arrested, charged, tried, convicted of thirteen murder counts and over thirty other felonies, and sentenced to death. His crimes were so vile they traumatized the world. He tortured people in their homes, raped children, mutilated his victims' bodies, and even kept parts of the corpses as souvenirs. A self-proclaimed Satanist, Ramirez would scrawl pentagrams on the bodies of his victims and on the palms of his hands while he sat in front of the judge in court. Ramirez is recognized as one of America's most horrific and prolific serial killers. DNA evidence has recently linked Ramirez to the murder of nine-year-old Mei Leung, who was sexually assaulted and killed in the basement of a residential hotel in 1984. William, who is in his thirties, was just a kid when the Ramirez murders headlined national news. Remembering my childhood impressions of Charles Manson, I asked William what he had thought of Ramirez then. William explained that back then he was mostly interested in teen killers like self-proclaimed Satanists Sean Sellers and Richard Kasso. "As a kid, I never really gave [Ramirez] much thought."

William draws a distinction between himself and other serial killer "collectors" who develop rapport with inmates only to satisfy a temporary or superficial need. Many people lure prisoners into false friendships in order to obtain information for a book or score a piece of artwork. When they get what they need (which often involves breeching an inmate's trust), they discontinue the relationship and move on to another project, another prisoner. But William made it clear that he isn't just collecting commodities; he's collecting pieces of people. "The inmates that I write to, they know that I am going to be there. We've had arguments – I've gotten into some serious verbal altercations – it's like any other relationship. Another person might stop, but I value the friendships." William told me that men in jail are still men. "I'm not saying that they should be released. Some of these guys are guilty; they belong right where they are, but I'm not breaking any rules by showing them a little bit of humanity, showing them what they kind of missed out on." In terms of the money he could make from his acquisitions, it is clear by the piles of pieces that reach his ceilings that William isn't capitalizing where he could. "It's certainly not about money; when you see my collection you understand that. I have a hard time parting with things. I've never sold a letter." William said that when he does decide to part with a painting, he'll price the piece higher than what he knows will sell. "People say, 'Why don't you lower the price?' It's because I really don't want to sell it."

I asked William when and how he got interested in Manson. He told me that, initially, "It was just a crime interest." William had been writing inmates convicted of murder all over the country, inmates ranging from the well known to the utterly obscure. Because Manson is the most famous American inmate, William's interest centered on establishing communication with him. Initially, Manson didn't write back. It took time, years, for William to compose himself effectively on paper. In 2005, he wrote Manson a letter that explained what kind of person he was, what kind of person his wife was, how they'd been wed with a Satanic ceremony. "I sent him a few pictures of the wedding, and I just told him, 'If you ever want to talk to somebody, you know, a neighbor, go ahead and drop me a line.'" Manson wrote back from the hole, and the two exchanged a few letters before Charlie suggested a visit. William credits Manson's willingness to meet him on his letter writing abilities and his pure intentions. "I mean, I was incarcerated myself, so I know how to write. And, as a matter of fact, I didn't ask him for anything. I didn't say, 'Sign this; I want that.'"

Manson called William in June 2006. Surprisingly, William didn't know much about Manson's biography, trial, and conviction before he'd initiated contact. Eager to learn more, he asked Manson which books he should read as part of a crash course. "None of them," Manson scowled. "They're all shit." So William respectfully abandoned the prospect of outside research and decided to let any information about Manson come from Manson himself. "He just became someone I talked to. I didn't know anything about ATWA, nothing about any of that. All I knew was that the man is highly collectible, and he wanted me to visit."

William met Manson on September 23, 2006. "I can remember waiting, looking around the room, at the microwave, and then the back door popped open and in he walked with his cane. He held up his hands like Jesus Christ and stuck his tongue out, then he gave me a nice, firm Indian handshake; we hugged, sat down, and just started talking."

William couldn't recall the specifics of that initial conversation, only that it was "light-hearted, nothing too serious." It was an introduction of sorts. "I was checking everything out," William said, "looking at his hands, his hair, the Swastika tattoo." Manson liked it when he found out William had done two years in a state prison and told him, "Most of the people that I've partnered up with, they may have done a little county jail time, but they never did state jail time like you." Charlie felt William could understand him better than most of his other outside connections could.

When I asked William about his stint in prison, he was a little reluctant to explain. "You see, most people don't know that about me," he frowned. William said he had gotten involved with drugs a long time ago and, well, "shit happens." When pressed, he explained further, "I've been to prison and I've been called a bad guy. People have told me, 'You're not going to make it.'" William cited the strength of his family's support as the reason he was able to escape the sort of situations that land a man on death row. "It could be any of us really; there are people who just get drunk, get in a fight, take someone to the back of the bar and beat them to death." William insisted a sheer lapse in judgment could earn a life sentence in California "real quick," at a facility where you'd be stripped naked, abused, and deprived of your possessions. "That was so long ago," William sighed. He took a moment to reflect before he continued, "It might sound pretty cliché, but I'm pretty much a fine, upstanding citizen these days. I mean I don't even eat meat."

I asked William to explain more about his connection to Satanism, and he jumped at the chance to set the record straight. "Satanism isn't about devil worship and all of that; it is very much aligned with environmental themes." It angers him to think that some people who call themselves Satanists are not simultaneously vegetarian. William was not only determined to align Satanism with positive and loving values, but he also had criticism for Christianity and other theisms that have misconstrued the essence of Satanism through time. Christianity, William confirmed, is the exact opposite of Satanism, but not in the way most people think. William believes that, while Satanism is "life loving" and "earth loving," Christianity is about "giving people domain over the Earth, and telling people, 'Oh, there is nothing to worry about because God has a plan.'" He told me that Earth isn't happy under people's negative influence, that it will go on without us, that, regrettably, the planet would be a better place without humans around. I asked William what kind of being he believed the devil to be. He laughed, "If the devil lived on Earth, I think he'd be living just like I am. I think he'd be wanting to eat good food, I think he'd be wanting to fuck cute girls; he and I would really get along. He'd have good taste in art, in music."

William explained that, when he eventually began listening to Charlie's ideas, he realized that a lot of his philosophy aligns with Satanism almost perfectly. Though William had been a practicing Satanist for years, he says Charlie really kicked his lifestyle into gear. "The more I became aware of myself, and the more I listened to Charlie, it just kind of hit me: I didn't really care about animals and I didn't really care about the Earth. I mean, I thought I did, but I didn't." At the time, William was eating meat and subconsciously craving a reason to realize his beliefs to their full extent. "I'd had these feelings all along; I just really had to be exposed to them in someone else."

"We play a lot of chess," William said of his visits with Charlie. "Charlie likes playing chess. He's whupped me a few times; I've whupped him back. We talk about girls. I use to ask him about the girls on the ranch, how they had sex, and which one he liked best. I always thought Leslie Van Houten was kind of cute. He'd tell me, 'Oh, she was a little bit wild.'" William has a Salvator

Asian, an extraordinarily huge species of lizard. Charlie always checks up on the reptile and routinely encourages William to rent a helicopter and fly his pet out into the wild where, Manson says, it belongs.

William's descriptions of the Charles Manson he visits paint a picture of someone that's part man, part mystic. Most times, they will engage in commonplace conversations about things like jail and women, while they distract themselves with games everyone knows how to play, such as chess. Sometimes, though, Charlie will act as though he's in on information no one else knows. Once, as William was getting ready to leave, Charlie nudged him and said, "You know, we could just walk right out of here." William protested that the point of jail was to ensure prisoners stayed put, and there was no way the guards would just let Charlie free. "Sure they will," Charlie smiled. "Nobody will stop us; let's go." William continued to deny the opportunity and Charlie just laughed.

William drew an interesting distinction: "The day Charlie went in, time kind of stopped. When I did my time and got out, it felt like two years was nothing. You don't progress; there's no conversation. It's the same thing all day long. With Charlie though, he has always had interaction. There have always been people bringing him the news. They are intelligent people; he picks them. Charlie is a good judge of character because he knows who is going to get stuff done, who is going to be able to help. He's been burnt a million times, so he knows whom to trust, and in that respect, I think he's been around, and exposed to a lot of intelligent, and influential people in and of themselves. He made it really clear that he does favors for other people. He says that people come to him; he doesn't go to them."

William doesn't take notes from his visits with Charlie and he records only a few of their phone calls. Theirs is an organic relationship that exists outside of artificial means of documentation.

William told me it was hard to endure Charlie's presence and a hangover at the same time. During his talks with William, Manson would rave about the Spanish Captain, the Pope, and his five snakes. "He'd get into these rants, and, keep in mind, it would be nine or ten in the morning. I'd have been drinking until one in the morning the night before, I'd be kind of hurt that day." When Manson goes off, William is just as speechless as I am. "Once he said to me, 'You think Richard Ramirez is bad? The Night Stalker? I'm as bad as they come; they don't make them more vicious or rotten than me.'"

I asked William how Manson regards the high demand for his paintings, his signature, everything he has ever owned or created, right down to the tube of toothpaste sitting on the sink in his prison cell. "He was telling me this today," William said. "He sent me a painting, and when I told him I'd received it he said, 'I just want you to know, William, I'm a terrible artist; I'm embarrassed to send this stuff out.'" William reminded Manson of the masses of people waiting in line to buy his artwork. "Well, that's just because I'm famous," Manson retorted. "They just want my signature." William told me he truly enjoys Charlie's creations, especially the pentagram necklace he treasures above the other items in his collection. But Manson dismisses his ability to create art out of toiletries as proficiency in mere "hobby craft." William, however, is adamant that Charlie's artistic talent, the way he breathes new life into the thread he unravels from his standard-issue prison clothes, is truly a gift. "The string art pieces he makes are unreal because of the conditions under which they're made. They are next to impossible to get, because it's so hard for him to make that stuff." William told me about a series of ship sculptures Charlie used to make. "These ships, they were something else. I've never been able to find one. I've only seen them in pictures." Manson makes dolls and sculpts scorpions, spiders—anything delicate, intricate, and small scale.

William told me he was scheduled next to visit with Tommy Lynn Sells, "The Coast-to-Coast Killer," convicted of six sexually motivated killings and suspected of dozens more. According to William, "He's a real rough one, a non-discriminatory 'man, women, and child killer,' the kind of madman who would walk into a house, get everyone together, and start killing them." Sells was a drifter who rode trains and stole cars as he traveled across the entire United States. He claims he committed his first murder at age sixteen, while employed as a ride operator for a traveling carnival. Sells insists he killed "at least" seventy people between the years of 1985 and 1999. He accomplished one of his most horrific attacks in the fall of 1987, when he murdered an entire family in rural Illinois. Sells shot the husband in the head and left him to die in a field. He then made his way into the family's mobile home, where he beat the man's pregnant wife and three-year-old son to death with a baseball bat. The fetus of a baby girl was pulled from her mother's womb sometime during or after the beating. Authorities revealed that the mother had been raped with the same baseball bat used to murder her family. Sells is currently on death row in Texas.

As I talked to William, I was overcome with ethical questions about his relationships. I wanted to know how he got past the reality of what his friends had done, enough to carry on normal conversations. Because looking past a person's irrational anger, hatred, and brutality is something with which I routinely struggle in my work every day. Some of the people I work with are, for the most part, people that society sees as dirt bags. And if it weren't my *job* to look past my patients' shortcomings, I might view them in the same, negative light. Some patients–pedophiles, sex offenders, psychopaths–have hurt others so horrifically that it's difficult for me to overcome my initial impressions of them as people, enough to put myself in a position to help. You truly have to "get past" what disturbs you, suspend judgment, and work with the presenting problem. Conquering the tendency, the temptation to dismiss a person based on his or her behavior is an individual process, so I asked William how he was able to generate empathy for the inmates he has befriended. How, I wanted to know, did he show compassion to someone who has none?

William said that question was tough and the answer uncertain. He recognized the connection between abuse endured as a child and violent crime committed as an adult, but he couldn't understand why the two conditions are directly and not inversely related. "I know Sells was molested when he was younger. It doesn't make sense: If you were abused, how could you go and murder children?" I asked if he'd ever confronted Sells about the issue. "I'm going to ask," William said, then hesitated. "I've got to be careful 'cause he gets angry and starts bashing his head into the glass if you piss him off." William told we all are, because serial killers commit the kind of violent crimes we all are, because serial killers commit the kind of violent crimes that happen everywhere, everyday. "If I saw someone beating a dog, I'd get up and try to put a stop to it. But sometimes things happen, and I just accept them, because there is nothing I can do about it. Right now wars are happening, buildings are being blown up, whole families are being destroyed. It's just the way it is. People have always killed each other."

By the end of our conversation, William had explained to me that, ultimately, his interest in dark art stems from his own stint in prison. "I'd been in prison," he shrugged, "so I had an interest in serial killers and crime and collecting was just a natural thing for me to get into." If there was an incident that incited his hobby, William said, it would have to be the first time he saw Ramirez's work, twelve color illustrations hanging side by side in an art gallery. "I just wanted one of those," he told me. "I wanted it so bad." William immediately went on the Internet to find more art by famous inmates and, when he discovered a wealth of beautiful hobby crafts pouring out of the state prison system, he said to himself, "I want to collect these."

"Very few people want these items, but the people who do will pay for them." William is part of a small circle of collectors, people few and far between, from vastly different backgrounds: former FBI agents, musicians, attorneys, and paralegals. The group convenes on Murderauction.com, the largest murder memorabilia auction site in the world, one William designates as "the melting pot where everyone meets." In addition to the feeling of community it contributes to his life, William's collecting is something he uses to "keep out of trouble." He spends a great deal of time writing and receiving letters, and because of his friends' rather unpredictable personalities each day brings something new and unusual. "When I go to the P.O box, I never know what's going to be in there. It's really exciting going to get the mail every day."

William reinforced the mostly benevolent nature of his friendships with those behind bars. "I know it sounds crazy, but I have best friends in prison all over the USA. And I know some of those I consider my friends might, if given the chance, rob, rape, or kill me. But they are in a controlled setting, one in which they couldn't kill me, even if they wanted to." Despite this disturbing reality, William seems to hold a high degree of importance in the lives of many of his incarcerated friends. Some who have been executed sent William their personal effects. He has been named next-of-kin on the lists of those still waiting on death row. William stressed what a huge responsibility it is to handle an inmate's final arrangements. "It ain't cheap, either," he grimaced. "In Texas, it costs eighteen hundred dollars to pick up a cremated body."

Though he doubts that many of his prison friends would remain friendly on the outside, William is unwavering in his belief that Charlie would remain loyal under any set of circumstances. "If Charlie got out today, I would have him over at my mother's for dinner. I wouldn't worry about him ordering people to kill me, or any such nonsense. If I had a baby, I would want Charlie to see him or her, to see the love and happiness I would have found. I would want him to rejoice in that happiness with me."

I told William that I wanted to meet with Stanton LaVey and asked if they knew each other. William said, "Of course we do," then pulled out an oversized, beat up yellow film canister. On its side was a piece of very old masking tape, with the words *Satanism: The Devil's Mass* scrawled on it. William handed me the canister. "Tell Stanton I still have this," he said. "I've been holding it for him." I asked William what "it" was and he told me it was an original print of the film made about Anton LaVey in 1970. He told me that this copy had once belonged to Anton.

William also collects satanic memorabilia. The last thing he would say about the film was that it came from a large collection he had acquired and he felt Stanton should own it. William took me over to his bookcase, where he showed me many rare first edition occult and satanic books. It was obvious William loved sharing this stuff with people. It was difficult to obtain most of the things he owned and I couldn't imagine the lengths he had to go through to piece together his collections. I asked him how one possibly obtained a tooth from Nicolas Claux, The Vampire of Paris. William laughed. "Man, it takes a lot of persistence and patience to develop relationships with these people." He added that collecting usually involves exchanging favors of some sort and that I wouldn't believe some of the connections he had to forge to make things happen. It occurred to me that just being able to obtain this stuff under such difficult conditions was the biggest thrill of William's collecting. This had nothing to do with money; it was the challenge involved in bringing an item home that made the effort worthwhile.

NOT
JOHN WAIN

Major

I used to have a horse named Major, and Major had his own mind. If he didn't like you and didn't want to give you a ride, he'd try to push you off on the edge of the barn. He'd run into fence posts, scare you, jump over fences. He'd do all kinds of crazy things. He had a wobble eye and he was kinda nutty. He'd get up next to the highway and run into the traffic, like the oncoming traffic, then he'd look back over his shoulder with that old crazy eye, and then he'd flip his hip like, "I'll throw you out front of one of these trucks, you motherfucker, you." He was a good horse for himself, I mean, you know, but he didn't like people that well. That's why I liked him so much. You had to be an experienced horseman to ride that guy. If you weren't up on all the tricks, he'd trick you. That's what this Irishman, Kenny, reminds me of. He's nuttier than a fruitcake. Whoever raised him, they raised him.

They didn't ever put a check on him, you know. Lying is his way of life, man. He'll lie about something one minute, then if you catch him, he'll apologize and then lie about that. Haven't been able to get him to tell the truth. [I] tell him how important it is but, you know, it just doesn't sit on him. He wants in on something. He wants to be with someone. He's got a need to belong somewhere. He just follows me around, man. I'm on the horns of a dilemma with this guy. I give him an amount of mail to write. And he writes and makes enemies every time. I like him, you know, but everybody else hates him. He causes trouble everywhere he goes. One ball of confusion. He's sad. He's a sad dude, man. He don't have nobody, but at the same time every time he gets somebody that might be right, he fucks them off, man. He's got a line of people that I've introduced him to and he'd just mess them over for a book of stamps. Stamps seem to be the biggest thing in his brain. If he got a hold of a guitar, it might work. I find things for him and look out for him as much as I can, but then I've got everybody mad at me because I'm helping him

Air

I'm walking the road and they're keeping their fucking mouths shut and doing what they're told 'cause if they don't I'll kill them. How can I do that? How can you do that? I'm an outlaw. I'm a crook. I'm a thief. I'm everything bad. I'm what you raised me up. I'm your bastard son, Jesus Christ. Jesus Christ was a bastard. Why do you think they crucified him? Because they loved him? You must be out of your mind, blind. Live and let live or die. You understand me? It's not just because of the shirt you wear; it's the tear drops that you've dropped already in the air, in the atmosphere that I have to breathe. If my atmosphere leaves, you can forget it, because I'm at the bottom of the ocean. I'm all the way down at the ground. I'm in the octopus's garden. The Beatles were eating my shit when I got out last time. Can you understand that? So that's how much of a chance you've got to survive. I told you forty years ago. It's coming. You won't listen. Weren't listening then and you ain't listening now. It took me forty fucking years to come from the hills of Kentucky. Telling you, "Don't build them fucking dams on the river. Stop using that fertilizer. Stop irrigating. You're destroying the planet." Nobody wants to hear it. If it's not making money, it's not popular. The best thing we could do is spray the garden. All the people that won't, get in line with the Bible, flush the toilet for the last time. We don't use toilets. Do you realize how many toilets are taking the water off the land?

Words

In prison, time is like an octopus, it goes out both doors; the back door, and the front door. Sometimes the back door is the front door, and the front door is the back door, and time doesn't really mean anything in the center of the thought, or the reality of the mind, or the grave, whatever you want to call it. Life and death. The word prison itself is a prison, and the understanding of the word prison *is the only way to freedom. I told everybody that in Universal Studios last time I got out, when I did a little interview with them. I told them the way out of the room is not through the door, 'cause you go through the door, it's just another room, till you get to the big room, and the way out of that big, big room is as small as a flea, a bug. They say first was the word, and the word was god, and then they put all their words in the word* god, *and live a life they call religion, and holy. It's stupid, asinine, in fact it doesn't even have a word that covers how ignorant it is, because it's just beyond belief. I met a man and he was studying Greek literature and I said, "What is Greek literature?" And he said, "It's a dead language." I said, "You spend all your days and nights studying Greek literature, never go outside, or go places or do things, just always study, study, study." I said, "Why are you studying?" He said, "I'm studying so I can get a job teaching it." I said, "Who in the hell would want to learn a dead language?" He said, "Somebody who wanted to get a job teaching it." So we teach people how to teach. They teach people how to teach. We got all these people that learn how to teach, to teach how to teach. That's pretty good.*

Experiences

You wouldn't know what a fight was unless you got into one. You wouldn't know what a jail was unless you walked inside of it. So, actually, bad experiences are really good experiences sometimes. You learn things from bad experiences. If you just stayed at home all the time you wouldn't know nothing. But you get out, you go out and experience life. Go drink in the bar, get in a fight, fall down, hurt yourself, and know what pain is. Get married, and you know what divorce is. All the things that you do are just experience, the life that you're living. And in here is my life, and out there is your life. So you go get a job as a correction officer. You come in, you don't know me. Someone says, "Oh yeah, that's the paranoid schizophrenic over there, watch him, he'll bite you. He's dangerous. He's no good. He's evil. These are his evil tennis shoes. We got his evil jacket over here." Then they retire. You watch them go through your life, eight hours at a time, and you can read everything they're thinking, everything they're doing. It goes around in circles. You begin to see just how everything is. The industrial revolution and the automobile society. It's perfect for society and the artificial environment.

Well, you haven't really missed anything because it's not important anyway. It's just a trip. It expands your consciousness; you know, the best thing for your consciousness is the Crucifixion. Imagine the Crucifixion. Be willing to go that far with life. And that's the best, the peak of, that's how you get in touch with God, that's how you become God, because your pain just opens up all the senses of your body to complete ecstasy. It's all right now, you got everything in your body, alive just turns on. The best experience I ever had was when my head was on fire. You think that would be the worst, but actually it just turned me on, just turned me completely on. You couldn't get turned on any more. You know, I was at my total peak. I'm still there. I'm still screaming like a maniac man, wow, far out. He set me on fire because he heard my voice and it scared him, and he seen Satan in my sound because when I open up my voice and music it sounds like it's coming from walls or something. It's Satan, and then I was singing too loud in church, singing on the cross, imagine dying on the cross and then singing. Can you hear it yet, Jesus with a guitar, man. I have a good day every day. I get to play a little music. I got a half-assed guitar. It's not that bad. I don't got no electricity, but you know that's cool, I don't need electricity. My music is a hobby. It's a habit actually, you know. I don't really play for attention or approval. I don't even think I know a song, man.

My image

I'm telling you, man, we're breathing the same air. All I'm trying to do is survive in my air. I'm not trying to run for office, I'm not trying to be a rock 'n' roll star. I'm not trying to ace you out of what you're trying to do, but you think acing me out of what I'm trying to do is going to help you do what you want to do. Everybody wants to be Marilyn Manson, and then they think I'm supposed to be mad at him. I'm saying, "Ah, he just saved me a trip. I don't have to do it, he already did it. That's cool." I get the credit for it. He built a great image around the world. He named it Manson and everybody'd buy it, whatever it is. I never heard any of his music but I heard it's pretty good. I heard he's pretty good. I'm so busy playing music I never have a chance to listen to what other people are doing. I make my own noise. I believe each person's got their own noise. I mean, make your own noise, I'm making mine. If people's listening, okay. I don't care if they're not listening, I'm listening. I know who I play for. I play for the music. I don't play for approval. I used to play for approval. I wanted attention, I wanted to be loved and I wanted attention, and I got good, I mean I really did, I got good.

I went to Frisco when I got out of the prison and I went up to the head gangster and I told him, "Yeah, I just got in town, I want to work at one of your clubs." He got a whole bunch of nightclubs and he said, "Yeah, what do you want to do?" I said, "I've been practicing guitar in prison and I'm pretty good and I want to play and sing." He said, "Let's hear what you can do, dig?" So I did a few songs for him and he said, "Charlie, that's nice but, man, Bing Crosby's been gone. You know Frank Sinatra's nothing anymore, that's not what they're playing." I said, "What do you mean?" He said, "Come on, smoke this. Come on to the Avalon ballroom." And I got a sports coat on and sports shoes, and my mind is running around in a '59 Oldsmobile 88 and all that, so the Grateful Dead come out and I never seen anything like that. I was on the Island. Twenty years behind in Washington State. And when those guys started playing and a strobe light came on, I freaked out, man, I jumped and ran out of that place. I said, "God." I threw my guitar over a cliff, man. I said, "That's it, that's the end of that, man." I didn't want none of that action.

X

HE'S ONLY THE DEVIL

*E*ven though it had been a couple of years since I last saw Stanton LaVey, I had a feeling we would reconnect somehow, that he would play a crucial part in my attempt to understand Manson. Stanton has many connections with all things underground. He has a refined understanding for the unconventional and the unorthodox. He speaks fondly of Manson and Manson's relationship with his grandfather, Anton LaVey, and through his understanding of that relationship he has come to see and appreciate what he recognizes as "genius" in Manson. I wanted to hear more of Stanton's take on Charlie and, since I was already in California, I decided to seek Stanton out.

Stanton is a very difficult guy to get hold of. When I finally managed to get him on the phone, I was surprised to find out he had left Hollywood to go into hiding. "People are trying to run to me," he said. "I'm trying to run away." I convinced him to meet me at his hideout, somewhere in California. Stanton was as enthusiastic and accommodating as ever. He couldn't believe I had the opportunity to meet Charlie, and we talked for a while about how my relationship with Charlie had started and since taken off. I told Stanton how the conversations we'd had about the Manson family stuck with me still. It was an opportune time for us to get together. Charlie is a central figure in Stanton's philosophy and belief system, and Stanton could shed light on Manson–the man and the myth–for me in a way no one else could. I could incorporate Stanton's knowledge into my state of mind, should I ever meet Charlie. Stanton had satisfaction in knowing that. We made plans to get together in the days following our phone call.

Stanton's apartment was, of course, deliberately tucked away and difficult to find. When I arrived, his girlfriend Sharon came to fetch me and take me inside. Sharon is slight with long black hair styled in a way that's part pin-up, part Goth. As we entered the apartment, Stanton greeted me and laughed when he introduced his girlfriend as "Sharon Hate." I squirmed a little as he enjoyed his own creative word play and my eyes slowly adjusted to the low lighting, the near darkness inside. Stanton took a seat in front of his computer, close enough to the machine that his face became illuminated, almost as if he were holding a flashlight under it to tell a ghost story, like a kid by a campfire. As I sat down on the corner of the couch, I thought to myself he wasn't really scary; he simply seemed like the devil. Stanton's belongings were packed in boxes as if he were in the process of moving. It became clear that this wasn't a home as much as it was a place to stay.

We briefly caught up on the previous years. It was good to see Stanton hadn't changed at all and continued to exude a unique youthful, mysterious quality. He asked me if I had mentioned him to Charlie and I said I had. Charlie had told me that he remembered Stanton writing to him. He confirmed that he knew Stanton's grandfather. When I asked Charlie what Anton LaVey was like, he told me the man was all right, basically a hustler who would do anything for a buck. Stanton's stepfather is Nicholas Shrek, the man who wrote The Manson File and produced the documentary Charles Manson Superstar. Because of who he is, it is easy to see why Stanton's knowledge of Manson and the Manson Family far exceeded mine.

Stanton told me: "I mean I've been listening to that Lie

[Manson's debut album, Lie: The Love and Terror Cult] album since I was born. I was rocking out to Manson's Lie album when Axl Rose was standing in the cafeteria line in elementary school. [Guns N' Roses recorded Manson's "Look at Your Game, Girl" on the album The Spaghetti Incident? as the unlisted thirteenth song.] I was Stanton LaVey when Brian Warner [Marilyn Manson] had braces on. In fact, I was evil before Ozzy Osbourne became Ozzy and started Black Sabbath. I've been here forever and Charlie will relate to this. There is a reason why Charlie's memory of my grandfather is sort of vague and empty as it may come off with that slight twinge of negativity to it, much like my grandfather. Charlie and I go together like fire and ice, like blue and red, like hot and cold, love and hate, good and evil, like everything we've been here forever; this is Abraxis, baby. 'We go way back, way, way back; isn't that right, Charlie?' Charlie is golden, Charlie is perfection, Charlie does no wrong. You cannot do wrong when you embody the truth in every drop of your blood. From the time I was able to say 'Uncle Chuck,' Charlie has been a beacon of truth, and a light bearer of the Luciferian order."

I asked Stanton to define "Abraxis," a term I had heard Manson use several times. During one of our conversations, Charlie told me Abraxis is balance, equilibrium between opposites. At his 1986 parole hearing, Manson identified himself by saying, "I am Abraxis, the son of God, the son of darkness, and I stand behind all the courts of the world." Charlie had also told me Abraxis was one God composed of 365 different gods and that every life form has its own God. I'd found the whole concept very confusing. Stanton told me Abraxis predates everything. It came before everything and will be after everything. It always is. Abraxis is all, it is nothing; it is the only thing that truly ever was. "None of this is really happening right now," Stanton proclaimed. "I can string together the words and the facts as we are calling them, but, not to sound too 1969, all we have, all we know, all we ever are, is the moment. Anything that ever was, never was anything that is yet to be, isn't and wasn't, and is already not, that folksy sounding 'I'll Never Say Never to Always.'"

Stanton began singing a Manson song:

> *Always is always forever*
> *As long as one is one*
> *Inside yourself for your father*
> *All is none all is none all is one*

Important to Stanton's appreciation of Charles Manson is Stanton's perception of truth, which he does not define in terms of "facts," but in terms of "illumination" and "existence." He explained that both Charles Manson and the memory of Anton LaVey are the two most powerful forces capable of changing the world's reality. "They were merely two children fighting over a little blob of clay, two honest children fighting for no reason, but for the thrill and fun of fighting over the blob of clay and watching it change between their fingers as it passed from one hand to the other."

I asked Stanton to start from the beginning and throw down what he knew about Manson and his family. And he told me that his theories are his and have been in development his entire life. His only apprehension stems from his respect for Charlie's ownership of his own story. "For the record," Stanton clarified, "this is the story as I know it, and whether or not it is completely true, or whether or not Charlie wants it to be put forth is yet to be determined."

Stanton would delve into a discussion of Susan Atkins and her role outside the Manson Family as a founding member of the Church of Satan. He told me that, around 1966, she participated in the Topless Witches Review, a striptease cabaret Anton produced at the Mitchell Brothers Theatre in San Francisco, as a publicity photo model on call for nude photo shoots. Between 1966 and 1968, she was featured in at least a dozen different men's magazines, pictured alongside Anton in the ritual chamber at the Church of Satan or "Black House" on California Street. Stanton claimed that Bobby Beausoleil (who was convicted of carrying out the July 27, 1969 murder of Gary Hinman, whom Beausoleil claimed had sold him a bad batch of mescaline) was another original and influential member of the Church. Stanton told me his godfather, Kenneth Anger, had also been one of the founding members of the Church of Satan, and that during the church's inception, Beausoleil had been studying occult practices and magic under Anger. Beausoleil could have been called Anger's high magic apprentice.

"It's not a coincidence that Bobby Beausoleil and Susan Atkins, these two key figures in Helter Skelter, were there for the creation of the Church. Bobby and Susan are the Adam and Eve of the Manson Family." Stanton described this time period at the start of the Church of Satan as the beginning of the end, or the beginning of the new beginning. "It's a glass half full, half empty type of thing," he said. "You say the end times; I say the start times." And, while he admits he doesn't know about everything planned and executed by the Manson Family and the Church of Satan between the years of 1966 and 1969, he is certain there was more going on beneath the surface bloodshed at the Tate and Hinman houses. Stanton assured me that the Tate murders, in which Atkins participated, were not executed as simple copycat murders to take the blame off Beausoleil for the Hinman murders.

"This is where fact turns into theory on my part. I'm quite positive that Bobby's incarceration for the murder of Gary Hinman was sort of something like the Dead Sea scrolls if you will: to the pre-planning and the very calculated staging of a world event, with as much emphasis and importance placed on Helter Skelter or the date as was placed on the victims and on who did the killing." Stanton insisted that, looked at side-by-side, it is impossible to seriously consider one murder the copycat of another. "That's just a built-in excuse. It's, 'Oh, we're hippies on LSD; this is as close as we could come to a copycat murder.' Come on. Maybe the DA, or the judge, or somebody bought that because of Helter Skelter and pop tabloid sensationalism. You know the mindless masses are going to believe whatever dish they are served, eat it up, and not give it a second thought."

Stanton suggested that every single aspect of the Manson Family murders is significant. He told me that if you took Helter Skelter and "trimmed the fat" from it, you would be left with a series of events that could not have happened unless they were intended to happen. Therefore, absolutely nothing was spontaneous or accidental, right down to who was killed, how they were killed, and at what place and time. "Since when is killing a pregnant movie star, putting an American flag over her head, hanging her from the banister, and scrawling 'death to pigs' on the wall just something that felt right at the moment?"

Stanton told me that Bobby and Anton were also featured in the same Kenneth Anger film called Invocation of My Demon Brother. It was during the making of this film, Stanton suspects, that his grandparents, Kenneth, Bobby, Charles Manson, and Susan Atkins were all in the same place at the same time. But from what he dug up by "badgering" his grandmother and repeatedly questioning Bobby, Stanton discovered everyone had a different story about how the ensuing events unfolded. The inconsistencies don't discourage Stanton. They fascinate him. "This was something I was brought up to prepare for. I may come off as self aggrandizing or something of the sort by saying this, but I really believe it to be the case that my presence here on Earth right now, or at least one of the reasons I exist is for this very purpose." Stanton's self-definition stems from the sequences, the coincidences that have come together just perfectly in his life.

I thought about all the events that had led me to this apartment to hear Stanton share his story. What were the odds? I was starting to believe that this journey had a momentum of its own. It was intense, and we both felt it. "It's about as heavy as it gets," Stanton said, almost as if reading my mind. "We are gnawing on the bone of human history as we know it; we are chewing at the bone right now because the meat is gone. We have torn away from that. We are vultures at high noon."

Stanton explained, "I was in no small way prepared and groomed for my role, by way of never knowing who my own biological father is." Stanton alluded to the story of his father, who he was or was not, and described it as an illustration of order that exists in chaos. Stanton told me chaos is everywhere, much the same way God is everywhere for those who believe. Stanton went one step further by suggesting that everything people see and label as God, that which Stanton says they "use as a dump site for all their fears and self doubts," is merely chaos. "It is the electricity that keeps the whole thing going." Stanton told me Anton possibly understood this idea better than anyone else ever has. "He [Anton] told me that when the pendulum swings in one direction for long enough and far enough, it is inevitable and necessary for someone or something–a movement, meme, religion, brand, ideology, icon, philosophy, magic–to push it back." Stanton attributed such things as the intensity of the events on August 8, 1969 or the collection of rock stars that died at the age of twenty-seven to this principle. "It's one of these spooky, uncanny, sort of paranormal unexplained truths that just can't be escaped or overlooked." Stanton acknowledged that what he was saying sounded crazy and promised me: "It's going to sound crazier and crazier."

Stanton supplied a unique take on the purpose of the Internet: "As far as I'm concerned, the Internet was made and designed with the express purpose of collecting information from history and purging or deleting stories like Manson's, specifically." Stanton explained this is why he is the only person he's heard of who is permanently blacklisted from having a reference on Wikipedia. "It's intentional," he said, "and it's because of what I represent, because of the voice and the reach that I have." He described a war between "dueling powers," wars within wars within wars happening as we spoke According to Stanton, the world is staged, all of the time. He told me there is a specific reason he has no Wikipedia page at the same time he is the subject of a five-page feature in SPIN magazine simply for recording half a song. Stanton was serious when he said, "Those two things just don't make sense, but there is a very important reason for it, and that reason brought you here tonight."

I already felt I'd been brought there that night. What Stanton was telling me didn't sound that crazy at all. I wanted to understand more about how the stars had aligned in Stanton's life since his childhood. Before my mind could finish formulating my questions about Stanton's beginnings, he began to give me all the answers.

Stanton's birth certificate reads, "father unknown." Anton assumed the task of naming Stanton, whose name is taken from the same novel as his mother's: Nightmare Alley. Stanton explained, "The two lead characters are the Great Stanton and Madam Zeena. She is thirteen or fourteen years his elder, as my mother is mine. And, throughout the whole thing, the two are in love at the same time they are at extreme odds." As a child, Stanton was told his father had been a fisherman who'd docked one summer in 1977 at Half Moon Bay, where his mother worked at her brother Bill's bait and tackle shop. According to this story, the fisherman came into the shop with his father and the two sold their catch to Bill before the fisherman spent the night with Zeena. He set sail the next day, never to be seen again. Zeena couldn't remember his name. "So I was told I had a nameless seaman for a father. That's the kind of funny you come to expect from Anton LaVey."

Stanton's now estranged mother hasn't spoken to him

since she rejected her father Anton. "She dumped me off on my grandmother Dianne [Anton's wife] and swore she'd never speak to either of us again. Which, considering I had never done anything wrong to her, is strange." Around this time, Dianne confessed the true identity of Stanton's father, which turned out not to be true at all. "I was told my father was really a local delinquent who dropped out of my mother's school." Anton painted for Stanton the picture of a young man who was a hood, car thief, drug dealer, and pot smoker. "I was seventeen years old at this point and I was already all of those things. Of course it was an easy sell; I was basically told that my father was me."

When I asked Stanton to elaborate on the idea of himself as his own father, he told me he exists as an early experiment in Satanic selective breeding, cloning. "I'm not telling this story because I give a shit about the fact that I'm a test subject; I'm way cool with all that. I'm telling this story only as a way of illustrating the kind of intentional information detours and roadblocks set up strategically at specific times and delivered by specific people for specific reasons." I could tell the issue was a touchy topic, so I didn't press Stanton to reveal any more. He left the subject by saying that the scheme of his life works as a miniature version of the "tactical diversion, mass manipulation, and Satanic ritual magic" behind some of the world's most notable people and events, namely the Manson Family murders of August 1969, Altamont, The Zodiac Killer, and the publishing of the Satanic Bible.

Stanton reverted back to the subject of the Church of Satan, circa 1966, declaring Susan Atkins its spokes model, and Bobby Beausoleil, Kenneth Anger, Anton LaVey, and Charles Manson its founders. Stanton told me the Church had only one official meeting. It was an all night event in San Francisco, during which the blueprint for the plan "The Start Times" was drafted. Church members gathered at the former Russian Embassy, a beautiful four- or five-story Victorian house complete with all the traditional trim and ornamentation. Stanton spoke of a famous photo depicting Bobby in front of the embassy. Scrawled in red on the door behind him is a bit of Aleister Crowley's moral law: Do What Thou Wilt. "This is Bobby, pre–Manson Family: not just a member of the Church of Satan, but a very special student, one that had special purpose and responsibilities." Stanton speculated that the building is one in which "secrets will forever be kept." Stanton had once spoken to Bobby about the mysterious meeting, but Bobby's memories were hazy from the LSD that undoubtedly influenced most of the evening. What Bobby does remember from that night, the night he was introduced to Charles Manson, is "surreal and psychedelic." Bobby could recall, upon entering the Russian Embassy with Kenneth, seeing Anton LaVey in full ceremonial ritual garb: his widow peak scowl, cape, horns, sword–the works. Anton's full regalia meant, according to Stanton, that he was performing some form of ritual black magic ceremony or satanic ritual.

"My grandmother has told me that she has, in a secret safety deposit box, the real identity of the Zodiac Killer [who committed a number of murders in northern California in the late '60s and was never caught] and that, during the murders, before, and after, he paid visits to the Black House. He wasn't out and out with it; he didn't come right out and say, 'I'm the Zodiac Killer,' but there was no mistaking him for anyone other than who he was."

Stanton said the killings committed by the Zodiac Killer and Richard Ramirez alike were all part of a bigger, more significant scheme, "a much greater, beautiful, powerful, illuminating cause than our simple little minds here on Earth right now are able to understand." Each Church member Stanton questioned about the night in the Embassy summed up the occasion in just a few brief sentences. Each summary was unique. "How they are able to cram an evening into a couple sentences explains a lot, leaves a lot of room for explanation that we are not going to get. But it's safe to accept that a pact was made; a deal unlike any other deal with the devil took shape that night."

Stanton leaned forward, his face a picture of sincerity. "I know there was only one topic and one topic only about which my grandfather ever contradicted himself in interviews and his own writings. There is only one subject that received at times positive, at other times negative, mixed conflicting opinions and sentiments from Anton LaVey. That one subject is Charlie Manson. There is a reason for that too. I'm going to fast forward thirty something years."

Stanton was once a friend of Marilyn Manson's. They were roommates for a time and at one point Stanton made a cameo appearance in one of Marilyn's music videos. Marilyn is a member of the Church of Satan and was ordained by Anton LaVey. Stanton recalled the nature of their friendship: "So, I'm living in Marilyn Manson's house doing something along the lines of a mountain of cocaine a day and washing it down with never ending wells of absinthe. I had been groomed for this too after ten years living in Hollywood, partying with the best of the worst." Around this time, Stanton invited his friend, musician Hank Williams III, over to Marilyn's house so the two could meet. As the two got acquainted, Marilyn played a tape he'd never shared with Stanton before: the initial police questioning of Roman Polanski, in Europe, upon his learning of the murder of his wife and unborn child.

Of the Church of Satan's deal with the devil, Stanton told me, "Something had to be done; a sacrifice had to be made, and not just any." Stanton described in detail his impressions of the Polanski tape. Polanski was in France, and the recording features a French interpreter translating questions asked by a French inspector. That night, Marilyn rewound the tape and played it over and over again. Stanton says he listened to the recording over one hundred times.

At that point, Stanton began researching the financing of Polanski's films and the people involved who might have been involved in other things. There is J. Paul Getty Jr., who financed all of Kenneth Anger's films over his entire career and also coproduced Rosemary's Baby.   Stanton insinuated that Polanski has a clear interest in the occult based on the movies his made. Stanton discussed the urban legend surrounding Anton LaVey's alleged portrayal of the devil in Rosemary's Baby, during the scene in which Satan rapes Rosemary. He said the stunt double that played the devil received no credit for the film, although witnesses remember Anton being there. "Anton LaVey is someone like myself: if you are in the same room with one of us, you are going to notice you are in the same room with an uncanny, strange character, who isn't just a stunt double putting on a mask." That Rosemary's Baby was made at all is significant to Stanton. "It doesn't really matter how much of it was carefully planned and orchestrated and executed perfectly. It's neither here nor there; fact is fact."

The fact for Stanton is that, essentially, the entire Manson Family is an offshoot from the Church of Satan. He said that Susan Atkins ended her association with the Church when she became a member of the Manson Family. This happened the same night Bobby Beausoleil renounced his roles as Kenneth Anger's understudy and apprentice and became, instead, Charlie's "star" family member. All of this, Stanton told me, was preplanned. Evidence to the higher order behind the murders of August 1969 is the fact that "Bobby effectively martyred himself." Stanton said no one has heard a complaint from Bobby since the beginning of his incarceration. He insisted it's highly unlikely that a man who's spent the last forty years in jail for a murder resulting from "one drug deal gone wrong" would keep so solemnly silent for so long. "Bobby Beausoleil is not in prison as a consequence or penalty; he's in prison as a form of protection. The same goes for Charlie." Stanton told me he was hesitant to ask Charlie about the real terms of his imprisonment. "It's like asking the president, 'Why isn't the Constitution abided by?'"

Stanton stopped speaking for a moment and seemed to reflect before he said, "Talking about this stuff and laying it out there like this has me feeling weird, dude, and it takes a lot to make me feel weird. I've never told this story this way ever." The feeling in the room as Stanton spoke was intense. Though I was aware that what Stanton was sharing was very personal and self defining, we both seemed to understand that his story was something that needed to be shared. Up to this point, Stanton's voice had been calm and controlled. I had a sense he was surprised at the smoothness of his delivery and how the facts had flowed from him exactly, it seemed, as necessary. We sat together in silence for well over a minute, a small moment in time that seemed more like an eternity contained within an eternity.

He smiled, a sort of mischievous grin, and continued: "My grandfather lit a torch one fateful night in 1967 and handed it to Charlie Manson. Now and forever, Charlie is that torchbearer, so how much of this story will find illumination is yet to be determined. Solely by Man-son, Uncle Chuck. By the way, I love you, Charlie. I don't care what my grandfather said about you; he was just jealous because he couldn't get up in the action, get his hands dirty. Well, from my family to yours, love always."

It had been a very long day and it was late. During our conversation, Sharon had been busy cooking, making spaghetti and meatballs. As she handed me a plate full of food, Stanton said, "It's human flesh, you know." The remark caught me off guard; it seemed more sinister than joking because, well, with Stanton, you never know. Stanton enjoyed a good laugh at my expense. "Here's a bit of trivia you'll love," he said. "The plate you are eating off of is from the Church of Satan. My grandfather used it thousands of times."

As we ate, Stanton talked more about Charles Manson, the man. He told me he believes Charlie is the voice of reason, the quintessential protagonist of the "I'm not crazy; you're all crazy" kind of story. Stanton remarked on the Charles Manson that made appearances on late night true crime television shows. "All his wild, crazy, dancing jive, his faces and reflections–yeah that's how fuckin' crazy all of you crazy fools drive us. I know all these fools, these mortals; they drive me ape shit crazy too, and I find myself making every crazy face imaginable, and spinning around in circles, jumping around, and banging my hands on the ground like a man who has gone completely mad, with good reason; you are all diving us crazy." Stanton said he felt confident enough about this idea to speak on behalf of Manson. "Any crazy ways he may have acted are only and solely due to how motherfucking crazy these goddamn motherfucks on Earth drive us, for how blindingly stupid, useless, annoying, and destructive they all are."

Stanton told me that Earth's biggest problem is its human population, that if this one problem were eliminated, all its other problems would cease to exist. "Problem is a word that should not be allowed to have an s on the end of it, because there is only one problem and that is humanity." While Stanton says he didn't quite learn this lesson from Charles Manson, it was Manson who instilled the spark in Stanton's passion for his preexisting beliefs about people. "He definitely fuckin' reminded me at a time when I needed that extra little push, that little bit of guidance, that spark, that fire, yes, that fuel. Charlie knows all; he's the closest we have, our own messiah. I only speak the truth. I don't need to lie because I'm open and I receive plenty, but there's frightening fucking truths at the end of the road. So many of these things would be disturbing to me if I didn't have the comfort of knowing it's all over anyways."

Stanton assured me that if people would just open their ears and close their mouths, they would not be able to escape the essence of the satanic philosophy espoused by Charlie. "There is a reason for the Satanic Bible, a reason for ATWA. My grandfather had a message not at all dissimilar from Charlie's, not at all. All it takes is just a little bit of patience, and when you open your ears and close your mouth, you will not be able to escape the essential, the essence of the satanic philosophy side by side with Charlie."

Stanton recited for me the Nine Satanic Statements of the Satanic Bible:

1. Satan represents indulgence instead of abstinence!

2. Satan represents vital existence instead of spiritual pipe dreams!

3. Satan represents undefiled wisdom instead of hypocritical self-deceit!

4. Satan represents kindness to those who deserve it instead of love wasted on ingrates!

5. Satan represents vengeance instead of turning the other cheek!

6. Satan represents responsibility to the responsible instead of concern for psychic   vampires!

7. Satan represents man as just another animal, sometimes better, more often worse than   those that walk on all-fours, who, because of his "divine spiritual and intellectual development," has become the most vicious animal of all!

8. Satan represents all of the so-called sins, as they all lead to physical, mental, or   emotional gratification!

9. Satan has been the best friend the Church has ever had, as He has kept it in business all these years!

Stanton continued to explain the teachings of Satanism. He condemned rules and laws and stressed the importance of self preservation and survival of the fittest. He told me might is right, that you either live or die, that you are either predator or prey "People don't like accepting or admitting stuff like that," he said. "It's fucking horrifying." Stanton shifted his focus, "You see, Marlin, what you are writing, what you are embarking on here, makes you the Mother Goose of the future. A thousand years from now, you will be remembered as Mother Goose, instead of someone recording history as it happened." Stanton said life is a series of cycles, through which fact and fiction become so intertwined in so distant a memory that it can be impossible to distinguish one from the other down the line. But the subject of our discussion, he said, is something other than fact or fiction; it exists above both, a concept that has yet to be explored and understood. "You may grow a greater understanding and awareness of it than most people," Stanton said. "It may prove to drive you mad or it may also be your saving grace. For me, that's where I've been this whole time."

Stanton continued: "I fully support and back up Charlie one hundred percent, until the end. Nothing will sway me. I love Charlie. I don't need to love Anton LaVey because I am Anton LaVey, and I love myself plenty. I have come to learn this with the use of a lot of LSD and self introspection because, you know, you can only go so far. You know very well because in your career you are dealing with people who went in, got lost, and couldn't find their way around, and that's coming from someone who was diagnosed as schizophrenic by nine out of eleven Viennese doctors. Remember: any crazy I am, you made me that way."

In the midst of this trip of self-discovery, Stanton came to believe in the Hollywood machine, "the latest sort of slime ball religion nouveau of celebrity faith that exists with Tom Cruise as saint and Ron Hubbard as modern messiah, both keepers of a powerful awakening in the human subconscious mind." Understanding Hollywood, according to Stanton, is the closest humanity has come to understanding how reality actually works. "So we have Earth," he explained, "and then we have Hollywood, the miniature version of Earth."

Listening to Stanton talk about Hollywood, I was reminded of a conversation I'd had with Charlie, during which he'd told me essentially the same things: "I am Hollywood; that's my town, man. That's my garbage dump. Hollywood is actually a really holy place, man. Look at all the images and the body that Hollywood has created around the world. It's spiritual–look at all the dreams. Look at all the soldiers, look at all the wars, look at all the dying. You can see a thousand million people die in Hollywood, man. You can kill people on the altar of a sacrificial pyramid for five hundred years–still couldn't beat Hollywood. They do that in a weekend.

Stanton moved on from the topic of Hollywood to a discussion of Satanism as a means for human beings to overcome their destructive nature. He explained that the human animal lives to torture itself, lives a masochistic existence from beginning to end. According to Stanton, the human species is programmed to be a self denying, self loathing, self punishing, pain-seeking lot. "I have to remind myself everyday not to work or pay bills, but to jack off, smoke a joint, slap someone when they're not expecting it, and laugh 'cause it's funny."

We talked about Stanton's ten years in Hollywood: the parties, the debauchery, and the crazy number of celebrities he'd met. "I've only been star struck once: when I met Pee-wee Herman. I was twenty-eight or twenty-nine years old and I was shaking like a little girl." Stanton believes Pee-wee's Big Adventure is and will always be the greatest movie of all time. Because, he explained, it tells all of our stories, the stories of our collective pain, stress, frustration, humor, absurdity, bewilderment, confusion, and craziness. Yet, somewhere amidst all the chaos, there is order. "Just look at Pee-wee himself. Never is there a wrinkle in his suit or a smudge in his perfect makeup but, yet, he embodies chaos." Stanton said Pee-wee's Big Adventure embodies its own philosophy. "It sure has shown me a whole lot more about the human condition–what to be prepared for, what to expect out of people and situations–than any book. I'm saying that I have personally gotten more out of Pee-wee's Big Adventure than even the Satanic Bible." Stanton asked me, "Have you ever been star struck?" And I told him, "Sure, when I met Alice Cooper for the first time." Stanton thought about this and said, "I could see that, he's sort of the Pee-wee Herman of your generation."

We finished our meal and Stanton offered to show me his personal picture archive. I saw shots from his childhood: his family, his grandfather and grandmother. There were pictures of Susan Atkins and Bobby Beausoleil before they knew Manson. At one point, Stanton stumbled across a photo of Marilyn Manson and scowled, grumbling, "This fuckin' poser extraordinaire, this guy, this clown–I got wise and realized that this guy is selling my identity for millions of dollars." Stanton lamented what he sees as human beings' limited capacity to make connections. He told me people lack more than imagination; they are completely devoid of basic curiosity. "Things were bad when chivalry died and God went with it. Then things got worse when love died and hate did too. There goes romance; good-bye, revolution."

I asked Stanton about the future, where he believed things were headed, how he thought all of this would play out. "I know what things are leading up to," he said, "and it's fuckin' big, really big." He told me there is a large satanic undercurrent brewing: a lot of rituals, sacrificial murders, and satanic ceremonies occurring constantly.

Stanton held little back: "There are definitely other people inside the planet. I also believe there's a governing system to this entire thing, and we really are all some sort of an ant farm. I've got dirt that goes all the way through and all the way throughout; it comes right out on the other side and I mean it's like one steady stream. All of this, all the people involved, everything–it's one big, grand, orchestrated, fuckin' satanic ritual, the whole fuckin' thing, man. That's why they don't want me talking to you, or anybody. But, at the same time, they can rely on the fact that everyone thinks I'm about ninety percent crazy."

I had no idea who "they" could be. I didn't press for details.

"There's a helicopter overhead, everywhere I go," Stanton insisted. "They follow me around. There's always a helicopter over me – I kid you fucking not."

Dennis Wilson

The drummer of the Beach Boys was in my band, The Milky Way. He comes from my heart there in Santa Claus and One Horse Open Sleigh. The sleigh is on a butcher man like a red on a suit. We were cutting an album when he changed the words to the songs and stuff, and I told him he shouldn't do that, but he had an Italian business manager and he had, like, 17 or 13, 14 million dollars he was playing with like that. He wouldn't pay that, he wouldn't pay what he owed. He changed. I couldn't get my money so someone grabbed both his legs and pulled him under the ocean. You remember that? Do you remember how Dennis Wilson died down in the water and somebody had grabbed his legs and he couldn't come up and he disappeared under the water.

A Bug

Look in the phonebook. You see all them people? All those people have the same person inside of them that you do. There is no they, they and them are we and us. We and us are not at all. We died a thousand years ago. There is only God, and God is not a religion. God is a bug, 'cause if the bugs don't survive, we don't survive, and the bugs are smarter than we are. I discovered that in solitary confinement, living with a cockroach for fifteen years. I found out that guy was ten times more intelligent than I, and he could count the stars, and I couldn't even begin to think about counting the stars. That's how smart that bug was. He was a Pharaoh at one time, a scarab, and he was on a ring on the Pharaoh's finger. The Pharaoh could see in his mind, and he could see in the Pharaoh's mind, because the Pharaoh was God, and still is God. There is no death, there never was death. Death is love's breath. If you're dead, you're alive. Alive is dead. There is only one, and you're breathing it, and not only are you breathing it, you're destroying it. You're destroying it as fast as you can, because you won't destroy the people, if you don't destroy the people you're going to destroy everything, because people are destroying everything. I don't think you are really here, I think you're trying to find it, but I don't think you found it yet. When you find it you gotta get right here, right now, that's all there is. Now take a breath, are you breathing? That's what we're working for, right there.

The Self

I don't think it's normal, it's normal to have a self. If you don't have a self then you don't have any problems, but you become everything around you. In other words, if you're out in the woods or you're up in a cabin like that, somewhere like that, and you don't have no external self programming...like TV or radio or friends, or you know something like that, you just automatically pick up everything. You know where the dogs [are] at all the time. You know where the birds are. Everything becomes a part of you, man. When everything becomes a part of you, you become a part of everything. You really wake up the God that's inside of you.

Do you know how much we're brainwashed? I don't think you do. You know if I put you in cell 51 and I give you a TV for a year, then I take you out of that cell and put you in a cell without a TV...you'll have withdrawal symptoms. Television is a narcotic. It's worse than speed. In other words, you go dangerously in jeopardy of losing your life with withdrawals of TV, and same thing with radio. Back on radio we had these guys who would lay up in their cells for ten, fifteen years, listening to the radio. You take that radio away from them, they get dangerous. They really get dangerous.

More Fear

What makes it real, you know? Kill a thousand people. Still doesn't mean it's real. It's only real in fear. Does fear make it real? And what's the difference between fear and love, man. How you going to say, well, I love you but I don't fear you. When you become totally fearless you realize. I see an old man lying in a bed and every time the cops would come in and scare him, so I said, "Old man, what you got to be afraid of them cops for?" He said, "You got to show them fear, boy, or they'll kill you." I said, "Well, you don't have to be afraid. Don't you believe in Jesus Christ?" He said, "I am Jesus Christ, you stupid fuckin' juvenile." He said, "I'm not showing them my fear, I'm showing them their fear." And I found out that night that's what's real. If you don't show somebody fear, they don't know how to be afraid. They drive right on over everything you say, man, so you got to show them a little fear. And here's another one. Because he realizes people ain't no good and they'll use it against you. You show them kindness and they'll take it as weakness. You show them decency and honor and they'll think they tricked you. They'll come back and foreclose, take your money, and leave you on the street corner waiting for a bus that doesn't run there no more.

I'm Safe Here

The safest place on Earth is right where I'm at. I got a prison built around me, man. Got a bunch of dumb people who think that this is their house. They're working to protect their slave masters. They're slaves, man. More locked up than we are. So should the associate warden or program administrator who can't do anything. He can't not do anything. All he does is come back and get a cup of coffee and a piece of paper and walks around with it all day. So he can take his paycheck back to his wife, who is his warden, she tells him what to do. The whole thing is locked up in mother. It's not really loving, there's no one there, just how much is that doggie in the window. You keep the dog in the window, like that's supposed to be me, that's my reality; everybody's pissing on me and everything's okay. As long as they pee on me it's all right. I could tell you that a flash of blue light's gonna come across the sky, and a flash of blue light will come across the sky and you wouldn't say Charlie said that. You'd say Al Gore said it. You're afraid of who you're kowtowing to, and I don't have enough of your fear. In other words, I need more fear. I need enough fear to bow you down. That's the only way you're going to do it. You ain't going to do it standing up. You're too proud. The world has a prison body. And I've been in the prison body of the world since the '40s.

Civilizations

Well, the kind of mind I have is I was making little paper balls and hanging them in my cell from string off of the ceiling. And somebody come by and said you know that's the exact configuration of the galaxy, da, da, da. Whatever I've been trying to figure out the Stonehenge for a long time, man, and I tell my mind if in my mind I was there, and I'm a part of this forever, I should know how that was done and I figured out how it was done. There could be no such thing as personality. You've got to give that up. All that personal thing. You know, that's why that Stonehenge, it was put there by everybody. Everybody did that. Everybody at that time. Everybody had a part in that, a place in that. That's why it was done; it was done by a group effort. It had to be. There's no way in hell they could have done it any other way. It's the same thing with the problem that we have with the world today. If it's not everybody, it will not work. It's got to be everyone, and if it isn't everyone one way, it should be everyone the other way, and I feel that the intelligent life forms should probably, all the people that won't go to work, go somewhere else, another world somewhere, fly them on a rocket ship.

It's the only way it could have been done. We got a civilization of ego maniacs, you know, those type of individuals didn't have all that ego, they were more like ants. You know, look at an ant. If we were as powerful as an ant, look at what an ant can pick up. The same thing with a mouse, a little tiny mouse. I was in a cage with a mouse for a long time and that goddamn mouse is tough. I mean he could do things that if I had his strength and power I could tear the door off the fucking cell, you dig? There's only one thing that matters. The air right now. That's it. Without that, the rest of it don't mean a shit. There's only one way to do it. There's only one way to do it. And it's got nothing to do with personalities.

And every son of a bitch has been doing all this shit that they've been doing. They have no idea what the devil's going to be like. None. If you tell them, they're going to want to take it out on somebody else.

Go down and look at the museums of Mexico and you see a whole different perspective towards the sun God. They was up on the orbit of the sun long before NASA. Those guys weren't stupid, and you look at some of the stuff they built down there and some of the stones they were just shoveling around like nobody's business. They're moving 3200-ton stones without cables or ropes, without wheels, you know, and it was, like, that was a pretty strong-minded people. See these people that are stuck in this time mode, that's going back and forwards with hypothesis of who built the Stonehenge. I told them I built it, and they said, "How could you?" I said, "I used my dog, T-Rex. He carried the stones around for me. Because I had the brain over his just like I have the brain over yours." If you don't want to accept that, then fuck it, I don't give a fuck. Do what you want to do but just get the fuck out of my way, because if you're in my way and you're doing what you think you're doing, you're not doing anything because I'm not doing anything. The weather's doing it.

XI

NEW RISING SON

I learned about Matthew Roberts the way I learned about most people linked to Charlie: a frantic phone call from Kenny.

One evening, Kenny called to inform me that Charlie was "flipping out"; he'd received a letter from an editor at Details magazine, inquiring about his DNA. Kenny told me he didn't have all the details, but he'd learned there was "some rock star" somewhere trying to prove he was Charlie's son. Kenny gave me the name and phone number of the editor and asked me to call him. I didn't, even though I'd grown accustomed to Kenny calling with names and contact information for me to investigate. He has referred me to countless people: prison staff, authors, researchers, friends of his. I often explain to Kenny that I hardly have time to keep in touch with my own friends.

At that point I had no idea if Charlie even had any children. The thought that he could have children out living and functioning with the rest of society had never even occurred to me. Charlie is sensitive and protective when he feels he needs to be. I find it extremely uncomfortable to bring up issues such as this when we're talking, and have learned it's much easier to let Charlie bring up the personal stuff. I asked Kenny what he knew of Charlie's alleged children. He told me about one of Manson's sons, Charles Manson Jr., who had hung himself in Texas when he was in his thirties. Kenny then cryptically dispensed a number for "Candy," a woman he said could tell me more of the story.

Intrigued, I called Candy right away and introduced myself as a friend of Kenny's. Candy spoke with a strong, comforting southern accent in a voice that was warm and inviting. She told me she'd heard all about my friendship with Charlie and laughed as she explained her unusual name. Charlie, it seems, could never remember Candy's real name. So, because she'd once worked at the Kraft candy factory and Charlie loves caramels, he initiated a new nickname. Candy's words were lively, and Kenny had told me she strongly resembled Liza Minnelli, so I could almost put a face to the voice I heard over the phone.

Candy said she hadn't known much about Charlie before she reached out to him in a letter. She was far more interested in Charlie as a personality, she said, than in Charlie as a criminal. Two years before, she'd extended her first thoughts to Manson in a simple note. "I just told him I do not feel that anyone who behaves so bizarrely is really that nuts. I said he had a pretty good act going on. I wanted to know why the act was there." Candy doesn't think Charles Manson is really the character he portrays. She professed a love for psychology and figuring people out. "I'm sixty-five years old. I can remember seeing him on TV for the first time, and the more I'd see of him, the more I'd wanted to talk to him because I knew there was a deeper story there. Never, in a million years, did I ever dream that would happen."

Candy didn't think Manson would even read her letter, but a week after she sent it, she received a reply. Since then Manson has called her over seventy-five times. "It's kind of a mixed bag of emotions whenever you have a conversation with him; you don't know which one is going to rear its ugly head." Candy told me sometimes Manson is funny and happy. Other times he is the kind of man with whom she'd never want to be in the same room. And yet other times he is confounding, perplexing, preaching and proposing the sort of ideas that make her question, "Wow, where did that come from?" No matter which side of himself Charlie reveals during any given conversation, he is never, Candy believes, the Charles Manson the world sees. "He's asked me a hundred times if I'm recording our conversations, and I always say, 'Why on Earth would I ever do that?' He's told me, 'Well, you are talking to history.'" Though she feels creating actual voice recordings would violate the trust she shares with Charlie, Candy does keep a journal in which she documents the discussions and writes about the feelings they arouse. Assessing her inventory of conversations, she can see absolutely no comparison between the Charles Manson that does interviews on TV and the Charles Manson that talks to friends on the phone.

I asked Candy what she and Manson talk about. "I didn't have the greatest life growing up, and people like that can usually pick each other out of a crowd. So, that was sort of the first place I went with him." Candy described Charlie as a kind of comrade and confidante. They identified with each other's upbringing because neither was "brought up in the greatest of worlds." Manson told Candy he wished he'd never left Indiana, where he'd spent time at a school for boys. "He loved Indiana and said if he had stayed he would have ended up being a farmer there, for God's sake!" Candy chuckled at the seemingly improbable idea. The Manson portrayed in the media seems an unlikely farmer. "But just talk to him," Candy insisted, "and you'll learn he knows a lot about farming: crops, cattle, horses." As well as she's gotten to know Manson, Candy is continuously surprised by the way he thinks, speaks, and reacts. For instance, Manson's mother is commonly thought to have been a neglectful, abusive parent, but when

Candy once mentioned the woman (she can't remember exactly what she said), Manson jumped down her throat. "Don't you ever talk bad about my mother!" he'd screamed, though Candy says her intention was never to speak badly about a person she'd never even met. "My mom done an armed robbery to pay for my tonsillectomy," Charlie continued to rant. "Never talk bad about my mom. She spent five years in prison, he'd gone on to say, for that offense alone.

I told Candy I'd talked with Kenny briefly about the death of Charlie's son. And she began to tell me about a man who'd worked with her in the candy factory and who had looked just like Charles Manson: "He had long hair and piercing brown eyes and displayed a great deal of pleasure every time someone said, 'Hey, you look like Charles Manson.' He would smile and say something like, 'Yah, far out; thank you.' The guy had a bizarre personality. Eventually, he committed suicide."

When Candy began communicating with Manson she started to research her new friend. When she stumbled across an article about an alleged son of Manson's who committed suicide, whose description coincided with that of the man she knew at the factory, she started to put the pieces together. The man had been born in Kentucky, in an area where Charlie had once lived. Candy asked Charlie where he was during May 1951, about the time the man would have been conceived. "He said, 'I was in jail; why do you ask?'" All that Candy knew about Charles Manson Jr. was that he died somewhere in Colorado. The mystery remains unsolved, but Candy has a good idea that her suspicions are correct.

I thanked Candy for all the information she shared with me.

She wished me luck with my book and graciously asked that I call if I ever needed anything. As I got off the phone, I was aware of how differently people, even those closest to him, perceive Charlie. It seemed as though Charles Manson connects to various people on distinctly different levels, so much so that it's easy to see why the world is filled with such conflicting information about him. Maybe, I thought, by surrounding himself with such an eclectic group of friends and admirers, he is better able to cultivate different sides of himself, able to wear various hats. Talking to Candy, I got the sense that in her life Manson plays the role of big brother.

I started researching the topic of Charlie's children and discovered several conflicting reports, none of which has ever gone public. One account described the method by which Charlie delivered babies at the ranch. On one occasion, he allegedly chewed through the umbilical cord and, with blood covering his face, handed the baby to its mother. It was easy to picture Charlie in such a surreal scene. Later, when I got the chance, I told Manson what I'd read and asked if it were true. Charlie laughed and asked if I'd ever seen a dog deliver pups. "It's no different than that," he said. "You just help the baby come out and tie it off with an old guitar string or something." I asked Charlie how many babies he'd delivered. "I don't know, a couple," he'd answered casually, and then moved on to something else, as though the topic weren't worth mentioning, as if it were not that big a deal.

In March 2010, Details published an article about Matthew Roberts, an aspiring writer, musician, and DJ who spins at

LA strip clubs a few days a week. The article was compelling: Matthew linked his conception to a 1967 San Francisco LSD-laced hippy orgy in which, his biological mother claims, Charles Manson participated. I was intrigued by Roberts' description of the "hellish" night terrors he routinely experienced as a child, by the comparison the writer made between Roberts' biological mother, who continued to drop acid well into her pregnancy, and Mia Farrow's character in Roman Polanski's Rosemary's Baby, who, post-conception, ingests a vile concoction intended to create the Antichrist. I discussed the article with Stanton LaVey, who said he knew Matthew Roberts, gave me his number, and urged me to talk to him. Stanton and Matthew became close friends when they once rented a "shitty ass motel room together on LA's skid row." The two were simultaneously experiencing hard times, "fucking really getting to know each other." Stanton told me that Matthew is complicated and composed of many intense layers: a "really deep cat." I asked Stanton about the possibility that Matthew might be Manson's son. "As far as I'm concerned," he said, "he is Charlie's son: there's no two ways about it. There are so many mannerisms, weird little ticks, things that Matthew does that he's not even conscious of that are totally Charlie."

I called Matthew from my hotel room and left him a message explaining who I was. Matthew called back almost immediately. We talked for a bit and made fast plans to get together in the following few days. Meanwhile, I was able to research more of his story through various other interviews he had given. My initial impression of his motivation for doing such press was that he wanted to find out, either way, if he was indeed Charlie's son.

Matthew and I eventually met at a Thai restaurant near his

apartment. Based on what Stanton told me about Mathew's likeness to Manson, I to notice an expected to see an immediate resemblance. But, looking at Matthew, who is built tall and solid, with long, wild hair and deep, wide-set eyes, I was reminded more of a friend I knew in Regina than of the masses of photographs I'd seen of a young Manson. Matthew seemed reserved, and quiet, in contrast to Manson's lively, often flamboyant style. We introduced ourselves and took a few minutes to get acquainted by talking about LA, music, traveling. He struck me as a person more interested than interesting, a quality I value in others. I felt as if I was immediately on the same level with Matthew. We share a love for music, psychology, nature. We both feel drawn to Manson; we wanted to help each other figure out the mystery. Our initial conversation was a feeling out process: while I tried to figure out if he was sincere, he tried to predict whether or not I would twist his story around to make him look like an attention-seeking idiot. It turned out we both had nothing to worry about. Matthew exuded honesty, and I immediately felt his commitment to speaking his truth.

Over dinner, I asked Matthew how all of this hysteria began. He assured me it had nothing to do with self promotion. "So I'm at a party in downtown LA and I'm drunk and I'm telling this guy my story. He just happened to be a freelance writer and he asked if he could shop my story around. I said go ahead. So he got it in Globe." At the time, Matthew had no reason to take the man seriously, no clue to the kind of contacts he had. Matthew said that, once his story hit Globe, he felt like a part of the butterfly effect. "The butterfly flaps its wings in China and it becomes a tempest in the United States. The story went from being in Globe to being the number one Googled story over Thanksgiving weekend. Over two hundred million people searched me and I never made a single phone call trying to pitch this story." Matthew told me he immediately took heat for self promotion from everyone, including those who wanted to promote the story themselves. "People would call me to do a story and at the same time accuse me of trying to advance myself or promote my band or whatever. I'm like, dude–you called me." Matthew assigns a lot of meaning to the fact that his story received intense international attention after a single, simple conversation at a party. "I had nothing to do with it, literally. So, to me, this is a story that wants to be told. It's got a life of its own."

Matthew isn't exactly in an ideal position to uphold any allegation. He acknowledged, "Can you imagine how I'm going to look if I get the DNA back and it's negative? I'm going to look like a complete idiot." For a burgeoning artist, garnering attention for falsely claiming to be the son of Charles Manson is not a smooth move. Matthew admitted that after buying Details magazine it took him three days to stomach reading the article. "I kept thinking in my head, 'What the hell am I doing? What am I getting myself into?'" He could have told the man at the party he didn't want his story told. The fact that he didn't is something, Matthew says, he wrestles with every day.

He may not have said no because of his overwhelming desire to know the truth.

"That's it. Ultimately, I want the DNA. I want the proof and I can't do it on my own. The truth is like God to me; that's the most important thing in my life because I've been lied to so much." Matthew assured me he could never lie about who may or may not be his father. Because he believes the truth is the truth, whether one likes it or not, even if the truth turns out to be the worst thing in the world. "It's the truth," he insisted. "You got to suck it up and live with it."

"I've never, ever, ever claimed to be the son of Charles Manson – not once." Matthew believes all he can do is field questions honestly and encourage people to make up their own minds. He resents headlines like "Man Claims to Be Son of Charles Manson" because he's become acutely aware of how the media tweaks a story to sell it. And Matthew has more than misrepresentation to worry about. Once, a reality show production company contacted him to buy the rights to his story and thus prevent him from speaking to any other media. "They wanted to own my publishing rights, they wanted to own my life story. For five years I wouldn't be able to do a single article, I wouldn't be able to mention the name Charles Manson. Basically, their intention was to shut me up and shut me down. It felt more like the FBI owned the company and they were trying to silence me." Since declining that offer, Matthew's felt as if he's been under surveillance. "It's like they're trying to set me up on shit or whatever, trying to get me on some kind of fucked up crime I didn't commit. I'm probably being a little bit paranoid, but who knows, man."

I asked Matthew to take me back to the start, before it ever occurred to him that he could be the son of the world's most favorite madman. He told me about the strip club where he spun and a porn star that performed there. She couldn't remember his name, but she seemed to have always known his face, and so she would seal the tips she'd save for him in an envelope labeled "Manson" and leave it in the back. Matthew said, "I really believe that Life magazine cover [the December 1969 cover featuring Manson's famous hypnotic stare] is just kind of ingrained in people's subconscious." He mentioned his appearance has evoked strange reactions his whole life, that strangers become instantly scared or intimidated at just the sight of him. This is a fact of life that Matthew has learned to live with but has never fully accepted. "People see me, they make the connection subconsciously, and then they get scared. I've always hated having that effect on people."

Matthew was born in Chicago in 1968 and adopted by a couple in nearby Rockford, Illinois as an infant. He spoke very highly of his adoptive parents, who raised him to go to church and play sports, as most typical midwestern parents do. But even in the midst of a calm, Christian upbringing, Matthew somehow felt drawn to Manson's mayhem. His first book report was on Helter Skelter. When he graduated high school, he moved to Los Angeles to pursue his love of rock 'n' roll and study at the Musicians Institute in Hollywood, where he met Clem, an original Manson family member who had allegedly cut a person's head off with a pocket knife. "When I talked to Clem, I asked him, 'What were you doing hanging out with this guy who is crazy?' He said he thought Manson was Jesus Christ because he watched him raise a bird from the dead." Matthew explained that Clem had served only seventeen years in jail, a reduced sentence because the judge thought him "too stupid" to have acted on his own with no orders from Manson. Matthew described Clem as an all around good guy: "Clem was a good blues guitar player. Everyone liked him, you know."

Matthew encountered much more Manson out west. He dated

a woman whose mother dated Roman Polanski. He worked with another woman who was friends with Curt Gentry, a coauthor of Helter Skelter. Eventually he met and became engaged to a woman named Gina. As the couple thought about starting a family, Gina suggested Matthew research his biological parents. He contacted an adoption-search agency and was given the name of his biological mother. But he was forewarned. Though the agent suggested his mother's mental health might not be in great shape, Matthew dismissed his mother's eccentricities, her decision to live without a phone or a car, her undivided interest in her vegetable garden, as simply the idiosyncrasies of an aging hippie. It took some time to realize that something was wrong.

Initially, Matthew's mother "Terry" alleged her son had been conceived as the consequence of a gang rape. Then she admitted she might have confused male aggression with male vigor, in which case the encounter might have resulted from miscommunication in a situation shrouded by drugs. "She was, I guess, like seventeen. I think it was just convenient for her to call it a rape, especially when she found out who was involved." Terry went on to tell Matthew she couldn't reveal his full birth name over the phone, but would have to do so in person for "security reasons." She alluded to her involvement in an "infamous hippie group." Matthew confirmed, "She basically admitted it was the Manson group." She disclosed that Manson had participated in the orgy that left her pregnant. "I don't know, but everything adds up. My mother looked like them, an attractive looking young girl. She lived in the same town as Mary Brunner." After his initial conversation with Terry, Matthew didn't need much more convincing to accept that he might have such an eerily recognizable face for a biologically based reason. Listening to Matthew, it became hard to believe I'd never thought of Charlie having children. "There's no telling how many kids are out there," Matthew said. "He was in jail. He got out. He was making up for lost time."

Matthew told me Terry promised to know exclusive details about Charlie's life. She claimed to have ratted Charlie out to the FBI. She said she knew of an investigation into Charlie's activities, initiated well before the murders, which, at one point, focused on a strange character named Steve who was a Charles Manson look-a-like. Steve turned out to be nobody. She insisted the idea of a worldwide race war was never part of Charlie's teachings. "That came out after he was in prison," she said. Terry once overheard family members talking about the Folger family. She couldn't understand why they were so upset with the Folgers; Terry really liked their coffee.

Matthew told me that when he'd heard the gist of Terry's story, "things really came to a head." He watched Charles Manson Superstar. "In that documentary, he talked about his children coming back, one of them coming back at around the age of forty." Manson was released from prison on March 21, 1967. Matthew was born March 22, 1968. Manson went back to prison in 1969 and has been there ever since. There was a small window of opportunity for a child to be conceived, and Matthew's timeline matches Manson's perfectly. It's alleged that Manson fathered another child around the same time, whose mother was Mary Brunner, Manson's first family member. She allegedly gave birth to their son, Valentine Michael, on April 15, 1968, just weeks after Matthew was born. That child's current whereabouts are unknown. Matthew was becoming convinced. "Then I started looking in the mirror; I mean, I look like this guy: my nose, my hair, my eyes. People have called me Charles Manson."

As he inquired more about his origins, Matthew's relationship with Terry deteriorated along with her emotional stability. "She got really upset and aggressive. In one letter she wrote that all I cared about was humiliating her, all I cared about was that her clitoris was violated. Those were her exact words." Eventually, Matthew sent his mother a photograph of himself. She was taken aback and insisted he looked exactly like Manson. "That," Matthew asserted, "is when she got crazy."

After cutting off contact with his mother, Matthew decided to write Manson to see if he remembered Terry. He did. In one of his letters to Matthew, Manson wrote about his relationship with Terry: "We took a super train to LA–what an experience to last a life time." Terry, of course, had come back from the trip pregnant, though neither could have known this at the time. And because of the circumstances surrounding Matthew's conception, Manson knew no more than Terry about the question of paternity. At one point, Matthew saw a picture of Manson's grandmother and described his resemblance to her as "uncanny." If, despite their physical similarities, Manson is not Matthew's father, there still exists something special between the two. "I feel like there's something that connects us and I think that he feels that too. I think it has to do with good and evil and our perceptions of the two." Matthew told me he understands Manson at a level most people cannot approach because he has experienced a similar set of circumstances. Except Matthew doesn't think he could handle incarceration "simply for being a subversive" as well as Charlie has. "One thing that's always fascinated me about him is that the man's spirit can never be broken. I'm not that strong. I'd have been crying like a pussy in solitary confinement, you know, and he has never wavered for a second in his conviction that he's right."

Charlie could still remember a few details about Terry and her family. He recalled a story Terry had previously told Matthew, about how her father had chased Charlie off his lawn, calling him a "white trash bandit biker." Matthew's biological grandfather was a six-foot-four heavily decorated marine who'd fought against the Japanese at Midway. "He wouldn't have been intimidated by Charlie or any of his cronies." Matthew told me there was no way Manson could have known these details if he hadn't actually stood on Terry's lawn forty years before. "He wrote [of their relationship] that it was free love and he paid the price. He told me how not knowing your father has its goods and its bads. He didn't know his father and explained how all men were his father, how it can be good to learn from more than just one."

As is his way, Matthew turned to science to explain the strangeness of his experience. He told me that if he is not Manson's son, the two could still resemble and feel drawn to each other through a phenomenon Einstein called quantum entanglement. Matthew explained: "You know, every now and again, the world sees a four-year-old child that plays Mozart perfectly. This is because everybody has a genetic code and a frequency by which they vibrate. Let's say you recorded all of those codes from the beginning of time and put them in a computer. You might find that kid has the same genetic code and frequency Mozart did and that's why he is able to play at four years old. He doesn't necessarily have to look like Mozart, because your environment dictates how your body reacts and how you grow up. Your genetic code is identical to that of a roach until almost the very last few digits, so let's say there are a finite number of possible human genetic codes and, every now and again, they repeat and the world produces a clone of a person that lived before. In the past, larger spans of time would separate these clones. People never made the connection. But now that we have over six billion people on the planet, the phenomenon might happen more frequently.

Matthew went on to describe his theory that, as our planet evolves, its electromagnetic grid is breaking down and introducing the possibility of another level of consciousness, in which synchronicity increases. He cited the coincidences and synchronicities surrounding the September eleventh attacks on the United States as an example of this. "I think the more you're kind of off that grid of collective consciousness, the more you're open to it and the more you're able to recognize it. Then, if you don't have fear of insanity or fear of being weird, you can incorporate it into your life in a reasonable, socially acceptable way. Because, in other words, it's nutty stuff, and people are afraid to experience things that are different."

Matthew hasn't communicated with Charlie in two years, since Manson stopped responding to Matthew's letters. Matthew told me he assumes Charlie won't write because Matthew's story went public. He is still hoping to someday unlock the secret behind his connection to Charlie, although, without DNA evidence, the chances of this happening are slim. And though he's dealt with a lot of criticism, he says he still cannot understand why. "Wouldn't anybody in their right mind, if there was a chance they were the son of Charles Manson, wouldn't they want to know if that were true or not?" Ultimately, Matthew says, he's stopped caring whether people believe his story or not, but this doesn't make him immune to the hatred people throw his way. "I honestly believe I've had assassination attempts. But I feel like I have some unique ability to survive, like Charlie does. He was sentenced to death and then they reversed it. He was lit on fire and his skin grew back. I once attempted suicide myself and it was a miracle I survived, you know?"

I asked Matthew about the night terrors the writer mentioned in the Details article. He described what he called "hallucinations" in which his eyes would be open and each bizarre sight would seem real. Matthew described an experience in which he found himself covered in spiders. In one recurring night terror, he'd awake to the torture of alien life forms. This, he told me, is significant, according to the theory he's developed to explain his experience.

Matthew has fervently researched his condition. He discovered that the frightening scenes disrupting his sleep could result from his pineal gland producing too much DMT, a naturally occurring hallucinogenic chemical, during his sleep. "Your brain produces DMT two times in your life: when you're born and when you die. It takes you into the world and it takes you out of the world."

Matthew told me about a psychiatrist who did experiments with DMT. When his subjects were exposed to amounts larger than those typically found in the human body, they experienced hallucinations centered on the same subjects that tortured Matthew. "They reported a lot of reptile stuff, a lot of alien sexual stuff," Matthew said. "These things were so traumatic to these people that the experiments had to be discontinued." The effects of the exposure to DMT were so disturbing, a support group was created to help the subjects cope with their shared experiences. Though the study was cut short and never repeated, Matthew believes it furnished enough evidence to suggest a trip on DMT doesn't provoke haphazard hallucinations like any other psychedelic drug. "These weren't just random experiences," Matthew insisted. These people were describing beings with common messages, shared themes." He referenced the fact that ancient tribes who took DMT recorded the experience of future technology they could not have possibly predicted. He suggested the possibility that DMT could induce another dimension of reality, a realm that has, as he put it, "a certain amount of reality to it, or at least repeatability, a consistency that exists outside of random chemical reactions." Matthew reinforced the trauma such alternate realities could cause fully matured adults, willfully participating in a scientific study. "Imagine now," he said, "a child, who has no idea what is happening to him, experiencing things so hellish and horrific, with nothing to explain it other than religion or demons."

Matthew and I talked about his interest in psychiatry. He half joked, "I'm fascinated with human psychology and human behavior; all of this couldn't have happened to a better person." Matthew told me that he'd once started medical school. "I was an intern and took classes, but once I got into it, I knew it wasn't for me." Matthew confided that once he saw how psychiatry really worked, he lost his passion for it. He didn't like the rigid labels placed on patients, nor did he agree with the field's heavy focus on medication. Matthew told me that during an interview, a writer once asked if he'd ever worried about schizophrenia. "I said, 'Well, yeah, I've thought about it. I'm not nuts but I'm a little nutty.'" The writer proceeded to publish an account that stated Matthew admitted to suffering from schizophrenia. Matthew said that kind misrepresentation is "the same kind of shit" the media has pulled on Charlie. "Like I said, if there's not a genetic connection, then I shudder to think what's going on in this fucking world."

We talked about our beliefs and experiences with mental health, and I asked Matthew what he thought about schizophrenia. He told me he thinks schizophrenia is a condition through which a person's mind advances enough to see the relativity of all things. Synchronicity will then seem to increase in that person's life to such a degree that he is left with the dilemma of deciding whether to believe he is the creator of his life's events or merely the observer.

Matthew elaborated: "We basically have two filters by which we perceive all of reality. The fear filter or love filter. Hate is not the opposite of love; it is still love, just to a lesser degree. Fear is the opposite of love. So where you have fear, that is a good indicator that you lack love in that area. The degree to which you hate one person or thing proportionately limits your ability to love another. So you can't love one thing while hating another. Likewise, the degree to which you hate or victimize another is in direct proportion to the degree to which you yourself can be victimized. Paranoid schizophrenia occurs when you perceive these events through fear. This condition can be cured, simply by perceiving these events through the love filter. Suddenly, then, you have the gift of intuition. Why would you ever fear someone harming you if you can't be harmed?

"Every event in our lives offers us an opportunity to learn something. The more adverse a situation is, the greater the opportunity to learn/advance. A perfect example of this is the story behind the movie A Beautiful Mind. I think I'm hyper intuitive and I think that ties in with the schizophrenic thing quite a bit because, ultimately, if you are synchronously experiencing things as a function of intuition, then you are simply living the life you are supposed to live, whether that's being in the right place at the right time or actually predicting things. A schizophrenic believes that he's predicting events, that he's creating reality."

I told Matthew about Stanton's experience with surveillance, his belief that helicopters follow him everywhere. "Really?" Matthew asked. "I moved into a friend's house for a while and he told me that the helicopters flying overhead went crazy; he hadn't experienced them that way until I moved in. All of a sudden they were flying right over us; it literally felt like they were going to land on the roof. I've moved near the airport and that doesn't seem to happen anymore." I asked Matthew to interpret this bizarre experience. He explained that, with thermal imaging technology, every person on the planet is visible from space. "Everyone lights up like a firefly," he said. "This might be my ego, or delusions of grandeur, but I believe I glow very bright. I do think they track me; maybe they think I'm some sort of threat."

THIRTEEN
UNCOVERING THE FINAL DETAILS

It was Stanton LaVey who told me about John Aes-Nihil. Stanton has known John since he was a kid, when John was his mother's and stepfather's (Zeena and Nikolas) roommate. Stanton and John were close and John used to drive Stanton to school. Stanton told me that what makes John unique, aside from the deep connection he feels wth the Manson Family, is the fact that he has been interested in Manson from the beginning: 1969.

John created the market for Charles Manson memorabilia, the now-popular nostalgia scene surrounding the stuff of serial killers, true crime, and all things underground. According to Stanton, "John Aes-Nihil is the original swap meet, flea market, smut peddling, bootlegging pirate." Most important, Stanton said, is that John does what he does for the right reasons, "taking care of people" along the way. "His intentions personally are deeper, philosophical; he wants to carry this information forward into the future, in one of the oldest, truest ways tested: through magazines, literature, books, and archives." Stanton said he could guarantee that John is the authority on all things Manson, that he "knows all." His archives have been accessed by virtually everyone attempting to discover or produce anything related to Manson. He owns every piece of video and the rarest photos. He has personally interviewed hundreds of people related to the Manson Family and documented it all. His interest borders on obsession; it's staggering.

I made the drive out to the Mojave Desert where John has lived for a while. He has since told me that the desert, out in the middle of nowhere and away from everyone else, is a haven for Satanists. John is pretty soft spoken; he has a deliberate way of talking, as though he thinks about everything first. In a way, he has the composure of an artist and, after spending about ten minutes with him, it was clear to me that this man was one of the being

Underworld

See the underworld, look at everything that everybody else has looked at from inside to out, from up to down. It's opposite to someone who lives in a basement all their life. So I have a sixty-three-year-old look at everything upside down and backwards. In fact, when my mom got out of prison, she got me out of first grade, made me roll my pants up and beat me all the way home from school on the back of the legs, to impress me. Do you know that...moonwalk, when you see people walking backwards? I've been doing that all my life. I was born on the dark side of everything, so I see why Kennedy got shot, because he wasn't the real leader of the world. Castro was, because the revolution is the leader of the world. That's when the world started, at the end of the old world. The new world order started with the Constitution and the Bill of Rights. And everybody else got their thing from it. And you learn that in prison because, like, every time you come up with something, if you come up with something different, not necessarily new in perspective to what new is in total and definition, but what is like beginning of a concept or an idea, like credit, you see where it comes from. It comes from the necessity, from the fear of dying. Someone will give somebody credit, so credit becomes a reality to the world, and they're using it and they don't even know what it is or where it came from.

Hypnosis

I have met a guy named Doctor Block from Arizona, in prison for five years, and I asked him if he would help me learn self hypnosis. And he said, yeah, he would teach me hypnosis, and he taught me *hypnosis. And I used to go to sleep and I'd practice this hypnosis, and I would go to sleep and I sent my soul unto the invisible, into the afterlife, and by and by my soul returned to me and said, "I myself was in heaven, in hell." Omar Khayyam wrote that, and I said if he can do that so can I, so I would practice the self hypnosis. Put myself in a trance, a sleep, and I would work on it. And I worked on it and I worked on it and finally in the middle of the night I woke up and said, "I sent my soul to the invisible," and by and by my soul returned to me and said, "Thought patterns are not important." What? He said, "Thought patterns are not important." I proposed a question and that's the answer I got.*

And I ignored it and went back to sleep. And two or three weeks later I woke up and...just thought, thought patterns are not important.... it's not important, so I went off into the pseudo-intellectual circle of humanity in prison, over on the grass, and I mentioned thought patterns are not important and everyone laughed. "That's crazy, Charlie, you don't know what you're talking about. How else are you going to think, Charles? You got to think in pattern or you're not thinking at all, you know?" And I said yeah, so I agreed with it. And then about thirty years later, I was sitting on a mountain and I seen the sun come up and the moon go down and looked at both of them, and I had the sun in one hand and the moon in the other and I said, "I've got it all, man. I've got all the line of the universe of the world forever."

Eternally and the pattern of my thought was a joke... ha, ha, ha. The pattern of my thought was programming, man, that's what someone had told me. I didn't know that. That was a bunch of junk that was running around in my stupid fucking head like a comic book. You dig? And then I woke up and where I really was, and I seen the starlit sky at night and I seen the moon. I said wow. I've been in prison, I've never seen anything like that before. I seen it and my mind just went whoop. Ha, ha and I became God. Yeah. I'll be goddam, man, I gotta hide this. If they find out they'll throw my ass down and put me in the nut ward, and that's exactly what they did. The cops couldn't whip me, so I was knocking cops out in the hallway. So all they could do was gang up on me and then medicate me down to where I couldn't move and keep me medicated for four or five years, until all the people that were doing that were killed.

In one way or another, they kind of all died of whatever, you know, so then they said that I was putting juju and I was putting voodoo and causing trouble with all the others because the thirty doctors ended up dying and the last one ended up blowing his brains out in a parking lot because he had got me handcuffed in a shower with two Negroes naked, and his wife ended up in bed with two Negroes. Isn't that strange?

I could have explained it, if I was given the position, the platform to explain it, where it could be official, but anything I say at this level is only going to get taken and twisted, make it be into other things they're not. The truth of the matter could have been explained, but they didn't want the truth of the matter and they still don't… they want the hippy cult leader guy. You know why? Because it's the only way they're going to survive. I didn't say it, the spirit of Avalon doesn't have a name on it, doesn't have a tag on it, it's just the spirit of what's known to be true. It's like that song I wrote: The moment is ever constant in the mind. Everywhere the blind lead blind. Here's your chance to step out of time, there's no reason, there's no rhyme, it's just the trouble you bring, it's the mind that you sing, it's the thought that you have in your soul, it's the thing that you know, the cold wind that *blows, it's that raven's wing of death that touches your cheek and the darkness and light when there's no one there, but your dreams are there.*

What is life worth on earth, what is life on earth worth? All of life on earth or all life on earth, how can you communicate that to people who just will not listen? Stuck in their own little minds, they'd rather die than accept the truth about what is reality. If you're truly for yourself, then you would truly realize what you really need to do. In the order of self, it's gotta be air. There ain't any way you're going to get off having air. You got to have that air. Anything you're doing to take that air is killing you. Anything you do that's destroying the atmosphere is taking your life. If you open up a can of bleach, to bleach some clothes, and you're putting all that anti-poison...Look in your medicine cabinet and look at everything in there that says kills 99 percent of the germs and figure that you're one in that 99 percent.

XII

WHERE THE TRUTH LIES

When I thought about my relationship with Charlie, his history was always, to some degree, in the back of my mind. This is a man who was convicted of seven murders. I'd never known much about the murders. The story behind the events of August 1969 has been told and retold and, somewhere in the retelling, the truth got buried and lost. The collection of fact and fiction surrounding the chaos is a conspiracy theorist's dream.

I think, on some level, the murder story was something I didn't really want to delve into. I was apprehensive. I'd told myself, "Well, he never actually *killed* anybody," so many times, that I managed to justify our relationship, while evading a major part of his past. With time, though, my justification lost its strength. I had to confront the issue. I had to attempt to find the truth. As I started researching the fine details of the murders, I realized that the more I learned, the less I seemed to really know. With so much conflicting information out there, it was a challenge just to figure out where to start. Charlie had once told me there are over one hundred and forty books about him, and he assured me every one of them is a "bunch of shit." Charlie was adamant when he told me that none of them told the true story, and that no book ever would. He had me convinced. Until, it seems, the truth–or part of it–found me.

Matthew Roberts told me about a woman named Vicki who had gotten in touch with him after reading one of his interviews; she was convinced that Matthew was Charlie's son. Vicki wanted to help Matthew find a few answers, fill in some of the areas of a puzzle that seemed to fall increasingly apart with every new piece put in place. The two spoke several times on the phone and developed a trusting relationship. Matthew told me that Vicki first met Charlie when she was just fifteen and visited him while he was in jail after the murders. Oddly enough, Matthew said Vicki didn't remember much of that meeting. Vicki was friends with several Manson family members and has maintained relationships with some of Manson's other friends. Through these relationships, Vicki has kept up with what's happening in Charlie's life. While Charlie was incarcerated at Vacaville Prison, Vicki began corresponding with him through the mail and the two started talking regularly on the phone. With the advent of the Internet, Vicki spent countless hours researching the Manson case and corresponding with other researchers through several online communities. She blogged tirelessly about her findings, until she came to the realization that there was nothing left to say or, for that matter, to know. Vicki has never given an interview and has kept her interest in Charlie and the family a secret. Vicki is not her real name.

Matthew and I both agreed that trying to make sense out of the Manson story was next to impossible. He advised me that Vicki was a wealth of information and gave me her phone number. I called Vicki and told her I was a friend of Matthew's and that I had contacted her at his suggestion. Vicki was immediately warm and welcoming and asked me, "How is Matthew? I haven't heard from him in a while." Vicki and I talked about our mutual friend. She told me she felt certain that Matthew was Charlie's son. She also told me that she hadn't spoken to Charlie in over a year. When I asked her if there had been some sort of falling out, she told me she had worked hard to help Matthew get DNA testing, an effort Charlie was completely against. This, she feels, is why the communication between her and Manson has altogether stopped.

I asked Vicki if she knew anything about Matthew's mother and she told me that when Charlie got out of Terminal Island he met Mary Bruner first and the two lived together in an apartment. "There was this girl, she was a runaway, and I can't remember her name. I believe she was Matthew's mother. She lived with Charlie and Mary for a few weeks. Mary got kind of jealous and asked her to leave. Charlie didn't know she was pregnant at the time, so he gave her a bus ticket to get back to Illinois." Vicki reiterated Charlie's absolute refusal to give any DNA to test Matthew's paternity. She lamented the hardships Matthew must be going through and told me how she hoped one day he would be able to find the truth. I asked Vicki if she knew anything about Charlie's other children. She replied, "One of Charlie's sons, Charles Manson Jr, went out to see Charlie, and on the way back to his home in Ohio, he pulled off on the side of the road, put a gun to his head, and blew his brains out." Vicki spoke solemnly about the suicide, almost as though she had just heard the news. "I've always wanted to know what happened during that visit."

Vicki lived in Virginia and she had a cool southern accent. Our first phone conversation lasted about two hours; Vicki loves to talk. It seemed like the whole Manson thing was such a big part of her and, since she rarely got to talk about it, she was happy to have me as her audience. I asked Vicki to start at the beginning, to take me back to her first introduction to the Manson family.

The summer Vicki met Charlie was the summer her parents

let her travel to California to visit family. She was fifteen. One day, her friends suggested they check out some nearby ranches and maybe do some horseback riding. They spent the afternoon walking around, checking out the ranches and the scenery. One of her friends pointed to a particular ranch and said, "That's where they filmed *Bonanza* [the TV series]." The teens were intrigued and decided to check out the area. "It was like walking into a ghost town," Vicki said. "It was all run down, not at all like any of the other ranches I had ever seen. There were a lot of pregnant women walking around and some of them didn't have any clothes on. I thought, 'This doesn't look like *Bonanza* to me.'"

I asked Vicki to go into detail about the ranch, which she called a *commune*. "There was a long saloon type building with what looked like a scarecrow on top. I walked inside of it and there were people over in one corner. They were playing cards and there was a television set up, like one in a bar. They did have a bar on the ranch, but no beer license. They called the bar 'Helter Skelter' and that was written on all the water bottles, everything inside. It was like a nightclub. It was only open for about four months before it got shut down. Everyone was nice and friendly there; everybody was really neat.

"There was this plank boardwalk that actually opened into a root cellar, what Charlie and I would call a root cellar because we grew up in the south, and you could crawl down into it, and you could hide maybe three or four people there. If your parents or whomever came to look for you, you could disappear! Many people asked us to stay but I said I'm going to have to get home sometime. I was staying with my aunt and if we didn't get home, my aunt would kick our butts. So, back down to the city we went."

This was Spahn Ranch in May of 1969. When Vicki met Charlie, she had no idea who he was or who he would become. "They were just hippies," she told me. "They were people with long hair who were smoking weed and living free. You didn't see that in North Carolina where I am from. I thought, 'This is so cool; I finally found a place where I can fit in.'"

Vicki described the ranch as a place in which it seemed no one was a leader, where everyone just did his or her own thing. She told me Charlie had just been one of the people there; he didn't stand out. Everyone called each other "brother" or "sis." There was a room the hippies called "the parachute room," which contained a red parachute used to store keys to their many old, dilapidated cars. "I don't see how anyone could drive any of those cars. They were in pieces, and tattered, and the motorcycles–it looked like maybe two of them were drivable."

Vicki assured me that, during her initial visit to the ranch, the family was living a peaceful, happy existence. The only drug on the property was marijuana. "Then they did LSD and, when speed came along, that was when it all went bad." Vicki went back to the ranch during Christmas break in 1970, when the Manson Family murder trials were already underway. She described the numbers of people protesting the trial. Many, she said, were her age, while others were a lot older. She described a woman known to the other protestors as "The Cat Lady," who had "a huge black car" and offered her home to people in the crowd who needed a place to stay. Vicki went back to Spahn Ranch each year through 1976. She told me, however, that it was never the same. Many of its ideals had changed and most of its original inhabitants had moved on.

Vicki took a few seconds to reflect, and went on to explain that "Helter Skelter," the idea that Charlie had been the leader of a cult and systematically brainwashed its members into committing crimes, was a defense theory designed to kill the hippie movement. The movement, she explained, was becoming too powerful–it came close to ending the Vietnam War and compelled people to demand equality. In Vicki's opinion, putting Manson up as the ultimate evil essentially killed the '60s: "Everybody knew it was just a set up. Hippies wouldn't have done that. Nobody that I hung around with would have ever thought of doing something like that. The government hated the hippies; they hated the drugs, the music, and the rebellion, the protesting. They wanted to put an end to us so people would take less notice of the useless killings in Vietnam. That bullshit Helter Skelter killed us; it was like they wanted to get rid of us, and they had a plan: 'We'll just take this Manson, he'll be the example of how awful these drug-infested hippie protesters are–he'll show what they can do!'"

Vicki spoke passionately as she unleashed her theory. I hadn't heard Helter Skelter analyzed like this before. I had to agree that her ideas made a lot of sense; many historians cite the Manson murders as the end of the hippie movement. Vicki collected her thoughts and continued, "Come on. If you were going to start a race war, would you pick the Beatles? Were black people listening to the Beatles? No."

Charlie began to call Vicki and they would talk about the people and things they shared in common. "I told him that when I was fourteen I use to run moonshine; he said he was only nine when he started running cars for his uncle." Charlie knew

Vicki's Uncle Jack and her ex-husband. Her Uncle Jack told her that Charlie was "crazy" but he was "fun" and would never do something like that [the Tate/LaBianca murders]. "They were into motorcycles, of course, and liked to throw knives into bails." Of her phone conversations with Charlie, Vicki said he was always nice and sweet. "He always asked about my mom."

I asked Vicki to delve more deeply into what she knew about the murders. She told me that "Tex" Watson, who was convicted of the Tate/LaBianca murders, got into drug dealing after he left the Manson family ranch and went to LA. Apparently Tex owned a wig store. He fell in love with a woman named Luella and she got pregnant, but Luella went to Mexico and had an abortion. Tex became angry with Luella for terminating the pregnancy and at the same time he grew upset over one too many drug deals gone wrong. So he relocated back to the ranch, a move Vicki described as "a huge mistake for everyone there." Vicki said that Charlie eventually moved Tex and Susan Atkins out of the main part of Spahn because "they were going out and starting their own little drug ring, and they would bring speed and all this other stuff to the ranch, which Charlie didn't like."

Vicki told me that the drug ring was "the beginning of the end." She assured me that, judging by the extensive interactions she witnessed at the ranch, Manson never tried to manipulate anyone's mind. "Charlie has always said, 'You gotta do this on your own.' I've never received any commands or orders. I heard things like, 'You wear too much makeup' and we'd all laugh at that." Vicki said that Charlie only spoke the truth: "Everyone thinks that Charlie wants to stay in prison, that he's happy there and never wants to get out; that's not true. He has asked me so many times if I could help him get transferred back up to West Virginia; he wanted to go back there so bad."

I asked Vicki about Susan Atkins, who was present during the Tate murders and died of a brain tumor in 2009 while incarcerated for her crimes. Vicki told me about her friend Linda, who was very close to Susan. "Linda was staying with Susan every day until she died and she would call me almost every day saying, 'Susan is so sick, it's pitiful.' You do have to have compassion; Linda was upset and crying–it was hard on her." Apparently Susan told Linda her version of what happened the day of the murders. The account goes something like this:

Family members Linda Kasabian, Tex Watson, and Susan Atkins went to Sharon Tate and Roman Polanski's house so that Tex could continue a drug deal with Abigail Folger's lover, Voytek Frykowski. Abigail Folger was a friend of Sharon Tate's, and both Abigail and Voytek were guests at the estate that evening. Voytek told the group to come back and subsequently turned them away on their return. At one point, Linda Kasabian entered the house, Abigail Folger took her to the bathroom, and the two did a couple of lines of cocaine. At one point Voytek got upset, there was a scuffle, and he threatened to call the police. Tex left the residence, angry, and went back to the ranch.

There was a call from Spahn Ranch to Sharon Tate's house. Tex gave warning on the phone that he was coming, which is why, according to Vicki, Voytek had his clothes back on. Abigail wasn't afraid when she saw one of the girls pass by her bedroom, and Sharon canceled the party she'd planned along with the visit from her sister, Debbie Tate.

Vicki said, "Well, right before Susan died, Charlie use to send me letters he wanted me to forward to her. He wanted her to know, that if she just told the truth before she died, she would have nothing to lose." Vicki said she tried to be the "letter passer," but no one wanted to bring the subject of Charlie up to Susan. The answer was always, "No."

I asked Vicki if the murders were simply part of a home invasion, and she assured me, "That's all it was." I was surprised to hear that the people murdered in the Tate house knew the people in the Manson Family. Vicki explained, "They knew each other. The Family was over there all the time; they were in and out and they swam in the pool at the Tate house." Vicki told me her friend Sylvia knew Jay Sebring, who was also murdered at the Tate-Polanski residence. She said Jay and Tex Watson were both hairdressers who knew each other. "Jay was into some really crazy shit, but it was the '60s and everyone was. It went on everywhere–drugs, orgies–what happened at the ranch, happened in Hollywood. In fact, people from Hollywood went to the ranch as much as the people from the ranch went to stay in Hollywood.

"My friend Sammy lives in Georgia and he believed he had Abigail Folger's car, but couldn't really prove it. He asked me if Charlie remembered anything unique about Abigail's car. Through letters, Charlie said to go into the glove box, pull the felt lining out, and look there for cuts in the glove box. If there were cuts, that was her car. Charlie said they use to cut up cocaine, eight balls inside the glove box. Sure enough, Sammy discovered the lining had been redone, and when the lining was taken out, the cut marks were there. Sammy traveled out to see Tex Watson and Tex told him 'the truth.' He said, 'Yes. It was all me.

Charlie never told anybody to do anything. I was in a rage and it was a drug burn.' Tex can't tell the truth now; he doesn't want to lose his ministry. He can't go back on what he said. God has forgiven him, and he needs to move on with his life. He said if he told the truth it wouldn't change anything. Tex is probably right."

Suzan LaBianca, Leno and Rosemary's daughter, attended Watson's 1990 parole hearing and told the parole board that, because of Tex's newfound Christianity, he was a new man, no longer dangerous, and should be released from prison.

Vicki told me a lot, and everything she said seemed believable. But, with this story, nothing is really what it seems. With every question answered, the number of further unanswered questions increased exponentially.

wakeup

Understanding

For me, Venice beach is a place in my head, you know, steps that I walked on. I'm living on the ground that I walked on. I've been out four times. Whatever out is to most people's minds is not really out, that's just what they've got in their heads. Out is not where they think it is.

There are some things that cannot be understood by the analytical mind. It's not possible to understand some things unless you've transcended the physical level, and that's on the level of impossibility, it just can't happen, it's beyond words. So when you explain something that's taken twenty or thirty years to transpire, and you try to explain it as common sense...it don't fit. I'm going to give you an example. There's an actor named Carradine who used to play all the monster movies. He was a hillbilly out of Kentucky. He was related to grandma, he was related to the Maddox clan, the Ku Klux Klan, all of those old sharp shootin' hillbillies, coons on their heads, shit like that. A lot of people don't understand the Ku Klux Klan. They understand the publicity of it. The Klan is an empty hood in a circle of colors; it doesn't have anyone in it. You can't explain something to someone when there's no such thing. How can you explain no such thing as being no such thing? If there is no such thing, then how can you explain no such thing is no such thing? But, there is such a thing, as no such thing, and in that chamber of no such thing is no such thing. Nobody exists to start with. So there's no complications, or confusion. It's only what it is, and what it is could go to the Dalai Lama, but actually he would be a bitch, 'cause he would do as he was told. In order to exist, you'd have to have words, and the words would need to be true, and how could the words be true when they're founded on shit to start with? The whole fuckin' thing is a big garbage dump, man.

My Life

My life is the only life I got to live in and I'm trying to live my life draggin' a lot of other people around with me, and it's not easy all the time. In order to succeed you've got to have the truth. If the truth is not involved, it won't work. All that morality, and all that garbage that they are preaching, and teaching, but they're not doing, because it doesn't exist to start with. It's all a big rerun, of a rerun, of a rerun.

I stand sixty-three years witness. I haven't done anything. The only thing I've done is fight to stay alive. I don't know anything. I haven't stood up for anything, or rejected anything. I haven't done anything. All I've been is a hard dick and that's it, man, all I've been is fuckin' feeling good and making weird sounds. I make some weird sounds, you know. Half the time, I don't even know what I'm talking about. I really don't care, it doesn't mean anything anyway. It only means something if I mean something to you. If I mean something to you, then I wouldn't be in here. All I mean to you is what you can make out of it, what you can get out of it. It's just the human condition.

I'm the money, I'm the card game, I'm a deck of cards. I was raised by those cards all my life. I've been running with those cards. Those are my only friends. Sounds kind of crazy, doesn't it?

Trying To Trick Me?

Why do I have to spend my life in prison because someone else wanted to use my life? The Roman Catholic Church have been using me ever since reform school. They recognized me as the devil right off. I wouldn't study their stuff. I threw their books at them. I refused to stand in their confirmation line. So, what they did is they tricked me. They send another inmate to me who said, "Let's run away." And I said, "How could we do that?" He said, "We'll go to the corn field down there, and there will be two bicycles there. We'll steal the bicycles, then we'll go out on the highway, and we'll hitchhike back to the city, and find your mom." I thought that was a good idea. When I was ready to do it, he said, "I changed my mind. I don't want to go." So, I ended up going by myself. It took me a lot of years to wake up, and they put me up to that. See it? They tried to beat me. There was a monk named Thomas. They use to pick on me when I was a kid, so he took me over to the gym and showed me how to box, told me how to hold my hands up. Took me to the boxing ring, showed me how to fight, so I went into boxing. I went to Chicago and won a jacket, that's at ten years old.

Religion

Well, you wake up. There's no ending to anything. That there's no beginning, that everything has always been and will always be, that the only reality is eternity. The eternal moment is all that's real. All the rest of it is a play or given to you by somebody that's already gone. They start giving it to you the minute you're born. They start piling it in your brain. See, I noticed that when I got out last time. When this kid was born they started putting shit over on him, you dig? And I wonder what the fuck are they doing that for? And then I seen that everything is one, everything you look at is you, so there is nothing else. Only if you allow it, if you let it into your existence, but you can only do what you've [learned] to do in that syndrome or that episode or that enclosure. You know that enclosure is you. Where that begun and where it ends is never. It only begins and ends in your mind. When you wake up all your thought patterns are just program implants that don't really mean anything because you're as much a robot as a robot is, because there ain't no such thing as no such thing. The universe travels around you. Everything travels around you because you've never moved, it's impossible, unless you were God. God never lives and never dies. God is always there.

Yeah, heaven was right there but you didn't know it. I mean all you knew is what they were telling you, and they were telling you, "You need this and you wanna buy that, we got that for you, and this don't cost lots." And you go through everything there is to go through, and you need to find the holiest most religious person in the world, and he wants to suck your peter. And you say, "Oh well," you don't know, you only know what you're told. I run back and say, "Yeah, this holy man wants to suck my dick and he beat me up, man, whipped me." [They] said I was lying and this holy man wouldn't do that, so then I find out that it's all about the thrill, all about those feelings that you get when no one's around, which all boils down to "don't give a fuck and why are you always helping those rich middle-class people." How come you ain't over there helping the poor like you say. You know, we tell the rich we're helping the poor. We're actually not helping the poor, we're helping ourselves. Well, you say that makes more sense than the other thing you were playing with. Because if you helped them other people they'll eat you up. If you want to give everything to the poor people then that puts you a couple steps under poor because they'll eat you up, man. Go back in that back alley and see if the winos don't pick your bones. So if the most holy want to go back, they built the monasteries high up in the mountain where no one can get to them. They send soldiers to die in war because they can't face the reality out the back door. The trash can reality of the garbage people. You know, they're the ones that have to work it all out and virgins are not sacrificed on the pyramids for good. They're sacrificed on the back streets for drugs and money and bureaucrats and politicians and preachers, double-dealing lying preachers.

XIII

UNCOVERING THE FINAL DETAILS

*I*t was Stanton LaVey who told me about John Aes-Nihil. Stanton has known John since he was a kid, when John was his mother's and stepfather's (Zeena and Nikolas) roommate. Stanton and John were close and John used to drive Stanton to school. Stanton told me that what makes John unique, aside from the deep connection he feels with the Manson Family, is the fact that he has been interested in Manson from the beginning: 1969.

John created the market for Charles Manson memorabilia, the now-popular nostalgia scene surrounding the stuff of serial killers, true crime, and all things underground. According to Stanton, "John Aes-Nihil is the original swap meet, flea market, smut peddling, bootlegging pirate." Most important, Stanton said, is that John does what he does for the right reasons, "taking care of people" along the way. "His intentions personally are deeper, philosophical; he wants to carry this information forward into the future, in one of the oldest, truest ways tested: through magazines, literature, books, and archives." Stanton said he could guarantee that John is the authority on all things Manson, that he "knows all." His archives have been accessed by virtually everyone attempting to discover or produce anything related to Manson. He owns every piece of video and the rarest photos. He has personally interviewed hundreds of people related to the Manson Family and documented it all. His interest borders on obsession; it's staggering.

I made the drive out to the Mojave Desert where John has

lived for a while. He has since told me that the desert, out in the middle of nowhere and away from everyone else, is a haven for Satanists. John is pretty soft spoken; he has a deliberate way of talking, as though he thinks about everything first. In a way, he has the composure of an artist and, after spending about ten minutes with him, it was clear to me that this man was one of the most fascinating people I have ever met. I was disappointed I had only a few hours to spend with him. I wished I could have spent a week out in the desert, learning as much as I could from John.

John started filming and directing The Manson Family Movies in 1974 while living in Oakland. The focus of the project was to reproduce the rumored films Manson family members made of each other's exploits leading up to and including the events of August 1969. John embarked on an immense amount of research before he began shooting the home video style footage. He tried to keep the reenactments as authentic as possible, using the same locations, and keeping the family's "feel." The film premiered in 1984.

John told me how the real Manson Family movies (if they ever, indeed, existed) might have gotten started. According to the story he was told, a TV station had been doing a shoot at Spahn Ranch when some of the crew's equipment was stolen. Filmmaker John Waters asked Tex Watson about the alleged theft, a crime Tex said never happened. Ed Sanders, author of The Family, claimed that the family filmed a satanic cult snuffing someone at Ventura Co. Line beach. According to Sanders, the filming of this event led to the family's filmed recreation of its own murders. Sanders' account alleges that a "famous New York Artist," which to some sounds like code for "Andy Warhol," acquired these films. John said he once asked John Waters if he ever talked to Warhol about this. Waters had; when he'd asked Warhol if Warhol owned the movie, his response was simply "I don't know."

John believes he got the real story about the family films from interviewing Robert Hendrickson, director of the 1973 documentary Manson. John said that Robert and his friend Craig had been working on a movie about Jesus, when they somehow ended up at Spahn Ranch and started making a movie about the family. Eventually, director Laurence Merrick got involved and told Hendrickson, as well as the family, that he could make everyone rich from the resulting documentary. "Apparently," said John, "Merrick never gave the family any money–and you know what happened to him." (Merrick was shot in the back by a deranged student of his acting school in 1977.)

John started the Manson Archives and the Archives of Aesthetic Nihilism around 1980. John coined the term "Aesthetic Nihilism," which is art or music so extreme it "verges on destruction." He then started work on the first of the Tennessee Williams Trilogy, while living with Nikolas, Zeena, and Stanton in Hollywood. John's next project was The Ma Barker Story, the prequel to the Manson Family Movies, to be filmed at Barker Ranch. He has also contributed volumes to the music and photography scenes; he's collaborated with everyone from Kenneth Anger to William Burroughs.

John told me he acquired a lot of his Manson archives from Bill Nelson. Nelson has self published a couple of books about Manson and Tex Watson. When John mentioned Nelson, I recognized his name but could recall little else. "Oh, Boy-Nelson," said John. "I met him when I lived in Hollywood and we started trading Manson materials. He said that he used to work for the Secret Service; he also said he had been a minister and a used car salesman." John told me he and Nelson used to meet at various Denny's parking lots to go through all of their Manson memorabilia. Once, Nelson showed up to one of their meetings and said his wife wanted him to get rid of his collection. John bought Nelson out–or so he thought. John told me that Nelson's sale was "the ultimate deal" because it included thirty-six slides of the photographs Roman Polanski took of Sharon Tate on the set of The Fearless Vampire Killers. John said the most amazing of these slides are all stamped August 1969; they are the photos that Voytek, Jay, and Sharon took of each other on August 5th, just days before they were slain.

John owns the original Tate murder crime scene photos, each stamped by the corner on the back. I asked John how Nelson ended up with such rare and exclusive items. "Somehow Nelson ended up with all of it." I told John about the crime scene photos I'd seen at The Museum of Death. "Oh yeah," he said, "I sold them a set of prints." I asked to see his photos and he pulled out a filing box filled with rare, many one-of-a-kind Manson pictures. I saw Polaroid photos of Charlie and the girls; some were photos from happier times, before all the madness. When John handed me the crime scene photos, he showed me the backs where they were verified. I was silent. There was really nothing I could say. I felt somehow connected to what had happened. I was shown the slides that came from Sharon Tate's camera, the pictures taken just days before she was murdered. The group of friends looked so alive. It was obvious that they were having fun and that they were all very close to one another. Most of all, they seemed oblivious to what would happen next. I commented on how beautiful Sharon was and John took me out to his garage, where he showed me a poster-size print of a shot Polanski took of Sharon nude in the snow. It was breathtaking: the most amazing photo of Sharon I'd ever seen. John said that, in the early '70s, he would meet random people at parties in Haight-Ashbury who said they'd been at the wild parties Polanski gave.

John has also talked with famed Hollywood journalist Paul Krassner about the home movies. Krassner allegedly told John that he has actually seen a film in which Charlie, Susan, Voytek, and Abigail are at the Tate house doing MDA and having sex. Apparently the Los Angeles Police Department seized pornographic films and videotapes found in Polanski's loft during the murder investigation. Krassner claimed the films also included Cass Elliot in an orgy with famous celebrities. Krassner believes that the secret celebrity sex tapes lie at the heart of the investigation's cover-ups. Krassner and others (notably private and police investigators) feel that the stars' actions could have been motivated mostly by the damage such tapes could do to their careers if they surfaced. John told me about additional movies that featured Sharon Tate with Dean Martin and Steve McQueen. Krassner wrote Charlie about the movie and received this response: "Sebring done Susan's hair and I think he sucked one or two of her dicks. That girl loves dick, you know what I mean, hon'? Yul Brynner, Peter Sellers...."

John affirmed, "The main thing about the Tate murder situation was the slumming, the movie stars converging with hippies." He talked about the "piles" of "insane" stories regarding the parties at the Tate house. He said Roman, Sharon, Jay, and movie stars from all over Hollywood would go down to the Sunset Strip to pick up hippies and take them back to their houses for drugs and sex. "Eventually," John pointed out, "that's going to blow up in your face." In his opinion, the murders were a direct result of all this wild interaction between the "rich and famous and the infamous and unknown."

John told me Nelson tried to get these videos from the same two cops who were in possession of the crime scene photos. Apparently the cops told Nelson the videos merely showed Sharon and Roman having sex. Allegedly the LAPD told Roman they would return his films if he took a lie detector test, the results of which compose part of John's collection.

I asked John about Polanski's polygraph. "Well, of course Roman passed the polygraph," he said. John doesn't believe Polanski had anything to do with his wife's brutal death, but he believes Polanski knew Voytek was trouble, and regretted the fact that he hadn't kicked Voytek out of his home before the horror.

I asked John what happened to Nelson. John said that Nelson had secretly held on to some of his collection. When he decided to sell what remained, John was on a European tour with his films and Nelson couldn't get a hold of him. So he sold to another collector from North Carolina, who'd previous bought items from John. When he received Nelson's compilation, the collector contacted John and sold him what he had acquired. It turned out that Nelson was having a nervous breakdown, undergoing various operations, and popping "piles" of drugs. John told me Nelson was "most likely nuts from the beginning" since he'd been a convicted pedophile long before John met him. John sees Nelson's interest in the Manson murders as a "voyeuristic obsession," a desire to live vicariously through the sexual exploits at the Polanski residence and Spahn Ranch. "He was insanely jealous of the sex orgies. While the family was partying at Spahn, Nelson said, he was preaching at a church in Canoga Park. The main thing is that Nelson was trying to be a normal Christian during the hippie era, and when he discovered the Manson family, he realized he'd really missed out." Apparently, Nelson's obsession knew no limits. He supposedly stalked family member Sandra Good for years.

I asked John to explain how he first got interested in Manson. He told me he read about the Tate murders in the paper when they happened and that, sometime before that, he had read an article in Time about a roving band of hippies ripping off tourists in Death Valley. He told me he's always seen the Manson trial as a witch-hunt. John believes Manson isn't responsible for the Tate murders. He told me, "I have always believed that you are responsible for what you do. Period. If these kids killed people it was because that is what they wanted to do. Any other belief about what happened is ultimately a dead end. Nowadays it is government policy that no one is responsible for anything and everything is someone else's fault and only the government can save you. So now you know why everything is a giant mess and Charlie is still in prison for your sins."

Now, John believes, the Manson story has turned into a "mass culture universal myth." John said no one knows what actually happened; even Tex Watson, who actually committed the murders, claims to have no idea what was really going on. Because of this, it's possible the public perception of Charles

Manson will someday shift. John told me about a writer named Wayne McGuire, who wrote a few articles for Crawdaddy and Fusion in the late '60s and then disappeared. McGuire predicted a future massive, worldwide schizophrenic breakdown, during which Charles Manson would morph into a major American folk hero.

I asked John to explain his take on the origins of the Manson murders. He would lay it out like this:

"When Charlie was released from Terminal Island and ended up in Haight-Ashbury, the hippies were attracted to him and he went with it. Constantly there were all these kids coming to him and asking him what to do about everything. Haight-Ashbury was being taken over by speed freaks and all of that. So they left San Francisco and went to LA. Then there was the spiral staircase, where the family spent a lot of time. The spiral staircase was a house located in the back of the Malibu Feed Bin at the intersection of Topanga Canyon Boulevard and the Pacific Coast Highway. Supposedly the family and Satanists and movie stars really got down there.

"Bobby Beausoleil lived in the Haight with his band The Orkestra. Ken Anger was there and dinged out on Bobby and told him he had to be Lucifer in his movie so Bobby said sure. So Ken and Bobby are living at a Victorian mansion called the Russian Embassy because that is what it used to be. While living with Kenneth Anger for four or five years, I taped every interview he did and he told the Bobby story at least twice. He said, "Bobby told me he needed to go to LA to buy band equipment, so he left in the van I bought him with the money

I gave him. Upon his return, I found a large square object wrapped in black plastic in the foyer. Our dog Snowfox was ripping at it, so I opened it and it was a bale of marijuana. I was outraged, as this could have gotten us all arrested. I threw him and the weed out. I subsequently went out, and when I returned the place had been broken into and all the footage of Lucifer Rising was gone. Bobby had driven my van to LA and the van broke down next to the Spahn Ranch, where he met those Manson people.

"Bobby knew Gary Hinman from when he'd previously lived in LA. Gary was selling weed that had been sprayed by the government with paraquat. The Manson people bought some of this and sold it to the Hells Angels who got horribly sick from it. This led to Bobby killing Gary, which led to the other murders.

"A number of points in Ken's version of the story are very unlikely. Bobby drove to Topanga Canyon. He may have met the family at the spiral staircase. He did stay with Gary; they apparently had a thing going on. The family was wandering around in a bus they parked at Gary's. The family and Bobby moved onto the Spahn Ranch. The family stayed with Gary Hinman, whom they met through Bobby Beausoleil. Gary was involved in some sort of drug situation.

"Jay Sebring and Voytek were trying to corner the MDA market. According to rumors, Rosemary LaBianca was somehow involved in the MDA deals (she did leave behind one million dollars), while Leno LaBianca was being hounded by the Mafia to pay up. (The FBI tapped his phone.) The connections between Leno LaBianca and the Mafia were well documented. In their initial investigation, LA police immediately looked into this angle. According to Leno's first wife, Leno had complained to her a week before the killings that someone had been in the house moving things around. Later, some of the girls in the family would admit to doing this. That's how arbitrary it all is; these drug deals involve like everyone in Hollywood.

"Vincent Bugliosi (prosecutor in Manson case, coauthor of Helter Skelter) was ordered to come up with a motive that did not implicate the rich and the famous—hence, Helter Skelter, baby. This idea basically came from Paul Watkins, a "member" of the Manson family—it was his take on things he heard around the ranch. As for August 10, I am rather certain that the plan was always to go to the LaBianca's. Apparently they did all this driving all over the place beforehand and maybe that was to confuse the passengers in the car: Linda, Clem, Susan, Leslie, Pat, and Tex, presuming that Charlie was driving. It is fact that the family had gone to parties at Harold True's next door and that the family had creepy crawled (broke in and moved belongings around) at the LaBianca's about a week before. Years later, Charlie stated that they were after Leno's 'little black book.' In a 1991 episode of Hard Copy, Manson admitted to knowing about LaBianca's Mafia connections when confirming that he in fact asked Leno for his 'little black book.' The family partied at Harold True's house often, and the LaBianca's daughter Suzan had a boyfriend in the Straight Satans, perhaps DiCarlo, who also hung out at Spahn Ranch. I have the original map hand-drawn by Harold True, showing the family how to get from

Spahn Ranch to his house.

"There's the idea that the LaBiancas were somehow involved in the same drug situation as Jay and Voytek. There is not really anything to back this up, aside from things that Charlie insinuated to Geraldo Rivera about the Mafia being involved with Leno or Rosemary leaving an estate of one million while Leno owed his bookie money and the FBI or some such entity tapped his phone. Then there's the idea that Leno was embezzling money from his grocery store business and cooking the books and possibly using it as money laundry.

"Tex Watson came to Hollywood to be somebody. He became a hairdresser and met the hairdresser to the stars, Jay Sebring. Tex met Terry Melcher, who was living at what became the Tate house. Tex met Charlie Manson. They both met Dennis Wilson. Everyone was driving around, hitch hiking around, even a big deal rock star like Dennis hitched sometime.

"Tex had been in the Tate house before he was in the family, because Terry Melcher lived there. There was a lot of involvement between the people in the Tate house and the people who were involved with the family before the murders happened. Tex partied there a number of times. Tex and Jay Sebring knew each other and they were both hairdressers. Tex was, at one point, renting a house that belonged to Leno LaBianca. There are massive connections between everybody. The free clinic in Haight-Ashbury had a benefit party. General Tate was there; Charlie, Susan Atkins, and Abigail Folger were there. An LA county fireman personally told me he saw Sharon Tate horseback riding at Spahn Ranch when the family was running the horse concession for George. There were no coincidences, no randomness; everyone knew each other. Tex created the Crowe situation by getting money for drugs from him and then running off with the money, leaving the girls there. Charlie had to rescue them. According to the girls' account, Tex and Voytek were involved in a similar situation.

"As far as the parties at the Tate house, now this depends on to whom you talk. Debra Tate stated that the family partied there. As I said, Voytek and Jay were trying to corner the MDA market, and they were working with these three drug dealers from Canada, who the LAPD interrogated. Mama Cass assumed these three guys did the murders because they were her drug dealers, and John Phillips called the LAPD and said the same guys most likely committed the crimes. In a very recent interview, Debra Tate just out of nowhere said, 'Those Manson people were here all the time; they used the pool; they used the bathroom...'

"As for "Helter Skelter," these killings brought out a pile of dirt that had to be swept under the carpet. The big deal was that movie and rock stars were slumming by picking up hippies on Sunset Strip and bringing them home to party with. Sex and drugs and Rock 'n' Roll and movie stars. The American Dream. One of the stranger stories I've heard is that Cary Grant was having sex with some boy in the bushes near the Tate house the night of the murders; when he heard all this screaming and stuff, he fled.

"I've run into several people who were in jail with Tex, and they all said the same thing. One of these stories made it into a Boston tabloid. Basically Tex would be in the chapel preaching against homosexuality; then he would go back to his cell and get a blowjob. I think he's a flat out sociopath, who is a genius at lying. Tex was a drug dealer and Tex killed everyone, which is what he told Pat Robertson on his show. Pat Robertson actually makes a statement at the end of my movie. It's one of the most amazing things anyone has ever said about this situation: 'You didn't kill a pregnant woman and smear her guts all over the walls, but this man did, and Jesus saved him; think what he can do for you.'"

Hearing John's analysis of the Manson murders, I felt in over my head. It occurred to me that the reason so many people are interested in the Manson murders might be the simple fact that there is really no way to figure it all out. I could spend the next five years trying to piece it all together, and I would likely end up at the same place I started. The more I talked to John and Vicki, the more I thought about Bill Nelson, how he'd relentlessly stalked and harassed Sandra Good and one of Charlie's sons—his obsession was a story all on its own. The Manson murders seemed to have taken over his life. I thought about all the secrets Nelson took with him to the grave and how, ultimately, he'd become another casualty in the Manson story.

When I think about the desert John calls home, I remember a lot of wind; it felt exactly like where I live, in the middle of the Canadian prairies. But somehow, out there, the wind had an emptiness to it. Everything I experienced on that trip had a momentum I really couldn't understand, yet things were coming together in a way that seemed almost necessary. It felt as though

I had to meet all of these different people and take from them whatever I could the better to prepare myself for what would happen next.

After my failed attempt to visit Charlie, I'd written the warden, and my visitor application had been approved. The day after I left the desert, I would go back to Corcoran for a meeting with Charles Manson.

I left the desert and began the trip back to Los Angeles. On the road, I couldn't focus on anything. I had serious doubts about what I was doing, but I managed to ignore them enough to keep going; part of me shut down. I went over in my head how the meeting should go, even though I'd convinced myself that it probably wouldn't happen anyway. There was a level of insanity involved in this visit, and I began to question how much sanity I had left. Because, though I had yet to understand fully why meeting Manson was so important to me, it was something I felt compelled to do. It took three hours to get to my hotel, but it felt like fifteen minutes. Once I arrived, I had no idea what to do with myself. I tried to catch up on emails but that was hardly a diversion. I couldn't possibly explain any of this to someone on the outside.

Sleep didn't come easy; it didn't really come at all. In the morning, I gathered my things and walked, rather like a zombie, into the cool morning air. As I made my way to Corcoran, I felt oddly at ease, as if a huge pressure had been lifted and I no longer cared what happened. I pulled up to Corcoran's first security point; that morning, the guard was chatty. He told me about some Manson movie he'd seen before warning me that I probably wouldn't be meeting Charlie that day. He wished me luck and patted my car twice on the roof. Inside the prison walls, the guards seemed shocked that the pending part of my application status had been lifted. I was cleared to go through. I think I was more surprised than they were, but I strolled outside to wait for the bus that would take me out to PHU.

It was ten A.M. when I cleared the final security desk. I was processed and walked through a metal detector before waiting outside with a guard for the gate to open. The early morning had developed into a beautiful day; a low-lying fog added to the quiet. "Is it always this quiet out here?" I asked the guard. "Yeah," he said. "It's kind of the opposite of what goes on in there." With that, the gate opened and we walked into an enclosure. As the first gate shut behind us, another gate opened in front and, once through it, we were on our way to the visiting room. As we walked, we talked about Corcoran and what it was like to work there. The guard told me he was thankful for his job, though he found it very challenging and stressful; he didn't feel like there were any other options for him. He told me his job was his own way of doing time, until he was able to retire. "Just go through there and walk straight ahead," he said. "Have a good visit." He pointed to a door and let me walk the final twenty steps on my own. I opened the door, paused for a few seconds, gathered my thoughts, and walked into a large room.

I was caught off guard. He was there, just as I rounded the corner. He was arranging a couple of chairs around a table. I interrupted him, "Hey, General." He looked up and walked over, and with a genuine smile on his face he said, "Hey, hey," and offered his hand in friendship. I slowly extended my hand too, though I'm sure the look on my face would have been the same if I'd seen a monster.

games to play

August 9

On August 9, they dropped an atomic bomb on Japan. That's the same date Sharon Tate was killed. There is this anti-Manson woman from Atlanta that's always writing stories about the family, and she wants to advertise August 9 as a historical date, or some kind of crazy shit like that. I said, "Why don't you look at August 9, as the day they dropped the atomic bomb." She said she didn't know that. I told her, "You don't know the shit you guys do, you only know how to put all that shit on me, man." It's funny how you tell somebody you know. They say you did 6, 7, and 8. You say, "No, I did 1,2,3,4,5,9,10,11,12,13 and the rest of it, but I didn't do 6,7,8." They say, "You did 6,7,8," and I said, "What the fuck reason would I have to lie. I did the rest of it but I didn't do 6,7,8. Why would I want to lie about that." There's no fuckin' reason you know, the time is done, the game is over, now that's already past, and they still won't accept the fact that I didn't have anything to do with that, not directly, like conspiring or conceiving, or thinking about that, you dig?

It's like you and I are doing things together, we do things together, we do whatever we want. And I take you out and I say, "Here's the way you use a knife," and I stab six people to death, and I say, "You see that." You say, "Yeah." And I cut their throats, and I say, "Now, you see how that's done." And you say, "Yeah." And I say, "Now, when I tell you to do something, don't hesitate, do it, you understand me?" And you say, "Yeah, I understand you." So, well, "Don't play me for a goddam idiot!" And you say, "I won't." So, later on, you say, "I'm going downtown." I say, "Well, you have a good day." And they say, "Well, Fish went downtown and killed ten people, you told him to do it." I say, "No, I didn't tell him to do nothin', man. Fish got his own head, he's got his own mind, you know." "Yeah, you're his leader." I said, "I'm no fuckin' leader, you're out of your fuckin' mind. If I gotta be a leader, I gotta be responsible for that. I'm not responsible for nothing, fuck you!" You dig? If I tell someone to go do something, it's worse than if I do it myself.

If I wanted that done, I would have done it. I didn't need nobody to do nothing for me. I can take care of myself. They keep saying I'm responsible for what you did; I'm not responsible for what you did. You come and you tell me, "Look, I'm having some problems with 1, 2, 3." I say, "Okay." You said, "Will you help me?" I said, "Sure, I'll be glad to, but now if I help you, don't forget you owe me 1,2,3." And you say, "Okay, I'll owe you." I say, "All right." And I go and take care of 1,2,3, then I come back to you and say, "Look, I need 6,7,8," and you say, "All right." I say, "You deal with it." You say, "What do I do?" I say, "Don't ask me, I don't care what you do, it's none of my business, I don't want to get involved in that." I don't want no conspiracy on me, I know what malice of forethought is. You know, I don't have malice of forethought against a pussycat, I don't sin against, I don't waste nothing. I don't leave camp fires burning. In other words, I don't make mistakes. The mistakes that somebody makes, that accuses me of making a mistake.

That's something that other people play, they play mistakes. I don't play mistakes. Yeah, I knew them (everyone at the Tate house), sure, that's my neighborhood, I knew everybody there. There is no doubt in my mind about anything. I know everybody there now. Who's not to know, sweetheart? When I go on the set it's me, I'm Mel Gibson, and Tom Selleck. I'm .357 Magnum, I'm Buffalo Bill, I'm Marshall Dillon, I'm Charlie Chaplain, I'm Shirley Temple, I'm everyone, I'm God, I'm you!

My So-Called Friend

See, if I got no say-so out there, pretty soon what happens is people come in to me and say, "Hi, I want to be your friend and la, la, la" and all that. And "I was going to commit suicide and then I thought, no, that you were my last hope and da, da, da, da and all that." And I end up in the fucking nut ward because they end up playing their suicide and bullshit on me, trying to put another psychiatrist in play with that goddamn lying stinking-ass Italian who's double dealing on the district attorney's office, who wouldn't give me my rights to start with. But me not having no parents and having no help, the system's always...able to do anything they want to do to me. I think the greatest philosophy I ever came across is when I decided I didn't give a fuck, and all stress left me because I was all tied up with the people that I love that was using me.

They didn't have any real concern for anyone but themselves and I had to recognize that inside myself too, as well too, you know. Because we're all looking out for number one. That's the only thing that really makes any sense. Your eternity is inside of you. Just like my eternity is inside of you. Because there is no me unless you're me and then, if you were me, that would be my me and then I would have tricked you. You would be possessed by the devil.

I mean, like seriously, seriously speaking there's only one in my world. There's only one I mean, you know. I get up in the morning with that and if someone wants to play-act like something, I'll play with them, you know. But basically I just live in a lonely kind of trip, man. I've been alone all my life. I was born alone. I've been alone forever, man. I mean the ranch was filled with people but they were all with themselves. I'm not, like I'd help them and do whatever I could for them, but like there was nobody there, man. Not even me. The only thing that I really worried about or thought about was the weather. The weather had changed so much since I was out last time. Every time I get out everything's changed. I get out and creeks are gone, the lakes are gone, it's all cement. There's hotels and motels and pancake houses and hamburger stands just covered with cement and concrete.

The beet farm is gone. The birds don't live there no more, this is gone, that's gone. Wow, man. Pretty soon it's going to be all cement. At one time I thought we could save the world, that's the joke. I don't think you can save anything because I don't think anything's lost. There's not going to be anymore. The universe don't need this little pile of dirt. And when you raise something, you learn to love it, you grew it, you take care of it, and then you cut it down. What kind of silly shit is that? I mean, what kind do you call that compassion or love or understanding? You know, then they give you a Bible to read and everything happened thousands of years ago and nothing's happening now.

ATWA

That's what I was thinking, man, that's why my message to all those people was ATWA. Without that you don't have nothing else. And they say, well order. What order, they want to bring back Hitler for an order. That's not order. Disorder you know, Hitler wasn't an order. He was a step towards order but that was only a step. And see, they tell so many lies and people get caught up in the lies. What does the word national mean to you? Well, yeah, national socialism. There isn't international socialism. I don't think that Hitler had the world in *his mind. I think he had the state in his mind. I met some of his youth movement guys in prison.*

And they weren't all that, they were on the chess board good, but off the chess board I don't think they were into parks and trees and animals and stuff like that. And you know, like, you got to be a pretty heavy dude to be in with that kind of stuff, because another animal is just like another world. You know, you get a rhinoceros, man, you got a whole existing being and a life form there that has wants and needs. Like dragonflies, I love those characters. I dance with them, you know. Yeah, when I'm out in the yard there, I dance right with them, man. And I love them, man. I tried to get one to land on my hand and this is how strict he is. He waited until my hand was on the other side of the fence, in between the fences, and....couldn't move in the direction towards him, and then he landed on my hand. That's how smart he is. Okay, something else, those crows are smart too. I had birds show me really intelligent stuff, man, stuff I can't even put in words.

XIV

A JOURNEY'S END

It had taken me almost thirty-five years to get here, seated across from the man who once gave me nightmares.

For a while, we just looked at each other. It was difficult to process and fully appreciate where I was and with whom I was visiting. Because it had been extremely difficult to have a visit approved, the clearance process and the walk to this room seemed extremely fast. I was tired, and so our introduction felt like a dream. We sat in two of four plastic chairs surrounding a circular table that was situated next to a series of vending machines. I asked Charlie if I could get us a couple of drinks because inmates are not allowed to handle money. I had a Coke and he had an orange juice.

It didn't take long for Charlie to get into character. In no time, he became animated and his hands flailed around as he made faces and tapped the table with his fingertips. I remembered what William Harding told me about going into the visiting room completely hung over. I smiled to myself at the thought; I had no idea how he could handle that. Charlie seemed to have more energy than he could manage. Even though we spoke on the phone a lot over the past two years, we were really still getting to know each other. I thought about Matthew Roberts, and I could see the resemblance to Charlie. It wasn't so much that they looked alike. It was deeper than that. They share a quality that is difficult to define, something beyond words. Matthew had told me he hated that people were scared of him. His likeness to Charlie frightens people so much that they can't contain their reactions.

As I thought about how difficult it was for Matthew to *look* like Charles Manson, I couldn't begin to imagine how difficult it was to *be* Charles Manson.

Charlie sat with his back to the wall and he seemed divided between his visit with me and his surveillance of the room. At times, he would stop speaking mid-sentence and sit still, silent, completely alert. He did this every time he sensed something was a little off. Charlie was rarely completely at ease. He was very observant and aware of his surroundings, almost as though he were constantly on edge. Yet he managed to exude the confidence that comes with his extraordinary kind of charisma. Even though he has almost nothing, Charlie carries himself with dignity and commands respect. At some point Charlie caught me staring at the swastika on his forehead. It's not carved into his head, as is so often reported. It's actually a dark green tattoo. Charlie told me that, when he was arrested, he was the most hated man in the world. And so, he came to identify with the swastika, the most hated symbol in the world. Charlie said he picked it up and made it his own. He went on to explain the swastika as an esoteric symbol used throughout the world to indicate different concepts. He told me the North American Indians used the swastika to represent a spinning wheel. "Come to think of it," he said, "I think it's the number fifty in Japanese."

I asked Charlie about the Manson Family girls and what it was like to have them following him around. He laughed and said, "You got that all wrong, man; I was following them. I had no idea what I was doing out there." I asked him if he was really a pimp. Immediately his mood changed, and I regretted asking such a sensitive question. Charlie looked at me with complete sincerity and explained that his mother didn't have any money and sometimes she had to hustle to make enough to buy him milk. He paused for a few seconds before he said, "So, yeah; I'm a pimp." Charlie rarely gave me the answers I expected.

I asked him if the story, the legend that his mother had once traded him for a pitcher of beer, was true. "Yeah, that's true," he said. He told me that, back then, there were no accessible abortions and his mother had never wanted a child; she was still a kid herself. A waitress had said how cute Charlie was, so his mother said, "Take him," and the waitress did. A few days later, Charlie's uncle tracked him down and returned him to his mother. Sometimes, when I ask what Charlie perceives to be a stupid question, I get back what he feels are equally stupid answers. I asked, "Do you have any idea why you're so famous?" Charlie snickered, sarcastic. "Because," he said, "I have a really big dick."

I learned that, for Charlie, getting to the visiting room is a bit of an ordeal. He has to walk almost two blocks, pass through several security points, and, depending on the guards on duty that day, submit to a strip search. Because he is such a high profile inmate, and because he is often met with such great degrees of worship and disdain, each of his trips to the visiting room, Charlie assured me, is a production. There were reasons why he'd refused to go down to the room for a year.

At one point, Charlie leaned across the table, so that he was maybe eight inches from my face and, through clenched teeth, he strained to speak in a menacing voice, "Do you know why I'm so intimidating?" I could smell his breath and I was silent. He fell back in his chair and awaited my response. "No," I admitted. I had no idea. Charlie relaxed and seemed to release the tension he'd been full of just seconds before. He sighed, "Because I've been intimidated my whole life." I couldn't help but wonder what Charlie could have become under different circumstances. From everything he'd told me about his life, it seemed he never really stood a chance. That seemed like a tragedy.

I remember Charlie drumming on the table with both hands, trying to compose a question he wanted to ask me: "So, how in the hell did you get in here?" I reminded him that he had sent me a visiting form and that I'd filled it out, sent it back, and it was approved. Charlie took a few seconds to gather his thoughts and looked over to the corner, where Kenny was sitting with his family. Kenny smiled the biggest shit-eating grin I've ever seen and began laughing and waving. He knew exactly what Charlie was thinking. Charlie asked, "So, what you're telling me is, Kenny did all of this?" With that, he started laughing, and I laughed as well. I got the joke.

This was Charles Manson, the most vilified, hated man in America. It would be easy to believe he was some "hippie cult leader," that he could threaten to kill me by ripping my heart from my chest and eating it, that his presence could induce in me a fear of facing death every second. None of this is true. Instead, the man I met had much in common with the people I work with. It would be easy to call him crazy, insane even, as if that label were somehow the answer to the questions posed by such a complex being. Instead, that label is a limitation most people struggling with mental illness have to overcome every day. Because the people around them don't want to delve underneath the label to see a person as he or she really is. Reaching past the way the world has labeled Charles Manson might require a man to risk his own sanity. Sometimes it felt as though I were doing just that. If it weren't for the history and the madness, Charlie could have been like the many people I've met who are simply trying to find their way through a world that seems completely alien, a reality they never fully understood. In some ways, he reminds me a lot of The Captain, one of my favorite patients. I can just imagine Charlie trying to control the world from his prison cell. In other ways, Charlie reminds me of Dwayne, who had such a unique view of the world and who truly inspired me. To a degree, Charlie even possesses some of The Claw's reckless abandonment.

When I asked Charlie what his psychiatric diagnosis was, he told me he has been diagnosed a paranoid schizophrenic with an antisocial personality disorder. He then proceeded to add every mental illness, every disorder he could think of, to his diagnosis. When he was finished, he told me calmly and with control, "I'm whatever you want me to be." Manson is a guy who defies definition; it's as difficult to say what he is not as it is to say what he is. And if you could diagnose Charlie, it would be beyond difficult to trace the origin of the illness. Most people in prisons are antisocial and some of them have good reason to be paranoid. It would be easy to call Charlie psychotic or delusional, but his character clearly has more depth than that.

Schizophrenia is a mental disorder that is characterized by abnormal perceptions and expressions of reality. Three of my favorite musicians [Roky Erickson; Peter Green, founder of Fleetwood Mac; and Syd Barrett, founder of Pink Floyd] are schizophrenic. They are also some of the most influential voices in rock 'n' roll and, sadly, three of rock 'n' roll's most tragic figures. Mental disorders are commonly treated with medications. But, because the side effects of these medications are so horrendous, many patients would rather deal with the symptoms of their illnesses than take the drugs that are supposed to help them. Charlie told me that three psychiatrists at Vacaville labeled him category "K," which, according to Charlie, is "as crazy as it gets." Charlie shared his experience with being heavily medicated, the five years during which his mind was hazy and his body was hardly able to function. In a lot of cases, medications are used as chemical restraints. I would suspect the guards at Vacaville determined Charlie to be an unruly and disruptive inmate. For a patient to be forced to take medication, he must be a risk to himself or others. But Charlie is neither. He is fully aware of his surroundings and he is in control of his behavior. I'm confident that he knows right from wrong.

Our first visit lasted five hours. During that time, four other inmates shared the room to spend time with friends and family. Kenny once told me people try to befriend other PHU inmates, just so they can get a glimpse of Charlie in the visiting room. I'd hoped to meet David Hooker, but he wasn't there.

As our visit came to an end, it became clear that we were both completely wiped. It takes a lot of mental energy to keep up with Charlie, and I was exhausted. Charlie was tired too; he hadn't been down to the visiting room in almost a year. As we said our goodbyes, I was still shocked that the stars had aligned and we'd been able to meet at all. Charlie said he would call me while I stayed at Graywolf's if he felt up for another visit that Sunday. I was very surprised, by the time I made it back to Graywolf's, to find that Charlie had already called to say he'd had a great visit and wanted to see me the next day. I would go back to Corcoran again.

The drive back to Regina from Los Angeles is a long one. Over the few days that brought me closer and closer to home, I thought about my adventure and everyone I'd met. I tried to makes sense of everything, but putting things into perspective was difficult. The trip hadn't brought closure. Instead, the world felt wide open, and things had a momentum of their own. I was just along for the ride. I began to welcome the uncertainty.

When I got home, I dropped my luggage on the kitchen floor and said hello to my cats. Minutes later I was back in the car, out to see Hank Williams III. It was a sold-out performance and when I got there he was already on stage. The show was amazing, as usual. It felt great to be with my tribe, getting soaked with beer and sweat. It felt great to be home. I hung out in the back until Hank finished, signed autographs, and took pictures with his fans. I approached him and we talked about some of the people we knew. I told him the story Stanton shared with me about the night at Marilyn's house, when they'd all listened to the Polanski interrogation tapes. Hank recalled the evening the same way Stanton had. "Yeah," he said. "That's exactly what happened." Hank wished me luck with my book, and as I left he said, "Send Mr. Manson my sincerest regards from the Williams family."

As I write this, Charlie continues to call. One day he told me over the phone that we were in the visiting room. I didn't know what he meant, so I asked him to explain. Charlie said that, once he meets someone, he is with that person forever. In his mind, we are still there in that room, at the table by the old vending machines, just talking. And he is still on the ranch, sitting around a fire, singing with his family. He is roaming the streets of Hollywood without a care in the world.

Charles Manson is a free man.

A Brief Biography of Charles Manson

Much conflicting information exists regarding Charles Manson. I asked Graywolf to put me in touch with someone who knew the truth. He hooked me up with a man called "Moorehead," who grew up and lives 200 miles from Manson's birthplace. Moorehead has been fascinated with Manson since grade school, when he first read Helter Skelter. Because he grew up on Manson's stomping grounds, Moorehead heard a lot of stories from people who knew Charlie's family and friends. An old school researcher and archivist, spending days in a library going through old census records is the way to uncover history, and he's perfected the process. He began doing research through court records, cemeteries, and old newspapers. Moorehead is a friend of Charlie's and he enjoys sending Charlie photos and accounts of his findings. He told me that Charlie has a lot of fond memories from his youth, memories of the way things used to be.

I met Denise Noe through Kenny Calihan. I was struggling to figure out the story behind the murders and told Kenny about my frustrations. He suggested I talk to Denise a friend of Charlie's and who wrote an essay titled "The Manson Myth." I'd never known Charlie to read anyone's account of the crimes, and so I was extremely interested in talking to her. Kenny promised to have Denise call me, and sure enough, a few hours later I received a call from her.

Pleasant and somewhat soft spoken. Denise was curious

about my book, and was direct with her questions. She wanted to make sure I had Charlie's best interests at heart before she helped me. Denise told me she has a very severe psychiatric disability. She is fifty-three, but has been living with her disability, formally diagnosed in her twenties, since she was fourteen. Although she is a person of fairly high intelligence, she has never been able to support herself, due to the limitations imposed by her handicaps. "I live–very frugally! –on alimony, because my ex-husband is a decent man," she told me. Denise first became interested in Charles Manson when she read the book Helter Skelter in high school. "I was utterly persuaded by its portrait of him as a kind of criminal mastermind and charismatic proto-Hitler who could convince others of his grandiose worldview and then persuade them to murder on his behalf." But Denise questioned what she read and started reading and researching to piece together the real story. She remarked, "I started to have a few nagging doubts when I read memoirs by Charles "Tex" Watson and Susan Atkins, and those doubts crystallized when I researched other books."

I asked Denise if it were true that Charlie read her essay, and she said she ran the article off, wrote "The Manson Myth" on the envelope, and sent it to Charlie with the hope that he would read it. He did, they began corresponding, and Charlie started to call. "The first time we talked, we talked about the weather. That shows that Charles Manson is human after all, since we humans tend to talk about the weather when we meet! During that first conversation, I had a coughing fit. He was quite gracious about it and urged me not to feel bad about having coughed in his ear." I asked her about Charlie's critique of her work. Charlie said, "It reminded me of an old Packard car I used to drive that had a couple of cylinders blown out and used to start and stop all the time."

The following biography is composed of information collected from Moorehead and Denise Noe.

Birth

Charles Manson's date of birth is up for debate. His birth certificate, on file in Cincinnati, Ohio, states that he was born on November 12, 1934, at Cincinnati General Hospital, now University Hospital. However, Manson has stated he believes his actual birthday is November 11th, which in 1934 was Armistice Day, and today is Veteran's Day. It is believed his birth date was deliberately changed so it would not "interfere" with such an important holiday.

His mother was Kathleen Maddox, widely portrayed as a party girl who rebelled against a strict, religious mother. The Maddox family was from Kentucky, specifically Morehead, where Kathleen was born, and, later, Ashland. Charles Manson's assessment of his mother varies with his ever changing mood. He has described her as an affectionate woman who did the best she could to care for her child. He has also endorsed books and other forms of media that have deemed her a neglectful, alcoholic prostitute.

Also up for debate is Manson's father: was he Colonel Scott, or the man whose surname Charles would eventually take, William Manson. It is widely recognized that Colonel Scott was Manson's biological father, while William Manson served as his stepfather.

Kathleen Maddox was never married to Scott; the two may have had a one-night stand or a brief affair around March 1934, before Kathleen moved to the Cincinnati area.

In August 1934, Kathleen Maddox and William Manson were married in Cincinnati. But, believing Scott to be Charles' father, Kathleen divorced Manson and returned to Ashland to attempt a marriage to Scott. She discovered Scott had already married, filed a bastardy suit against him, and obtained a settlement in 1937. Kathleen would claim that Charles Manson had known Scott and spent weekends with him and Scott's other child. According to Kathleen, and in contrast to other accounts, family surrounded Charles Manson early on, and he spent a lot of time with his grandmother, aunts, and uncles.

In 1938, Kathleen and a young Charles moved to McMechen, West Virginia, leaving Scott behind. The two moved in with Kathleen's older, married sister. A year later, Kathleen and her brother Luther Maddox were arrested and sent to prison for the armed robbery of a service station located just outside of Charleston. Charles spent the next few years living at the home of his aunt and uncle in McMechen.

School Years and Youth

Which school Charles Manson attended during his grade school years is unknown, but it is very likely he received his early education in McMechen. After his mother was paroled, the small family lived in various hotel rooms around the area; Charles may or may not have attended school at this time. In 1947, at the request of his mother, Charles was placed in the Gibault School for Boys in Terre Haute, Indiana. He escaped after ten months to find his mother who, as the story goes, rejected him.

On his own at the age of thirteen, Charles Manson survived any way he could. As a teenager, he burglarized various grocery and retail stores. He was caught in the act of one such burglary and sent to a juvenile center in Indianapolis, from which he escaped after one day. A subsequent recapture sent Manson to Father Flanagan's Boys Town in Nebraska, where he stayed for four days before escaping once again.

Reverting back to theft for survival, Manson and another boy committed armed robberies at service stations and grocery stores. During one robbery, Manson was caught and sent to the Indiana School for Boys in Plainfield, the place where Manson endured much abuse at the hands of guards and other young inmates. After four years in Plainfield and many escape attempts, Manson and two other youths finally succeeded in fleeing the facility in 1951. The three were headed for California when they were stopped in Utah for transporting a stolen car across state lines. Convicted at seventeen of his first federal offense, Manson was sent to The National Training School for Boys in Washington, DC. His incarceration at this facility initiated the series of psychological evaluations and I.Q. tests by which he would be analyzed for the rest of his life.

From 1951 to 1952, Manson was moved to increasingly more secure correctional institutions due to behavioral and psychiatric problems. After improving his commitment to his education and work ethic, Manson was granted a stipulated parole, which required him to live with his aunt and uncle in McMechen.

However, Manson also spent time living with his mother, who at this point also resided in McMechen. Charles and Kathleen had previously improved their relationship through an exchange of letters while Charles was in prison.

Marriages and More Trouble

Free from a long stint in various juvenile facilities, Manson attempted a normal life. In January 1955, while living in Wheeling, West Virginia, he married Rosalie Jean Willis, a waitress who was four years his junior.

The couple's first few months of marriage were pleasant and uneventful. For the most part, Manson worked honest jobs and made a decent living. But, once Rosalie became pregnant with Charles Milles Manson Jr., Manson reverted back to old habits. He stole a car and headed for Los Angeles. Once again he was caught, this time in Indianapolis, and charged under the National Motor Vehicle Theft Act. His probation was revoked and he was sentenced to three years at Terminal Island Penitentiary in San Pedro, California. After a few initial visits, Rosalie ceased to return. Eventually Kathleen had to tell her son that his young wife was living with another man and filing for a divorce, which was finalized in 1958.

In September of the same year, Manson was paroled in California. He became a pimp to a few underage girls and forged a US Treasury check, a crime for which he received a ten-year suspended sentence. In order to evade being charged with pimping, Manson persuaded one of his prostitutes, Leona, to marry him so she wouldn't have to testify against him. Once again on the move and still on parole/probation, Manson took his girls from California. He was eventually arrested in Laredo, Texas and charged under the Mann Act for transporting women across state lines with the intent to prostitute them. He was sent back to California to serve his ten-year sentence for breaking probation. Although the Mann Act charge was dropped, he was convicted of forgery and sent to McNeil Island Penitentiary in Washington State.

Manson's second wife petitioned him for divorce in 1963, after alleging the couple had had a son, Charles Luther Manson. In 1966, Manson was sent back to Terminal Island in California to prepare for an early termination of his sentence. In March 1967, Manson was released from prison, against his own wishes. It's alleged that Manson requested not to be set free, citing his belief in his inability to adapt to the outside world.

Freedom and Formation of The Family

On March 21, 1967, Manson walked out of Terminal Island Penitentiary a free man. But his newfound freedom would last just over two and a half years. According to Manson, he never wanted to be in the real world. On the outside, after spending seventeen of his thirty-two years inside a prison cell, Manson perceived the world as a whirlwind. He eventually found himself in San Francisco around the start of the Summer of Love, a time of unrestrained release and, thus, a stark contrast to the climate inside jails and reform schools.

One day, while sitting near the entrance to the University of California, Berkeley, Manson met twenty-three-year-old Mary Brunner, a Wisconsin native who worked there as an assistant librarian. The two began an affair and moved in together. Shortly thereafter, Manson discovered San Francisco's Haight-Ashbury: the magic district where hippies from around the world congregated and enjoyed the pleasures of free food, sex, drugs, and shelter. An unprecedented social phenomenon was happening at Haight-Ashbury, and soon enough Manson sat smack dab in the middle of it.

Soon after meeting Mary Brunner, the two began to travel around California, picking up other young women. They recruited Lynette "Squeaky" Fromme from Venice Beach. They picked up Patricia Krenwinkel on Manhattan Beach, then Susan Atkins at a house party in San Francisco. Slowly but surely, Manson acquired a following of mostly female devotees who were entranced by the philosophy he preached: a way of thinking, described in most accounts as a version of the scientology he'd studied in prison.

The early Manson Family lived a peaceful existence in a house in San Francisco. Eventually, Manson grew tired of the Summer of Love scene and he and his following set out in an old school bus Manson had gutted and converted into a group home. All the while, Manson, an aspiring artist, had music on his mind. The school bus traveled up to Washington State and down to Mexico before finally settling in Los Angeles. On September 11, 1967, Manson recorded his infamous LIE album. The rest of 1967 would prove uneventful for the Manson Family, which would live out a daily grind of dumpster diving, drifting, and having fun.

On April 15, 1968, Mary Brunner gave birth to Manson's son, Michael Manson. In the late spring of 1968, Dennis Wilson of the

Beach Boys picked up two of Manson's girls, Patricia Krenwinkel and Ella Jo Bailey, while they hitchhiked around California. Wilson brought the young women back to his house on Sunset Boulevard where the three allegedly talked for a while. Sometime during the conversation, Wilson invited the girls to crash at his place, while he went out to record at his studio. Later that evening, Manson and the rest of his Family occupied the Wilson residence. When Wilson arrived home, early the next morning, he was more than surprised to find the large group in his home. Scared, the famous musician asked the gang members if they would hurt him. As the story goes, Manson addressed Wilson's fears by replying, "'Do I look like I'm going to hurt you, brother?" At the same time he knelt down to kiss Wilson's feet.

Manson and Wilson became fast friends and the Manson Family stayed at the Wilson home for the rest of the summer. Through his relationship with Wilson, Manson met record producer Terry Melcher and manager Gregg Jakobson, the men who would arrange Manson's first recording session. Because of his developing relationship with Melcher, Manson and the rest of his Family often visited the producer's home at Bel Air's 10050 Cielo Drive. When Wilson moved out of his home in August, the Family was forced to find a new place to live. They eventually stumbled upon Spahn Movie Ranch, 500 acres of open space previously used in the filming of classic Hollywood westerns.

Spahn Ranch and Murders

After meeting the elderly owner of Spahn Ranch, George Spahn, Manson convinced him to allow the Family to crash at the ranch for a few days. Those few days turned into the better part of a year. The Family worked around the ranch to earn its keep, tending to the horses and keeping up the grounds. The Manson family girls also slept with Spahn to sweeten the deal. Not long after the family moved to Spahn, a drifting, drugging Texan named Charles "Tex" Watson join the group.

In the fall of 1968, some of Manson's family members, including Manson himself, ventured out on a field trip and discovered the Myers and Barker Ranches contained within California's Death Valley. Each ranch was owned by an elderly woman, easily persuaded to assist Manson in producing his music by providing him and his group a place to stay. During the winter months of early 1969, the Family occupied a home rented on Gresham Street in Canoga Park, California. After spending only two months in the Gresham Street house, the Family moved back to Spahn Ranch.

On March 23, 1969, Manson made a visit to 10050 Cielo Drive. He was looking for Terry Melcher who, allegedly unbeknownst to Manson, was no longer the tenant of the property's owner, Rudi Altobelli. Manson was met at the door by one of Sharon Tate's friends, who advised Manson that the home had become the Polanski-Tate residence and directed him away from the property. Manson examined the property and then left to spend the rest of spring and early summer back at Spahn Ranch.

On August 9, 1969, Tex Watson, Susan Atkins, Patricia Krenwinkel, and Linda Kasabian drove to 10050 Cielo Drive. When Tex and the girls arrived at the house, they found it occupied by Sharon Tate, who was eight and half months pregnant, and her friends, Abigail Folger, Voytek Frykowski, and Jay Sebring. The family members proceeded to stab every person in the house to death and shoot Steven Parent in his car, parked in the driveway.

The following day, August 10, Watson, Atkins, Krenwinkel, Kasabian, Manson, Steve Grogan, and Leslie Van Houten drove to the residence of Leno LaBianca, a supermarket executive, and his wife Rosemary, a dress shop owner. The house was located in the Los Feliz section of Los Angeles and situated next to a home at which the Manson family had attended a party the year before. Manson allegedly entered the house first in order to restrain the couple; he then left the property, taking Atkins, Kasabian, and Grogan with him. The three remaining family members entered the residence and stabbed Leno and Rosemary LaBianca to death.

The Aftermath

Authorities raided Spahn Ranch on August 16, 1969, seven days after the Tate/LaBianca murders. Manson and his Family were taken into custody, but were released shortly after, due to a misdated search warrant. After the Spahn raid, most of the Family fled to the Barker Ranch in Death Valley. On October 10, 1969 the Barker Ranch was searched; authorities became alert to the location after several members of the Family burned up a heavy equipment loader down in the valley. Soon enough, the Manson family members, minus Tex Watson who had returned to Texas, Patricia Krenwinkel who'd fled to Alabama, and Linda Kasabian who'd traveled to New Hampshire, were arrested and put back behind bars. The three would eventually be extradited back to California, where they were indicted for their crimes.

On June 15th, 1970 the jury was selected for the Manson Family murder trial. Until the murder trial of OJ Simpson in 1995, the Manson trial was the longest and costliest trial in California's history. The trial proceeded in the manner of a circus. Manson family members protested the proceeding outside the courthouse. Manson and his girls were responsible for many outlandish courtroom outbursts, disruptions, and distractions. Manson and his girls would show up to court with Xs carved into their foreheads.

The trial focused on exposing and dissecting the motive behind such seemingly random acts of violence. The prosecution pinpointed Manson's belief in an impending, cataclysmic race war, "Helter Skelter," as the group's main motivation. The murder investigation uncovered Manson's alleged obsession with The Beatles' White Album and his belief that the music contained coded messages directed at the Manson family. The Beatles, Manson believed, espoused Manson's exact vision of a future "black uprising" during which the black race would overcome the white race, with the latter "self-annihilating" as a result of its division between racist and non-racist sects. Evidence from the crime scenes–references both to the White Album and to war written on the walls in blood and carved into the victims' flesh– was used to support the theory that Helter Skelter sparked the Manson Family killing spree. Linda Kasabian would even testify that Manson had wanted to plant some of the victims' personal effects in black neighborhoods to make it look as though Helter Skelter had begun.

On November 16, 1970, the prosecution rested its case. Three days later, on November 19, the defense rested its case. On January 25, 1971, Manson and the girls were convicted in the Tate/LaBianca murders. On March 29, 1971, the jury handed down the death sentence for those convicted in the Tate/LaBianca case. On April 19, 1971, Judge Charles Older officially assigned the death sentence to Charles Manson.

Manson and the girls spent ten months on death row. In 1972, the Supreme Court of California abolished the death penalty, ruling it unconstitutional. The death sentences were reduced to life sentences with the possibility of parole. Since then, Manson has spent time at various state prisons throughout California, including San Quentin, Folsom, California Medical Center, Vacaville, Pelican Bay, and Corcoran. The bizarre nature of his crimes continued to draw extensive media coverage throughout the 1980s and early 1990s and there still exists a barrage of anything and everything Manson: TV and magazine interviews, books, movies, music, T-shirts, and other merchandise. His case has been cited as one of the most infamous in American history.

Other Violent Manson Family Crimes

Bernard Crowe Shooting: In 1969, Tex Watson ripped off an African-American drug dealer named Bernard "Lotsapoppa" Crowe. Crowe proceeded to hold Watson's girlfriend, Luella, hostage until Watson either returned Crowe's money or delivered his drugs. On July 1, 1969, Manson went to the home of Crowe with his friend T.J. Walleman, who brought a gun. An altercation ensued, during which Manson fired the gun and shot Crowe. Manson allegedly worried he had killed Crowe, a fear that seemed to be confirmed when he read reports of a dead Black Panther soon after the shooting. Although Crowe was not a member of the Black Panthers and had not died from the gunshot wound, the event significantly increased the air of paranoia at the Manson ranch.

Gary Hinman Murder: On July 25, 1969, family members Bobby Beausoleil, Mary Brunner, and Susan Atkins went to the house of Family acquaintance Gary Hinman to retrieve money they felt Hinman owed the family. It is not clear why they sought the money. Some accounts report that Hinman had recently acquired an inheritance, part of which Manson felt was his. Other accounts suggest Hinman had sold Beausoleil some bad mescaline and that Bobby had returned either to get some good mescaline or retrieve his money. Beausoleil, Brunner, and Atkins kept Hinman hostage for two days, a time during which Hinman went to great lengths to prove he had no money. At one point, Bobby hit Hinman twice with his gun, before placing Hinman under the girls' surveillance and proceeding to search the entirety of Hinman's house. After struggling with Hinman for the gun, Bobby was able to reach what seemed like a settlement with Hinman, who would give Beausoleil the title of his two cars, a VW bus and a Fiat. At this point, Manson and friend Bruce Davis arrived at the house, Davis with a gun and Manson with a sword. Unaware of the agreement between Hinman and Beausoleil, Manson sliced Hinman's ear off and left. Shortly thereafter, Bobby finished Hinman off, stabbing him to death.

Donald Shea Murder: Donald Shea was a stuntman and horse wrangler on Spahn Ranch. Manson blamed the Spahn Ranch raid on Shea, believing that Shea had turned the Family in to the police. Manson may or may not have placed the blame on Shea due to the fact that Shea had committed what Manson considered "sin" when he married an African-American woman. On August 25, 1969, about one week after the raid, family members Bruce Davis, Steve Grogan, and Charles Watson took Shea for a ride on the outskirts of the Spahn Ranch. Grogan hit Shea on the back of the head with a lead pipe and Watson stabbed Shea to death. Shea's body was buried in a shallow grave, which wasn't discovered until 1977, after a confession made by Steve Grogan.

Dear Mothers of men in prison - I've lived + played Handball Chess Sports Cards Games + LIFE with the people in prison ever sence I was 12 + even before that in Boys schools - I've watched your Sons come in + go out for over 60 years So its not like I just Drove up - you chave been in your World befor I got them in your mind thought + dreams - SAME as I was there befor you wrote + let me know that you know about what I Call me - I'm already taken up by LOTS Of others: "Other thoughts, wierd ways, FAR FAR out in the religous, + governars + Controls, Crime, Drugs,

...art cars & memay te models -
I'm no spring Chicken but
I do Know Death & all its
travels & how to Low RIDE
& stay Cool & not git Convoluted
by the subjugated people who
are in to all that do or die tuff guys
trying to prone they man to mona s
plans - I see your photo you Look
nice but you realize I'm not
OUT FROM Under a HOST [LOTS] of
PAST Commitments as my
word is Bond & Bond is my
life in Chambers of Courts, &
Stars, men of War & peace
Soldier, of truth & honor - I'm a
OUTLAW Croak & Gang king
being - I was razed to my
Survine & not to git
Caught up in Games. I Make

games to play — I don't know
where to start with you — I
know you know but you Don't
know what I know & I don't have
time to do all you may need — I'm
TOTELY & compleetly comited to
A–T–W–A– for 4 years I brought
the TROUBLES of the world, I
LEARNT from from your words
untold 4 reasons of no
one could understand + would
be a wast of time that I don't hang to
explain. I came from Mixico in 1959
with the problems in my mind about
Air Die ing + Cruaty no one could drink
& it was barred out of my mind
to some a world later to be
found gone, + had been gone
before I was barred — I'm NOT
JOHN WAiN – That world was i

he back doors + [...] BEHOND Whats
real to your thought patterns + on LOOK & that
get Caught + TRAPED by this thing that
gone far behond My (what ever) Im in
way over my head + the got TONS
of pauls who wont let me do anything
+ when I start or do anything they
take it + run to say they are me + that
they are doing this + to give them the Money
+ they are bigs, betty + tent sweety + all
the games You + I know are played by a
lot of people who beg to die + I cant do
but just a little — Ive been to Death Row
3 times NOT for Crimes of passion
or greed but for ATWA + a need
given to me when I was raseing
up in LIFE to be a what ever you
People that live are no good for, or to them
selves, or anyone els — I Cant keep
going through people's whos to TRUST
over + over one at a time — it
keeps me in the Hole all the time
40 years in Lock up + I Cant
git out of the FEARs of
Rats turn Coats phonies + warped
People who want to prove
or be some one by useing
some one els — If you had a job